To William Devanney

With every good wish

Sincerely

Matthew Luckiesh

Sept. 17, 1949

TORCH OF CIVILIZATION

by Matthew Luckiesh

TORCH OF CIVILIZATION, 1940
COLOR AND COLORS, 1938
THE SCIENCE OF SEEING (WITH F. K. MOSS), 1937
SEEING AND HUMAN WELFARE, 1934
SEEING—A PARTNERSHIP OF LIGHTING AND VISION (WITH F.K.M.), 1931
ARTIFICIAL SUNLIGHT, 1930
LIGHT AND HEALTH, 1926
LIGHT AND WORK, 1926
LIGHTING FIXTURES AND LIGHTING EFFECTS, 1925
FOUNDATIONS OF THE UNIVERSE, 1925
PORTABLE LAMPS, 1924
LIGHT AND COLOR IN ADVERTISING AND MERCHANDISING, 1923
ULTRAVIOLET RADIATION, 1922
THE BOOK OF THE SKY, 1922, 1933
VISUAL ILLUSIONS, 1922
LIGHTING THE HOME, 1920
ARTIFICIAL LIGHT, 1920
THE LANGUAGE OF COLOR, 1918
THE LIGHTING ART, 1917
LIGHT AND SHADE AND THEIR APPLICATIONS, 1916
COLOR AND ITS APPLICATIONS, 1915, 1921

TORCH OF CIVILIZATION

THE STORY OF MAN'S CONQUEST OF DARKNESS

Matthew Luckiesh

D. SC., D. E., DIRECTOR, LIGHT-
ING RESEARCH LABORATORY
GENERAL ELECTRIC COMPANY

G. P. PUTNAM'S SONS   NEW YORK

COPYRIGHT, 1940, BY MATTHEW LUCKIESH

All rights reserved. This book, or parts thereof, must not be reproduced in any form without permission.

Second Impression

Designed by Robert Josephy

MANUFACTURED IN THE UNITED STATES OF AMERICA

ACKNOWLEDGMENTS. *The author is indebted to the Pacific Gas and Electric Company, San Francisco, for six of the illustrations of early light-sources and to the General Electric Company for the others.*

TORCH OF CIVILIZATION

I. TORCH OF CIVILIZATION

IT WAS MIDNIGHT on a Western desert. The last lingering flush of earthly light had disappeared long before. Only the eerie light of other worlds suffused the darkness of that expanse of desert waste. A young man walked alone in company with the stars. Civilization was so far away that he might have been walking on the moon or on any other distant darkened world. Far to the left and to the right vague mountains cut the horizon into faint wavy lines. Occasionally the mournful howl of a coyote emphasized the stillness—and the loneliness. The bleached sands underfoot, vague and watery in the starlight, faded away into distant ghostliness. Hours had passed since the delicate colors of the desert sunset had faded quickly away. And the stars, waiting all day long behind the veil of bright sky, came forth as good friends do, to serve when darkness fell.

The monotony of the day had been broken only by slow changes in lights and shadows, and by mirages, as the glaring sun traveled through the thin blue sky. After dark the monotony was intensified by a vagueness which descended with the starlight. But the young man also felt the enchantment of mystery which aroused a kind of expectancy. Only the continual crunch of his footsteps seemed real and earthly as he maintained his course by the stars. Darkness also aroused a feeling in which mystery was emphasized. Suddenly this became intensified, for the expanse of ghostly sand became one of water. Everywhere ahead the faint sheen of its surface eventually lost itself in the mists of a thin fog.

Unexpectedly a light appeared somewhere ahead, like a lighted window in a distant cabin. But there were no cabins anywhere in that desert waste. No one lived in that expanse of desolation. The light moved, rapidly for a moment, then it stopped again. Was this a will-o-the-wisp which, according to folk-lore, lured travelers to destruction? The young man looked upward to the friendly stars, still faithful guides penetrating the misty veil which hung over the water. As the young man trudged on through the shallow water another light appeared from nowhere. It seemed to hang stationary for a moment, then moved away rapidly. Another and another came weirdly into existence. Soon there appeared to be hundreds of these vague lights moving in disorder. Tantalizingly vague in outline and out of reach in the darkness, there was no way of estimating their size or distance away. For an hour as the young man continued walking in the water, this unearthly display continued. Indeed this was a world of unreality—of mystery.

The young man was the author. That overwhelming display of will-o-the-wisps was never to be forgotten. After many years it still remains a vivid picture, rooted deeply in memory by the thoughts, speculations and emotions it aroused. Of course, none of us believes that the *ignis fatuus*, false light, or will-o-the-wisp lures lonely travelers to destruction. But I have often wondered whether or not that remarkable display—its mystery and apparent chaos—did not help to lure me into the realms of the mysteries, fascinations and services of light. I like to feel that by accident or coincidence that great display of elusive lights on a lonely Western desert was prophetic of a life work. Certainly

This oil-lamp furnished light in Babylonia 6000 years ago as its ancestors probably did in the Stone Age.

throughout the ramified realms of light there have been mysteries on every hand. Certainly there has been the loneliness of pioneering along the frontiers of knowledge. Certainly there has been a succession of fascinating adventures. And along the entire journey, the lights of established facts or knowledge have been trustworthy guides as the stars are.

The story of light is as old as the universe and as far-flung. In this sense it is timeless. It has no known beginning and it has no comprehensible end. But as far as human beings are concerned, the story of light begins with their first appreciation of it. In their primitive state they worshipped it, with much justification, and ever since have woven it into many rituals and other ceremonies. In this sense light always bears the mark of a blessing and has acquired many favorable meanings. Worship and primitive practical uses long preceded any understanding of it and of its endless service and beneficence. All these many aspects are blended into a story unexcelled, and perhaps unequaled, by anything else in the physical universe or in the lives of civilized human beings.

Light from the stars reveals their motions. Without knowledge of these the starry sky appears to be a chaos of disorder. But knowledge has revealed a superb orderliness and the realization of this has supplied the most powerful incentive for mankind to learn to understand Nature. Without a deeply rooted faith in the dependability of socalled natural laws, we would not be much encouraged to understand light or anything else in Nature. Without such established faith, the task of building a structure of knowledge would be a hopeless one. No mere opinion can alter the orderliness of Nature. No political party can repeal her laws. Nothing can repeal the facts revealed by science.

TORCH OF CIVILIZATION

No aspect of Nature has done more than the heavens above to establish this faith and to encourage mankind to believe that Nature could be understood and is worth understanding. We cannot prove that the Sun will rise tomorrow morning, but the overwhelming evidence of orderliness of Nature and of dependability of natural laws gives us an abiding faith that it will do so. Similarly, we have great faith in Polaris, the North Star. For ages it has helped to guide mariners across uncharted seas just as it guided the author as a young man through the darkness on that sea of desert sand. We have faith that apples will continue to fall to the ground due to the invariable law of gravitation. We are quite assured that stones will not roll up hill tomorrow. Such faith in orderliness of the inanimate things of Nature is the sound foundation upon which modern science and material civilization are built. And this faith is not shaken whether we are concerned with the enormously great realm of the universe with its orderly stars or with the extremely minute universe of an atom with its orderly electrons.

Light from the stars reveals much more than their motions. It tells us what the stars are made of, also something of their age. Those far-off crucibles, where temperatures and pressures exist far beyond those attainable at present by man, serve as laboratories for modern scientists. By delicate measurements of the character of the light coming from them, something is learned of the constitution of minute atoms as well as of immense stars. And beyond the stars at incomprehensible distances are nebulae, probably other universes in the making, evolving ever so slowly through eons of time. Out there, time is of no such importance as it is to a human being whose life-span is only a tick of the cosmic clock. All these celestial bodies reveal something of themselves and of the plan of the physical universe through the peculiarities of the light which comes to us from them. Thus pigmy man with unlimited Mind defies distances so inconceivably great that light traveling at an enormous speed sets no limits upon his understanding. And he depends upon light for these journeys and for the fruits of them.

Coming back to Earth, we find the Sun the dominant factor in our bit of the universe. The Earth and other planets revolve around it just as the Moon revolves around the Earth. The daily cycle of the Sun has fashioned our days into periods of work and rest. The seasonal course of the Sun from high altitudes in the summer to lower ones in the winter determines the cycle of growth, fruition and dormancy of plant life throughout the year. Thus all living things on Earth are dominated by sunlight. And even many things that are not living are the result of sunlight of long ago. Our coal beds, for example, may be considered to be sunlight or solar energy stored for eons in the remains of a tremendous plant growth of an age long past. Thus when we burn coal to provide us with heat and power, we are turning on the sunlight of eons ago. In a sense, sunlight is the life-blood of all living things on earth. It is intimately woven into life and health processes probably much more completely than we even suspect as yet. At any rate, we are as truly enslaved by sunlight as the Earth and its sister planets are chained to their courses by the force of attraction of the Sun.

How life first began on Earth is still a matter of conjecture, but how it altered and persisted is largely a matter of sunlight. Before modern science came into existence, knowledge was superficial and it was distorted by superstition, mythology and other products of primitive minds and knowledge. It was not uncommon to consider that the physical world consisted of four elements—sunlight, air, land and water. The need for air and water is obvious to the most primitive beings. Land and water furnished the other essential—food. The need for sunlight is not so directly obvious, still it has been widely recognized as essential by all primitive people. Widespread worship of the Sun or of Light is a powerful testimonial of this recognition. Human beings turn toward light as naturally as plants do.

About a billion years ago simple living things existed on earth. During the course of the ages which followed, many changes occurred in climate and in other factors upon which life depends. Among these, sunlight is the most universally important. Glacial ages came and went. The earth's surface raised and lowered. Even a tilt to the north or south alters the supply of sunlight as much as a change in latitude does. Some places became deserts and others received an abundance of rain. These and many other changes took place from time to time. Thus living things gradually had to adapt themselves to these changes in order to survive. Thus evolution took place and continued in countless directions. Various branches of the tree of life developed. But no living thing escaped from the need for sunlight either directly or through the living things it lived on.

As living things became more complex, crude senses began to become separated from each other. The sense of touch aids living things to detect objects within actual reach. The sense of smell extends this reach but still involves actual contact with a part of the object. Actual particles emitted by the object, whether it be a gardenia or a goat, come in contact with the sensitive surfaces of the sense of smell. The sense of hearing developed along a similar principle of physical contact with the object through vibrations in matter. The shriek of a distant whistle sends vibrations through the air to the sensitive parts of our ears. Likewise, the rumble of a distant train may be heard through vibrations in the steel rails if we place an ear close to the metal. But the sense of sight developed along an entirely different line which extended the limits of sight enormously.

Through the visual sense, contact with the object is not made through matter in the ordinary sense. We can see through a vacuum of a tungsten lamp bulb. We can see stars through enormous distances of practically empty celestial space. None of our other senses can span these really empty spaces. The visual sense evolved to utilize radiant energy emitted by the sun through a vacuum, through celestial space and through many material things. Light from the sun had been showering over the earth for eons, vitalizing plant and animal life and entering into life-processes. Living things were already using it in many ways—in a sense were completely enslaved by it even though it is a kindly slavery. Why should not a sense evolve which used sunlight? This did happen. The sun emits radiant energy of various wavelengths just as radio sending-sets do. Through ages of evolution the visual sense adapted itself best to the use of sunlight.

The retina at the back of the eye is sensitive to the more dominant wavelengths of energy radiated by the sun. Objects reflect or transmit this energy in varying degree. Thus a pattern of invisible energy flows from the objects toward the eyes. The eye-lens focuses an image of this pattern or scene upon the sensitive retina. Through delicate chemical and electrical processes the sensation reaches the brain. Then through complex mental processes which involve a long period of learning while we are babies, we see things out in space where they are. This is the most marvelous sense in many ways. Two eyes add further refinements. Thus we have a visual sense outstandingly different from our other senses, but it is eternally chained to sunlight or to other light-sources which emit energy within a limited range of its wavelengths.

Thus it is seen that Nature shackled us to light in many ways. Sunlight provides a world in which we can live and which supplies energy and food. More specifically, we are bound to light because it is an essential partner of vision—our most important and educative sense. Without light we would be as blind as we would be without sight. Certainly our usefulness, welfare and happiness depend largely upon our ability to see. But light is even more important than sight because the limitations and abilities of sight are fixed. Our control over light is relatively unlimited.

A great variety of light-sources is now available and by controlling light with optical systems the horizons of visibility can be extended enormously. For example, light can be so controlled by microscopes and telescopes that we are able to see things far beyond the limits of unaided sight. By breaking up light into its various wavelengths, things are discovered far beyond the limits of chemical analysis. In this manner we look into minute atoms and into distant stars, both far beyond the limits of unaided sight. In countless ways we can examine the worlds beyond the reach of our senses by harnessing light to extend our sight and by understanding the messages which light brings back to us from these worlds. And these horizons will be pushed back steadily in the future.

Traveling around the world along the highways of civilization, it becomes obvious that the material world of civilization is largely built by, and for, seeing. To a great extent its progress has marched hand in hand with progress in the production and use of artificial light. This is emphasized still more as we visit the byways of this world of human beings. We find the Eskimo sitting in his crude hut or igloo with his activities and progress as restricted as the feeble smoky light from the spluttering blubber in his lamp. Similarly, the flickering light obtained by burning crude natural materials represents very well the comparative level of civilization of primitive tribes everywhere. In the hinterlands of many progressive countries the character and use of artificial light illustrate very well how the level of living recedes with distance from the centers of progress. And even the most complex civilizations reveal, through artificial light and lighting, their rank in the scale of material progress. From these journeys, whether actual or imaginary, we see light leading the procession of civilized progress. Civilized activities are no longer bounded by sunrise and sunset. Night is turned into play-time. Trains and planes plunge through the night guided by man-made light. Industry, education, recreation do not retire unless they want to. Indeed, artificial light is the torch of civilization.

Primitive beings first came indoors into caves or crude huts to escape obvious dangers of enemies and obvious discomforts of Nature such as rain, wind, cold and ice. They had to admit daylight in order to see. This entered through the mouth of the cave or openings provided in their huts. They were still almost completely slaves of Nature for their activities were almost entirely bounded by sunrise and sunset. But the first primitive being who seized a flaming fagot from the open campfire and carried it indoors laid the foundation of the modern home. He performed an act whose civilizing influence was destined to be immeasurable. His mate and his offspring followed him and this near-animal family was the forerunner of the eventual human family. For the first time it sensed something of the cheer and comfort of a home. The heat and light from the crude fire drove cold and darkness from it. Privacy and intimacy gradually changed the crude ties of mated animals into the bonds of family. Leisure hours in comparative safety and comfort strengthened these bonds and the roots of civilized progress were nourished. Thus dawned our present civilization. Thus our artificial world was born and blessed by artificial light. These efforts toward self-determination clearly distinguished mankind from other animals.

From that lowly beginning human beings have struggled slowly up the ladder of civilized progress. But for thousands of years they learned by the painful process of accidental experience or by the costly method of cut and try. Those methods are still fairly prominent in our political and sociological worlds because of the dominance of politics and narrow self-interest and the absence of modern scientific attitude. For a long time learning was confined largely to what the unaided senses revealed. Thus progress was limited to what was more or less obvious. With the advent of modern science, great unobvious unknowns were revealed. Hidden forces such as electricity were discovered and harnessed. The production of light by burning materials advanced by refining the materials but flames greatly limited the service of artificial light. The harnessing of electricity enormously increased the possibilities of artificial light. Bottled light has no such limitations as flaming material. It can be used anywhere in countless ways. Its cost has so diminished that more than a hundred times more electric light can be purchased for a dollar than if we were still using candles. Notwithstanding great advances in light-production, modern civilization was generally satisfied, as the first primitive families were, to banish darkness. Artificial light continued to play the role of a competitor of darkness.

Long ago it seemed to the author that the proper role of artificial light should be as a competitor of daylight. We human beings are the products of Nature—of the outdoors. Biologically speaking we came indoors only yesterday. We—and our visual sense—evolved under daylight and the brightnesses outdoors. As we apply the great principle of adaptation—of evolution toward fitness to the conditions under which human beings evolved—it seemed unreasonable to make an exception of eyesight, the visual sense, and seeing conditions in general. Many years of intricate research have revealed much proof that this exception is unwarranted. The visual sense is most efficient under brightness-levels outdoors. These are hundreds and thousands of times higher than those commonly encountered or provided indoors. It has also been proved that seeing is done most easily when brightness-levels compare with those outdoors. In other words, the science of seeing reveals that the proper role of artificial light is to compete with daylight, not with darkness.

In the role of an essential partner of sight, the job which light has to do is almost infinite in variety. It follows sight everywhere into the realms of usefulness, safety, comfort and happiness of human beings. It has services to render everywhere throughout the realms of work and of recreation. But its possibilities do not end with revealing things for the purposes of work or play. It has possibilities directly

TORCH OF CIVILIZATION

concerned with health and with life. Some modern lightsources not only provide light of various qualities including that of daylight. They can provide the invisible ultraviolet energy which had been left outdoors. This energy prevents and cures rickets, kills germs, and is valuable to human beings in other ways. Thus artificial sunlight in the fullest sense is now available for our artificial indoor world.

Modern artificial light is so controllable in every respect that it may be considered as a relatively new medium of expression. For centuries artists have used various media, such as paints, to beautify the artificial world and to please and intrigue human beings. With the advent of bottled electric light the possibilities of the use of light as an expressive medium increased enormously. Already many uses have been made in many appropriate fields. The expressiveness of light is only limited by the knowledge, skill and taste of the user and by the capacity of human beings to enjoy this use of light. Considering that light also has the unique factor of mobility, effect can follow effect rapidly and without end. Material civilization has progressed far from a lowly beginning and artificial light has been a powerful force which in many respects has led the parade of progress. May it not be possible that the use of modern light, so controllable in brightness, color and mobility, may even evolve into a new fine art? If it does it may well be man's most abstract achievement in art, even finer and more ethereal than music. If its use attains such heights, artificial light may well deserve to be known in still another and a finer sense as the torch of civilization.

II. DRAMAS OF LIGHT

PROMETHEUS IS THE legendary individual in Grecian mythology who, at great risk and eventual sacrifice, stole fire from heaven and bestowed it, its light and other blessings, upon mankind. Such an arduous task could scarcely be executed successfully by a weakling and it was too important to be trusted to an underling. But the imagination of the story-tellers who evolved the myths took care of such matters. Prometheus had good connections and was strong, wise and crafty. He was a son of a Titan and was a brother to several Titans, including Atlas who had the titanic job of holding the heavens upon his shoulders. He joined with Zeus against his brother Titans and his craftiness was largely responsible for placing Zeus upon the mythical throne on Mount Olympus. But as is still not uncommon in politics, henchman and ruler came to a parting of the ways. Prometheus eventually rebelled against the tyranny of Zeus who ruled the universe with an iron hand. Accordingly when Zeus planned to destroy the human race and to create another, regimented more to his liking, Prometheus stole a bolt of lightning from Zeus who had denied fire to mankind. Thus the human race became strong with the new powers arising from the control of fire and light and other byproducts. It was also greatly enriched by the benefits therefrom.

If electricity had been as commonly in use when these myths evolved as it is now, doubtless the stolen lightning would have been presented to mankind directly as electrical energy. Prometheus might well have been the heroic giver of the manifold benefits of electricity which is the life-blood of modern civilization as fire was the life-blood of the primitive civilization. By using other names and altering some details, a great variety of myths of many primitive peoples could readily be presented with sufficient accuracy to reveal the overwhelming importance of fire and light in the thought, attitude and lives of early human beings. Journeys over the earth today beyond the vague boundaries of civilization reveal the same awe and worship. And even in the language, literature, and ceremonies of the present time are found countless remnants of the impressions which became deeply rooted in more primitive times, minds and practices.

Before writing was invented, myths could only be handed down to succeeding generations by word of mouth. Thus they are the products of countless story-tellers. As someone has stated, myths were born, not made. They were born in the infancy of people when knowledge was meager and imagination was rife. They arose from joy, fear, gratitude and various human sentiments and emotions. They were childish attempts to interpret the events of Nature and to explain the common facts of observation. As such they afford an excellent means of learning something of the knowledge and attitude of earlier peoples, some of whom had progressed far in certain directions but not in the direction of understanding Nature. For example, ancient Greece and pagan Rome were far up the ladder of civilization in some respects, but the understanding of causes hidden from their unaided senses was almost non-existent.

Mythology contains many powerful dramas of light, dark-

Physical light for the eyes, symbolic light for the mind and sacred light for the soul.

DRAMAS OF LIGHT

ness, and fire. Down through the centuries to the present time, these have inspired poets, dramatists, composers of music and various other artists. The myths had been copied and modified throughout the earlier periods and eventually evolved into realistic dramatic presentations with suitable settings and properties throughout the theater, grand opera and other realms far beyond the limits of ritualistic ceremonies. In the early myths and worships, it is not always possible to separate the significance of light from that of fire. Apparently the benefits of both were often blended. Of course, the association of fire and light was obvious and until less than a century ago the sole practicable source of light was fire—burning material. Notwithstanding the importance of fire as a source of light and of other benefits, the importance bestowed upon light in myths and ceremonies throughout uncounted thousands of years has been overwhelmingly greater than that given to fire.

Light is the forty-sixth word in the Bible. It is followed by 773,700 words according to somebody's count, which doubtless will not be seriously disputed. According to the first few sentences of the Bible, the achievement of the Creator immediately following the creation of "the heavens and the earth" was the creation of light. In other words, after there was a place upon which human beings could live, the first gift was that of light. These simple facts and myths indicate the extremely high place which light held in the minds, attitude and practices of people before the Christian era and during the period when Christianity was being born.

Uncounted symbolic uses of light are found in the Bible and in religious ceremonies. Many of them are powerful dramas indeed. Probably without a single exception these

TORCH OF CIVILIZATION

symbolisms have their roots deep into pre-Christian practices and in the mythology of peoples who existed during the misty childhood of mankind and of knowledge. During the early years of Christianity, it was struggling for existence against socalled paganism. There was much controversy over ceremonial uses of light, for many Christians condemned them as pagan practices. But eventually they came into extensive use and the drama and pageantry of light became an important part of the settings and ceremonies of the Christian churches. They were likewise retained and refined in other ritualistic churches.

Considering the far-flung benefits of sunlight, it was logical for light to become sacred, life-giving and symbolic of divine presence. The sun, Ra, was one of the chief gods of the ancient Egyptians. The Assyrians, Babylonians, Incas, Aztecs, and more civilized ancient Greeks and pagan Romans are well-known examples of the many peoples who gave a high place to this deity. The name of an ancient Persian god, Mazda, has distinguished certain electric lightsources for several decades in the present age. From this usage this ancient name is being reborn. It is acquiring more extended meaning which may give it a permanent place in modern language. In many cases, the sun or light has been the sole object of worship as the god of all. Primitive worshipers commonly considered fire as the purest representation of heavenly fire, the origin of every living thing. The same has been true of light.

In the more primitive periods, light was not used in a symbolic sense. It was actually considered the deity. Lamps were burned in temples and buried with the dead for actual use of gods or spirits. The crude material attitude gradually

DRAMAS OF LIGHT

gave way to a finer poetic meaning as human beings became more intelligent and developed and refined their sensibilities. Thus deeper and more imaginative symbolical meanings became attached to light, oil-lamps and candles. These meanings or usages need not possess the slightest taint of superstition or of idolatry. None of us in this age needs to apologize for symbolic uses of light, color or anything else. Symbols are in use on every hand in language and elsewhere. Knowledge is the "torch" of civilization. The Statue of Liberty holds high a torch. Pioneers of civilized progress carry the torch. Most virtues, progressive movements, and humanitarian enterprises wage war with their "light" against the evils of darkness—deceit, injustice, oppression, prejudice and ignorance. Politicians, despots, and others, regardless of party, motives or practices, are self-appointed torch-bearers. Many adopt the halo of light commonly surrounding Christ and saints or the flaming radiance of the "sacred heart." Sometimes they attempt to create and to nourish new myths which reveal them as great and good gods but none overlooks entirely the powerful symbolism of light.

The Bible contains many symbolic uses of light. Christ is the "true light" and Christians are "children of light." All are battling against the evil powers of darkness. It is logical that darkness acquired symbolisms or meanings quite opposed to those of light. It represents chaos, ignorance, danger, anger and sorrow. It became the abode of evil spirits and all the evil practices and effects emanated therefrom. When Saint Paul was converted by Christ "there shined about him a great light from heaven." In Nature the impending thunderstorm approaches with a threatening and foreboding frown. Daily we see faces lighted up with knowledge, beclouded with bewilderment, frowning with displeasure and darkened with sorrow or with anger.

In the early struggles for a right to worship Christ, the intolerance of their enemies drove Christians to burrow into the ground as animals do for safety. In the catacombs of Rome, lamps have been found in niches in the walls. Obviously, these lamps were not buried with the dead, so they are assumed to have been ceremonial lamps. A great struggle was going on between pagans and Christians and their practices. Naturally the early Christians were intolerant of pagan practices and there is little doubt that there was a great controversy among themselves about continuing the long-established ceremonial uses of light. During those early centuries of Christianity there were many uses of light in this manner. For example, history records that elaborate candelabra were kept burning in the tombs of saints. However, it seems to be true that not until the beginning of the fifth century did the ceremonial use of light in the Christian church become very extensive and well established.

Any fundamental interest in the dramas of light necessarily follows the course of usage in religious settings and ceremonies. Here they became standardized and deeply rooted in modern civilization. During the Reformation in the sixteenth century the ceremonial use of light was generally abolished in the Protestant churches which arose from that upheaval in Christianity. In this branch, ceremonial lights were considered to be relics of superstition, of the Pope's authority, and even of paganism. They were retained in the Lutheran churches notwithstanding the fact that Martin Luther, a German monk, was a leader of the Reformation and was excommunicated by the Pope in 1520. In the Church of England the ceremonial uses of light have

DRAMAS OF LIGHT

been subjected to many changes through the whims of kings and queens and, one might add, some jacks or knaves. Officials of the church have been indicted and impeachment cases have been brought before the House of Commons for disobeying the edicts.

Many uses of light in religious settings and ceremonies were revived in English cathedrals after the Restoration of King Charles II after the death of Cromwell in 1658. They became widespread in England in the nineteenth century. In the present age of greater tolerance in democratic countries, only a rather dull poetic sense can fail to see the beauty of many of the symbolic uses of light. Such dullness must be heavily reinforced by deeply rooted prejudice if one is to be immune to the thrill of light and color in the impressive dramas and pageantry of the ritualistic churches. Certainly there is ample justification for employing the expressiveness of light for its impressiveness upon human beings in religious services as well as in any other civilized activities. In the realms of sentiment, most adults are still children. The excuse for growing up lies largely in the development of mature judgment, tolerance and wisdom. Certainly adulthood should not curtail too much such opportunities for stimulating the imagination and arousing fine sentiments. These are distinguishing characteristics of *human* beings.

One of the simplest, oldest and most common symbolic uses of light is the sacred or eternal lamp. There are many references in ancient Grecian and Roman literature to sacred lamps burning continually in sanctuaries and tombs and before statues of gods and earthly heroes. In ancient Rome the Vestal Virgins maintained the sacred fire in the temple of Vesta. They were very carefully selected in early childhood and were bound by vows of chastity during their period of

TORCH OF CIVILIZATION

service. Their guardianship over the god-sent fire, if enacted before us amid appropriate settings and in actual detail, would be an impressive drama of light as it must have been in reality in ancient Rome. According to the Bible, the perpetual fire which came from heaven was to be kept burning on the altar. It was holy and those whose duty was to keep it burning were guilty of a grave offense if they permitted it to be extinguished. If ordinary human hands touched it, drastic punishment was meted out. The two sons of Aaron who "offered strange fire before the Lord" were devoured "by fire from the Lord." In early centuries the seven-branched candelabrum was lighted eternally and through the centuries remained a necessary accompaniment of worship.

In Catholic and Jewish churches today the sacred or eternal lamp hangs conspicuously over the altar. Its tiny flame connects the present with divinity, with the beginning of the creed and with those who suffered martyrdom. Its symbolism is far more impressive than mere words, just as a picture or actual demonstration is more powerful than many words of description. Originally rather crude materials burned in the sacred lamps. Throughout the centuries many successive refinements have been made in the oil in use, but notwithstanding these changes the lamp retained its symbolism. Even electric light may eventually replace the flame without altering the use and meaning. I know of a case where the Catholic caretaker of a Jewish temple obtained oil from his priest for use in the Jewish eternal lamp with which he had been having trouble. The lamp burned without a flicker and the church remained standing, testimonials, perhaps, to the progress of tolerance. Where the symbolism demands that something must be actually burned,

DRAMAS OF LIGHT

electric lamps cannot replace flames. However, where light is the sole factor it should make little difference in many cases how the light is obtained. Of course, the gentle non-uniform flicker of flames is an unique quality and distinction compared with which the steady light of electric lamps is so obviously steady that they have no place where this mildly unsteady quality is important. However, it appears inevitable that electric light will continue to be adopted for more and more of the purely symbolic uses of light. Already there are many electric lamps in symbolic usage surrounding statues of Christ and saints, on Christmas trees and elsewhere. Nevertheless, flames are so thoroughly tied to the past that they will remain traditional barriers in many cases against the advance of modern methods of light production. This is quite proper where the change would unnecessarily destroy sentimental value or unduly becloud the poetic meaning.

These are a few glimpses of the historical paths along which many dramas of light have come down to us from the still more remote infancy and childhood of the human race. They could be multiplied many times and so could the details of a great variety of uses of light in these realms of ceremony and fancy. But these should suffice to awaken the interest and to increase the understanding necessary to enjoy the use of light in these realms of appeal. Without such interest and understanding the dramas of light encountered in our daily lives have little significance. In fact, many may be received with indifference because they are commonplace and others may not even be recognized. They are found on every hand and they range throughout the realm of dramatic appeal or effectiveness. They may express a variety of sentiments and aid greatly in arousing or

TORCH OF CIVILIZATION

emphasizing such feelings as joy, sorrow, tragedy, respect and piety. They may even range far beyond the boundaries of what may generally be considered to be strictly dramatic uses and purposes.

The impressiveness of dramas of light may depend largely upon light alone as a lighted Christmas tree does, or a lighthouse in the dusk, a symbolic eternal lamp, or an eternal flame in memory of someone or something. Naturally such uses are not entirely without a setting or occasion. Usually these dramas of light are aided greatly by appropriate settings and well-established customs and occasions. Common examples of such combinations of these are church ceremonies, religious festivals, and many other rituals. Sometimes the dramatic powers of light are aided still more by the accompaniment of music as in a church, or by noise which accompanies a thunderstorm at night, a torch-light parade, a fireworks display or a night battle in modern warfare. There are more delicate displays of light and color which are impressive in their appeal. These vary from the changing elusive colors of the opal and the bold glitter of diamonds to the variety of sunsets. Such may be considered to be symphonies of light and color but all may be included in the broad category of dramas of light. Let us briefly consider a few of these.

Dusk is settling over a great modern amphitheater. A colorful pageant has been completed on the large oval field providing a suitable prologue for the religious ceremony now in progress. Tiers upon tiers of human beings rise in a solid mass surrounding the central ceremony. Lights begin to come to life here and there amid the great throng. Rapidly thousands of them spring into being. In a few moments a hundred thousand lighted candles are in the hands of that devout multitude. Those great embankments of humanity are seemingly replaced by myriad living lights. These are now a vivid part of the setting. Organ music begins softly and so do the myriad voices. The music swells as the great mass of humanity joins in singing appeals and praises to the Lord. All have become more than an inspiring setting. All are a part of an overwhelmingly impressive ceremony. Injustice, oppression, brutality, war cannot live in that mass of devoted humanity. They are pushed back into the darkness where they hover among other evils, awaiting the extinguishing of the lights of religion and of civilization. To the poetic sensibilities of that great crowd the myriad candles radiate divine presence, heightening the religious feelings of everyone and aiding the myriad voices to radiate their piety and devotion more fervently. Those tiers of humanity become a vortex of deep emotions which flow outward, challenging darkness but also leaving their good imprint upon all who are a part of the impressive ceremony. The effect of the enmassed ceremonial use of light is dramatic indeed. It is enhanced enormously above and beyond the effect of words and music alone. It is a great impressive drama of living light whose effects cannot be adequately described in the limited language of words.

A contrasting drama of light—not of joy but of tragedy—may be constructed from an early edict regarding the use of light as a part of the ceremony of the excommunication of a priest. In the basement of a cathedral or monastery a group of twelve grim priests is arrayed in a circle, each holding a lighted torch. In their midst is a solemn bishop and before him stands the convicted priest. The torches illuminate the faces of the priests with severe highlights. Grotesque shadows are magnified on the walls. They move

TORCH OF CIVILIZATION

weirdly and some disappear through archways down dark passages. Amid earthly shadows it is drama of the light of truth, integrity and divinity opposed to the evils of darkness which seemingly waits to engulf the outcast. As the bishop concludes the ceremony with the sentence of excommunication, the lighted torches are hurled to the ground and trampled underfoot. Thus the drama of spoken words is greatly enhanced by the powers of lights and shadows in the setting and by their symbolic meanings for the occasion. If the excommunicated priest is eventually reinstated, a lighted torch or candle is placed in his hands as an appropriate recognition and symbol of reconciliation.

Festive lighting has been a practice since earliest times. When Saint Paul was preaching the gospel of Christ at Alexandria "there were many lights" suggesting a festive illumination. King Constantine commanded that the entire city of Constantinople be illuminated on Christmas eve. What a meager display those feeble flames would be compared with the elaborate lighting of the present age outdoors during the Christmas holidays. In 1802 England celebrated the Treaty of Amiens and this gave an opportunity for a public display of gas-lighting which had just been born. The exteriors of a series of factory buildings were ornamented with a large number of gas-lighting devices. The display on this occasion was described as "one of extraordinary splendor." It was a great novelty at the time and the populace came from far and near "to gaze at, and to admire, this wonderful display of science and art." In the midst of the present electrical age that display would appear insignificant indeed.

Each of the great modern expositions has used more light more ingeniously, and with greater variety, than its predecessor. The earlier use of electric lamps was confined chiefly to outlining buildings and architectural details. Later the lamps were concealed and buildings and ornaments were floodlighted. With present light-sources providing great control of light and producing colored light in abundance, recent expositions at night are largely expositions of light. Everywhere light is used to reveal and to enhance the architecture, to provide color and decoration and with its mobility even to augment the beauty and subtlety of flowing water. In present-day expositions light stands out as the torch of progress—of civilization. Dramas, awesome in their magnitude, silently and subtly changing, even grotesque and humorous, greet one in these worlds of today and tomorrow. And fittingly on a hilltop in New Jersey stands a high tower surmounted by a great beacon of electric lights. It shines perpetually in memory of Edison. It is a modern eternal lamp.

Naturally the theater has utilized some of the dramatic powers of light and in a lesser manner some of the symbolism of light and color. In general these uses in the theater have not risen to great heights nor have they more than touched the possibilities. There is commonly the argument that everything should be subordinated to the play and the acting. Indeed, this must generally be true but there are many occasions where the powers of light have a right to be used to their utmost in enhancing a setting or in providing atmosphere which aids the action and impending action subtly or suggestively. Many successful uses have been made of the dramatic powers of light and color. Among the best have been those where action, music, and setting are well harmonized as in the ballet, in grand opera, and in allegorical plays. Here myth, fancy, fantasy and allegory provide the basis for great opportunities in the dramatic use of light and color. Maeterlinck in his poetical drama, *The Bluebird*, appropriately made Light the faithful companion of mankind. The palace of Night into which Light does not enter, is the abode of many evils. The poet has played upon primitive or basic instincts toward light and darkness. No producer has as yet utilized modern light as effectively as the poet has utilized words. But, of course, spoken drama has been practiced for thousands of years and great control of words and experience with them were achieved long ago. Great control of light became possible only recently and dramatists of light have much to learn.

Considering its limited opportunity, the use of light in the production of silent motion-pictures has contributed relatively more to the drama of light than the theater has throughout its thousands of years of existence. The silent motion-picture had to tell its story largely through acting and action in an appropriate setting. As motion-picture production improved, light was often called upon to do much in aiding the setting and in suggesting what it could. The harshness of lighting as the miser counted his gold or of the attic home of the struggling artist may be powerfully dramatic. The concentration of light and the crowding of darkness centers or directs the attention. The light which makes darkness barely visible can do far more than mere setting to perfect a scene for dirty work. In the entire gamut of settings, actions, emotions and sentiments, light and color are handmaidens whose powers are used indifferently or skillfully according to the ability of the producer. There is enjoyment in watching the play of light and color as well as the play itself. Examples are everywhere in the dramas of stage and screen as well as in the dramas of life and of civilization.

Surrounded by a cyclorama of darkness, the steel mill at night, with its shadowy buildings and grimly busy men, with an accompaniment of clanking iron and rumbling machinery, is a dramatic spectacle of light. The flashes of light from fiery flames, the sparks from the white-hot metal, the billowing smoke and hissing steam provide a drama of light in the peaceful warfare of men against raw materials. On a battlefield this powerful drama is multiplied infinitely. Great fingers of light projected from searchlights score the heavens. Tracer bullets search their targets high in the darkness. Flares floating downward from parachutes illuminate areas with an unearthly light. The lightning flashes of guns near and far complete the powerful drama of light amid the rumblings, booms and crashes of impressive sound effects. And the drama of light lives vividly in the memory of those who survive, for we are impressed more through the sense of sight than through other senses—and it has the best memory among the senses.

War and memory bring us to the tomb of the Unknown Soldier—one beautiful thought and achievement arising out of the World War. Politicians who have driven countries to war, kings and queens who have sent armies to die on battlefields, and good and bad leaders of armies have been more than amply applauded in history and remembered by monuments but the common soldier soon entered oblivion. In a tomb in the capitals of several countries rests an Unknown Soldier. In one capital the tomb is a plain cubicle of severe lines. The soldier lies under a dark marble slab directly underneath a rectangular orifice in the flat roof. Through it the sun shines and the blue sky is visible. At night the stars keep their vigil. And all the time gas flames silently emit their eternal light at the top of large pipes which flank the grave. Here is a drama of light perpetuating the memory of those who died while civilization was blacked out temporarily and in the grip of the evils of darkness.

For relaxation we may turn to Nature toward the end of the day. Clouds may drift lazily in a serene sky as the sun approaches the horizon. As it sinks deeper into the haze, its color changes from yellow to orange and then to red. The clouds cut the light into great streamers. As the sun sinks to the horizon the tips of clouds are tinged with red. Sky-light and sunlight mixed in the shadows become delicate tints of purple—pink, lilac, lavender and mauve. The sun sets blood-red. The sky is painted with diluted colors of the spectrum—pink near the horizon, then orange, yellow and blue-green until beyond the zenith and toward the east its natural blue darkens. Lights, colors and shadows change gradually as a powerful symphony of light as mobile as music. The sun disappears below the horizon and twilight begins to fall. On tomorrow evening the sunset will be different as it has been different on all the countless evenings throughout the ages. This great drama of light varies throughout the entire gamut of infinite possibilities.

Twilight deepens and the colors intensify, then fade. The more powerful stars appear from behind the darkening veil of sky. Nature's noises quiet down. Far away the lights of civilization twinkle in increasing numbers. Only a faint flush of the sky remains. The great canopy of darkness overhead is pierced with many pin-holes of light. Away to the north sometimes the Aurora Borealis appears. Diaphanous curtains may hang in the sky and move as if disturbed by a gentle breeze. Great streamers may shoot across the sky and disappear. This is a dreamy drama of light.

The last lingering flush of the sky disappears and Night rules. But the stars are there to assure us that Nature is orderly even though civilization may be temporarily disordered. We contemplate the drama of light overhead and our imagination carries us far off into the realm where other universes are in the making, where numberless stars are being born. In this infinity of interstellar space where light is literally, as well as fancifully, the music of the spheres, worlds are dying and other worlds are being born. A brilliant trailing flash, like a tracer bullet, heralds an erratic traveler entering our earth's atmosphere. The meteor vanishes in the fires of friction, its ashes mingling with the cosmic dust. But its atoms continue their eternal journey sometimes in inert matter, sometimes in living things. And perhaps eons hence they may be drawn into a giant nebula to be born a part of another star in a timeless universe. The great drama of light overhead had no conceivable beginning and for us will have no end.

III. SWIFT AND SILENT LIGHT

OVER THE RADIO comes the voice of a king abdicating his throne. Four thousand miles away we hear each word only a fiftieth of a second after his companions do. The radio message travels with the tremendous speed of light. Earthly distances are shrunk into insignificance and time is also telescoped. We tune in another station and hear orders going forth to a Canadian Mountie far off in the Barren Lands near the Arctic Circle. News also goes with the speed of light to prospectors far beyond or to isolated explorers ten thousand miles away in the icy isolation of the Antarctic. We need only turn a knob to hear a voice formally opening a great Exposition of many other modern miracles of science. We may hear a click as light from the North Star, Polaris—446 million million miles away—operates a switch which converts the exposition into a fairyland of man-made light. Tuning in other stations we may hear the minute explosions of atoms in a far-off laboratory, dedicated to the method of modern science; or we may hear the ominous crashes of distant cannon, modern relics of the method of the Stone Age. For us our radio receiving-set enormously extends our sense of hearing and television adds its extension to our sense of sight.

The marvels of radio still thrill us and, quite properly, because they are achievements of ours—of human beings. We are proud of them and of the great new powers they give to our senses, to our activities and to our ambitions. But these

SWIFT AND SILENT LIGHT

radio sending- and receiving-sets are not unique. Everything around us, from minute atoms nearby to enormous stars far off, are Nature's radio stations sending forth the same kind of electromagnetic energy—swift and silent—as man-made radio stations. Our complex visual sense, of which our eyes are a part, is an astonishing example of Nature's receiving-sets. In the long course of evolution it has been tuned to receive a certain range of wavelengths of radiant energy just as the radio receiving-set in our homes may be tuned by us. Our receiving-sets of sight are selective to radiant energy of certain wavelengths or frequencies just as our man-made receiving-sets are. This is more than an analogy. The messengers in both cases are fundamentally identical in character and obey the same general laws.

As we commonly consider it, light is both a cause and an effect. We look at a tungsten-filament lamp and say it emits light. As a matter of fact that lamp merely emits radiant energy of many wavelengths or frequencies. Whether it produces the sensation of brightness or accomplishes other results depends upon the receivers. Our visual sense is sensitive only to a limited range of wavelengths of this energy. Only when radiant energy of proper wavelengths reaches the retina at the rear of the eye do we experience the sensation of brightness. The sensitivity of the retina is very important. Here is where the selectivity of the visual sense really takes place. In other words, the retina is sensitive to—tuned to—radiant energy of a narrow range of wavelengths. Energy of those wavelengths must reach the sensitive retina, and certain effects must be transmitted to the brain, before we experience the sensation of brightness. Only then does the source of radiant energy, such as a tungsten lamp, become a light-source. That part of the energy which appears as light, the essential partner of sight, may be properly termed, visible energy. I shall loosely term it light, as is commonly done for convenience.

As human beings, our primary interest in light is in making things visible to us. In order to understand this we need not know much about light itself or how radiant energy is produced. It is more important to go back in our imagination to the early beginnings of life on earth. Evolution is the magic result of the perpetual process or tendency for living things to adapt themselves to their surroundings and to utilize the things in the environment which surrounds them. As the environment changes there is need and opportunity for changes in the living things. If the former changes are not too great or too rapid, evolution takes place for generations through adaptation and the survival of the fittest of each generation.

Let us imagine a time, perhaps more than a billion years ago, when the only living things on earth were the simplest kind of living organisms. These had no separated senses or organs. We need not speculate upon how life began or pursue the devious and complex courses of evolution throughout the eons of time. It is sufficient to realize that there are countless evidences and many examples of the processes of evolution through adaptation to suitably guide our imagination. The simplest forms of life gradually led to more and more complex forms. Organs began to develop—mouth, stomach, lungs—to handle food and fuel. Senses began to develop to guard against and to utilize things in the environment.

With one exception all our senses developed on the basic principle of contact. Touch, taste and smell depend upon contact with the object or with a material part of it. Obviously this limits the range of those senses. The sense of

As art outranked science 2000 years ago, Greco-Roman ornamentation dominated the feeble flames of this Pompeian lamp.

SWIFT AND SILENT LIGHT

hearing has a greater range, but it still depends upon contact with the object through vibrations of a material medium such as air. A distant whistle sets up vibrations of certain wavelengths or frequencies in the air. These vibrations travel in all directions until they reach our ears. They cause a mechanism in our ear to vibrate sympathetically and we hear a sound characteristic of the wavelength and waveform of the vibrations. Thus, the range of our sense of hearing also depends upon a material connection.

Vibrations which we hear as sounds cannot pass through empty space, whether it is the vacuum of a lamp bulb or that between us and the stars. But there are no such limitations on radiant energy such as light and radio waves. All the time that living things on earth were evolving organs and senses in their perpetual adaptation and refinement, the sun was emitting a flood of radiant energy upon the earth. The moon and the planets reflect it, thereby becoming visible. Stars emit this energy which can travel through empty space not occupied by a material medium such as we know as matter. Fire emits light and so do all sufficiently hot bodies and many sources developed by modern science.

The radiant energy from the sun travels in straight lines and is more or less reflected or transmitted by objects and all material media. Obviously, if a sense could be developed to utilize this energy, the living thing possessing this sense would have light for seeing things at a distance without the usual material connection. If an organ could be developed so that patterns of energy reflected from objects and scenes could be reproduced with fidelity and focused upon a properly sensitive part of the sense-organ, those objects and scenes could be seen. Through the long slow process of evolution and adaptation, the optical system of our eyes developed so as to focus the patterns of energy upon the retina at the back part of each eye. The retina may be likened to a telephone exchange. It consists of tiny nerve-endings which are the sensitive receivers. There are about 130 million of these tiny receivers or "telephone" connections in the retina of each human eye. The grand scale of Nature's works is emphasized by the fact that there are only 40 million telephones in man's entire artificial world at the present time. The retina, through a chemical reaction to the radiant energy in each minute section of the pattern or picture, provides the first step in the making of a final record on our consciousness. The receivers are at the ends of nerve fibers which are bundled into a cable—the optic nerve—leading from each eye to the brain. The chemical changes which take place in the retina are altered in some way into electric impulses or signals which are transmitted by the optic nerves to the brain centers. They then become sensations and we see the objects or scene as a pattern of brightnesses and colors.

In the realm of Nature there are many wonders which eclipse the achievements of mankind. But Nature has had almost infinite time compared with the very brief period during which man has been at work learning to understand and trying to apply what he has learned. In fact, Nature is the fundamental textbook for mankind. It contains many illustrations which man may copy but it is largely filled with hidden facts and laws concealed from our unaided senses. As rapidly as they are discovered they may be put to work in an infinite variety of combinations. In the long process of evolution in countless directions, many kinds of eyes were developed. We learn from these that human eyes are superb for our use. The visual sense in lowlier forms of living things is merely a brightness sense; that is, it detects brightness, not form. Such a visual sense does not possess the refinement of eyes with adjustable lenses for focusing images of objects upon a sensitive surface such as the retina. Many living things, such as insects, have compound eyes consisting of a great number of stationary eyes packed close together. These are arranged so the insect can see throughout a large solid angle. Apparently the crude and confusing images suffice for the relatively crude needs of the insect. About every variation that we may imagine is represented in the uncounted kinds of eyes and visual senses in existence. Ingenuity in adaptation to environment and to need is very impressive and extensive.

Higher forms of life eventually evolved two single movable eyes. This does not necessarily mean that all two-eyed animals enjoy the advantages of binocular vision. In many cases each eye is used more or less independently and alone. However, human eyes are movable in their sockets and may be focused accurately upon objects throughout a great range of distances. They move together and provide binocular vision which gives depth to a scene. Human beings are provided with a relatively long infancy and early childhood during which to perfect their use of their endowments. During that period we learn how to use our eyes and particularly to see things out where they are instead of on the retina where their images are focused. Thus, through early years of learning we actually make a marvelous contribution to the abilities of our visual sense.

Having acquired the sense of sight and the ability to use it, we depend upon it far more than upon any other sense to read Nature's textbook. We use it to study the visual sense itself and to study its partner, light. Such studies lead us far afield but we return with knowledge to make better use of

TORCH OF CIVILIZATION

light and even to make better light to aid our sense of sight. This is an illustration of the spiral progress in any field of knowledge and invention. We use sight to learn more about light, in order to invent more things to aid sight, in order to learn more about light—and so on perhaps to the end of the unknown and the uninvented. This is my excuse, if any is needed, for a few glimpses into the hidden recesses of light.

Notwithstanding the overwhelming importance of light in the lives of human beings, it remained a mystery until the method of modern science began to probe below the surface a few centuries ago. Of course, much was already known of its behavior from ordinary observation and simple experiments. Obviously it traveled in straight lines. Certain laws of reflection, refraction and diffusion had been unraveled many centuries before. However, Roemer in 1675 was the first to discover that it takes time for light to travel through space. He determined its speed approximately by observations of the moons of Jupiter as they appeared and disappeared in their regular revolutions around that planet. Light itself remained almost a complete mystery until the great Newton first took it apart in 1666. He placed a glass prism near a slit in a window shade and dispersed light into its various wavelengths. Thus he produced what is termed, the spectrum, in which the energy of different wavelengths is seen by us as different colors. He saw only the visible spectrum with its colors arranged in order: violet, blue, green, yellow, orange and red. Actually more than one hundred different colors may be distinguished in the visible spectrum of sunlight.

Until about 1800 it was not known that invisible radiant energy accompanied visible energy emitted by the sun and other sources. Newton when he viewed the visible spectrum more than a century before, saw the principal colors arranged as in the rainbow. He did not know that there was invisible radiant energy beyond the violet and beyond the red. Many simple means are now available for detecting and measuring ultraviolet and infrared energy as those two parts of the spectrum of radiant energy are termed. Here again we see that our sense of sight is a selective receiver. It utilizes only a narrow band of wavelengths of the total spectrum of radiant energy. This also illustrates the primary problem in producing efficient artificial light-sources. Obviously the aim is to have the source emit as much visible energy as possible accompanied by as little invisible energy as possible. The efficiency of a light-source is determined by the amount of light produced by the total energy emitted by, or supplied to, the light-source. The rate at which light is emitted by a light-source is measured in lumens. The rate at which energy is supplied to the light-source is measured in watts. Therefore, the luminous efficiency of a light-source is measured in lumens per watt.

When sunlight is dispersed into energy of various wavelengths—its spectrum—by means of a prism or other suitable means, it is found to supply most abundantly the radiant energy to which our visual sense is most sensitive. There is some invisible ultraviolet energy which kills germs, prevents rickets, and is important in other ways. There is also some invisible infrared energy which helps to heat the earth but much of this is strained out, by the water-vapor in the atmosphere, before it reaches the earth's surface. The human visual sense evolved throughout eons of time to utilize best that part of the sun's energy which is most abundant and also the most nearly constant part of the entire solar spectrum. This is not surprising, for evolution is the result of the tendency to adapt, as perfectly as practicable, to the environment and to the need.

One might wonder why human eyes are not sensitive to the sun's energy throughout the entire spectrum or entire range of wavelengths. The explanation is very simple. The optical system of the eye is equivalent to a simple lens. The power of such a lens—the focal length—varies with the wavelength of light or radiant energy. It cannot accurately focus energy of various wavelengths on the retina at the same time. Too great a range of wavelengths would result in a fuzzy image. Therefore, the range of wavelengths to which our visual sense is sensitive had to be limited if a simple optical system for the eye were to be satisfactory. This aspect of the selectivity of the visual sense is still another striking example of adaptation during the process of evolution of living things and their organs and senses.

Extensive researches dealing with eyesight and our ability to see various objects under a variety of conditions, reveal other powerful evidence of adaptation through the slow but certain processes of evolution. It has been proved that our sense of sight is most sensitive and capable under the levels of brightness outdoors in the daytime. It is to be expected that in evolving a visual sense it would become best fitted for the kind of light and even the quantity of light outdoors. However, the significance of this fact has long been generally ignored by those interested in eyesight and seeing. For many years the logic of adaptation has impressed me as a sound basic philosophy. To me this has been a basic force for many years in planning and prosecuting researches which have established the importance of abundant light and how to use it best. Translated into our artificial indoor world the results indicate the desirability of levels of brightness comparable to those outdoors. The amount of light falling on the earth's surface outdoors in the daytime is hundreds and even thousands of times that falling upon our desks and other work-places indoors. Thus to the obvious importance of light is added the unobvious importance of abundant light which was present during the eons of evolution of human beings, their eyes and visual sense.

Outdoors a white surface appears approximately white under daylight illumination. Through eons of adaptation of our visual sense outdoors, daylight became colorless or nearly so. Thus average daylight has become approximately neutral, favoring no colors, and naturally we accept it as a basis for our appraisal of colors. It has also acquired other basic characteristics. The lighting outdoors has left its imprint upon our faces as other factors have. Our nose is turned downward so we may not be threatened with drowning in a rainstorm. If the human race walked on its hands for ages the nose would probably be turned upside down eventually in the long course of survival of the fittest. The eyes are in sockets for protection from physical injury as well as for mechanical operation. The eyebrows and forehead shield the eyes somewhat from the vast expanse of bright sky. In many directions we find evidences of adaptation to outdoor light, brightnesses, lighting and seeing conditions. These, added to countless other details of living things, have established the great principles of evolution and of adaptation to environment. They reveal the important fact that human beings and their organs and senses have followed the same course as other living things and are the result of natural environment outdoors. To accept this general fact is to accept the facts that Nature's light, lighting and abundant light should be our guides for the use of artificial light in our artificial world of civilization.

Our knowledge of light itself, as is true of other complex phenomena whose details are deeply hidden from our senses, is a series of great contributions of geniuses in science superposed along the course of a continual growth of knowledge of details. After our modern age of science began a few centuries ago, Newton in about 1666 was the first great genius to apply himself to an intimate study of light. He first theorized that light was a substance of very fine particles emitted by the sun and other light-sources. About the same time Huygens developed the idea that light was energy emitted as a succession of waves somewhat analogous to the waves seen on water. For a long time there was a controversy between adherents of the two theories but evidence continued to come to the support of the wave theory more and more. In about 1875 Maxwell assembled all the available facts into a mathematical generalization which included not only light but all other radiant energy regardless of wavelength. In fact, the mathematical picture which he constructed anticipated radiant energy of wavelengths as yet undiscovered such as radio waves and X-rays. These were destined to be discovered and put to use before the century came to an end. Then Planck developed the quantum theory in which light and radiant energy of other wavelengths were assumed to be emitted in discrete entities or bundles of energy. Many others have made valuable contributions and the present picture is a combination in which radiant energy consisting of discrete quanta, or bundles of energy, appears to travel in accordance with the wave theory and to act as though it possessed wavelengths and frequencies.

SWIFT AND SILENT LIGHT

We are not concerned here with more than brief glimpses into the inner realms of light. Apparently radiant energy differs from anything we are familiar with. It travels through what we consider to be empty space devoid of matter in the common sense. In order to form a conception of energy traveling in waves it appeared necessary to invent a peculiar medium which was termed, the ether. This was assumed to fill all space not occupied by what we ordinarily consider as matter or material substance. It was even assumed to pervade all matter. Thus a perfect vacuum as well as stellar space was assumed to be filled with this socalled ether in order that light and other radiant energy might travel through them. Notwithstanding many ingenious experiments, no one as yet has been able conclusively to prove the existence or absence of the socalled ether. Nevertheless, this does not alter the facts known about light. It merely leaves another of many annoying unknowns for scientists to ponder over and to explore if possible.

If we had to depend solely upon our everyday observations we would conclude that light traveled instantaneously. As we toss a ball or drop a stone we see that it takes time for these objects to travel from one place to another. The difference is merely one of magnitude. Things travel fast or slow in relation to our own speed or to speeds we are familiar with. So it is with size. An atom is very small and the earth is very large compared with us and with most things we deal with. Sound seems to travel fairly fast because the waves travel about 1100 feet per second in air. When we see the steam rise from a distant whistle and hear the sound a few seconds later we are conscious that it comes to us not instantaneously but with a finite speed. We can make no such simple experiments with light to demonstrate that it travels with a finite speed. Its speed appears infinite to us in our daily lives, still it is very slow when measured by distances out in the enormous universe of heavenly bodies. It travels to us from the sun in eight minutes. When an eclipse of the sun takes place, the sun continues to shine for us for eight minutes after the black-out actually takes place.

Sirius, our nearest star, is 500,000 times farther away from us than the sun is. It takes nine years for light to reach us from that star. It takes light seventy-six years to reach us from Polaris. But these are very small distances in the universe and even still smaller compared with the distance to the boundaries of celestial space as they are known at the present time. Light travels about 186,300 miles in a second or 5.87 million million miles in a year. The latter is termed a light-year and is a common measure of distance in modern astronomy. Distances to known nebulae and star clusters far out in space are measured in thousands of light-years. Distances spanned by eyesight aided by telescopes and photography are already measured in millions of light-years. Some idea of these distances may be obtained from the ticking of the second-hand of a clock. It would tick a million million times in 32,000 years—a tick for each year back to the Stone Age. Light travels a million million miles in two months.

The speed of light is more than a thrilling fact to us. It is the most prominent fundamental factor in our present knowledge of the scheme of the physical universe. The speed of light is the maximum speed attainable by anything which possesses mass or the equivalent of mass. Incidentally the mass of an object is that factor which, when pulled by the earth's force of gravitation, makes the object appear to

SWIFT AND SILENT LIGHT

have weight. The force of gravitation depends upon the distance from the center of the earth. Therefore, the weight of an object is not the same at various places on earth. However, the mass remains constant—provided the object is stationary. Actually the mass of any object increases with its velocity and becomes *infinite* at the speed of light. In other ways the speed of light is intimately interwoven into the mathematical equations representing great natural laws which modern science has discovered and will continue to discover. Thus the speed of light is seen to be extremely important in the entire realm of physics and the physical world.

Just as light is overwhelmingly important to all living things on earth, it, or rather the radiant energy which it represents, plays a stellar role throughout the physical universe. In fact, as we study the constitution of matter by penetrating deeper and deeper into the miniature universes which we term atoms, matter apparently gives way to energy. In other words, the latest picture of atoms and, therefore, of matter, is that each atom is a systematic arrangement of energy which behaves like mass or matter. Certainly the ultimate source of radiant energy such as light is from within the atom. Thus light and radiant energy associated with it may be considered the life-blood of matter throughout the entire universe, from within the atom to beyond the stars. And the speed of light is a fundamental constant or factor in the entire plan of the creation.

Indeed, light is the torch of creation. Light-years and the speed of light reveal the limits of distance and time in the universe to be inconceivable. Our earth becomes merely a mote of dust and our lifetime only a tick of the cosmic clock. Modern civilized human beings learn these crushing facts and still are not crushed by them. Why? Because our earth, our history, our civilization, our lives comprise the universe of human beings even though our minds and our explorations know no bounds. The things we learn anywhere have only one ultimate practical end—in the service of mankind. No explorations have led science further into the universe or deeper into the atom than studies of light. No scientific expeditions have brought back greater additions to knowledge. No applications of knowledge have done more for civilization than the production and use of light. This swift and silent messenger brings to us most of our knowledge in all our pursuits—even in the pursuit of light itself.

IV. MANKIND COMES INDOORS

A GREAT EUROPEAN capital lies under the pall of a black-out. Stone-Age brutality has temporarily extinguished the torch of civilization. Artificial light, the life-blood of civilized activities, has been reduced to a mere trickle outdoors. Traffic gropes in sudden unfamiliar blindness. Human beings creep and stumble, and even die, in their helplessness. In effect the black-out has robbed them of sight. Those civilized human beings had long taken artificial light for granted, as most of us have. Immersed in the enjoyment of the independence which it has bestowed upon us, we become unconscious of its beneficence. In the last century artificial light extended the civilized day to the full limit of twenty-four hours. Most of us forget, most of the time, that without modern artificial light, activities are largely bounded by sunrise and sunset as they were—and still are—for primitive human beings. Instead, we work, play and travel as independent of daylight as we choose. Only when the light fails temporarily do we realize that artificial light is literally the life-blood of modern civilization.

We take a trip into the wilds, back to Nature. Long before the sun sets, we make our camp. As twilight falls we sit by the campfire. Our activities are almost as restricted as those of primitive beings. We go to sleep and awaken with the dawn. Temporarily we have become slaves of Nature. Under those conditions we realize how far civilization has traveled on various roads toward independence. In our mind's eye

TORCH OF CIVILIZATION

we see primitive beings, feasting or starving according to Nature's bounty, and sweltering or shivering according to the weather. When night fell they sought shelter with the animal instinct of self-preservation. Thus the natural cave and later the crude artificial shelter were adopted for protection from obvious things—wind, rain, cold and animal enemies. By coming indoors, into shelters however crude, these early beings made the first important declaration of independence from Nature.

Primitive beings came indoors for obvious reasons, and, as far as they were concerned, they left outdoors only that which was obvious to their senses. They knew nothing beyond the horizon of the obvious. They let light indoors in order to see, but they had no idea how much light they left outdoors. They left outdoors abundant light and were totally unaware of the ultraviolet and infrared energy because it was invisible. They left natural lighting outdoors and had indoors the accidental lighting from a hole in the wall. Eventually while indoors they lived largely by the light from the fire on the floor or hearth. As ages passed the light was furnished by crude flames located wherever convenient. This artificial light differed greatly from daylight. It was extremely feeble and quite deficient compared with sunlight. And the restricted space indoors became a world of near-vision. The comparative safety provided leisure to develop skill with the hands. Unnatural burdens were placed upon the eyes. As a consequence, primitive beings had exchanged the natural benefits of the outdoors for the obvious safety, comfort and leisure of the indoors. But this exchange involved great changes in light and lighting and in the use of the eyes.

Guided by primitive practices of the present and historical

Lard oil in this Betty lamp and tallow in candles supplied the torches of the pioneering civilization of Colonial America.

periods and by relics of crude light-sources and means of making fire, our imagination can penetrate the fog of prehistoric times. Today in the Northern icy wastes, Eskimos sit in their stone huts or igloos by the feeble smoking flames of sputtering blubber. Other primitive families may still be using a burning fish held in a split stick. In relatively recent times natives of the Orkney Islands used the fat carcass of the stormy petrel for a torch by placing a wick in its mouth. Somewhere in the tropical jungles natives may still imprison fireflies in a perforated gourd or other suitable receptacle. Fireflies in the West Indies and elsewhere emit a continuous glow and a few of these little lighting-plants are better than nothing.

The simplest observations of burning wood reveal the fact that some kinds or parts burn better and give more light than others. Resinous knots of pine and some other woods are still in use today by primitive beings and through necessity even by civilized persons far from civilization. In the hinterlands of Europe and Asia burning splinters of wood and sputtering wicks in crude grease are probably furnishing light tonight as they did a century ago. These are some of numerous examples of the use of Nature's raw materials. It is reasonable to suppose that their use extends backward a very long way toward those earliest human beings who first used fire for artificial light. These more or less obvious ways of providing light are crude compared with candles of the past thousand years and even with the oil-lamps of earlier historical periods. However, those apparently crude primitive light-sources in which natural raw materials were used are great advances in the progress of mankind.

It is likely that animal instinct led human beings into caves and other natural shelters long before they had advanced

TORCH OF CIVILIZATION

far enough to use fire. It may be difficult to visualize a human being without sufficient intelligence and initiative to fashion tools and to use them. The monkey is skillful with its hands but it uses only the raw materials of Nature. It does not fashion tools or use them. An enormous period must have elapsed before even the crudest artificial shelter replaced the natural shelters in which primitive human beings were driven by animal instincts. When they learned to use fire is solely a matter of conjecture. Probably it was early in the beginnings of the tool-using era of the human race. It may well be considered the beginning of civilization.

We may be certain that Nature first introduced early human beings to fire, long before they acquired the skill to make it. Lightning had shattered trees and set fire to them long before the earth was inhabited by early human beings. This awesome electrical phenomenon with its nerve-shattering sound effects was a common one over much of the surface of the earth. Volcanoes were other natural sources of fire in a few places. But wherever the early human beings obtained their fire, we may be certain that they were awed by it. After they became familiar with its usefulness in lighting, heating, cooking and signaling, we may be certain that these benefits enhanced its powers in religious ceremonies.

Fire became a treasure to be maintained because it was difficult to rekindle. We may readily imagine the careful banking of the fire by ashes which preserved the glowing embers for a long time. And we need not stretch our imagination to see natives borrowing fire from each other. The importance of fire and the difficulty of rekindling it doubtless led to the maintenance of a public fire burning continuously. Here primitive beings could come for embers with which to kindle their own fires. Naturally around the public fire crude civil, political and religious affairs were born. Certainly many quaint customs developed in the course of thousands of years. Thus we are able better to understand the importance of the public fire and of the ceremonies associated with it even during the heights of Greek and Roman civilizations.

With matches as common as they are now, perhaps most persons never give a thought to the primitive art of making fire unless reminded by the curriculum or skill of the Boy Scout. Twirling a stick between the hands or by means of a string bow is a familiar stunt. The friction at the end of the stick as it rubs a hole in a dry piece of wood transforms the mechanical energy into heat. Dry inflammable material soon begins to smolder and by supplying more oxygen by blowing upon the feeble embers, and judiciously adding material which readily burns, this high achievement of primitive beings is performed in an era flooded with matches.

Making fire by friction was a great achievement in the early periods of mankind. Probably it was widely used but there were other methods. Far back in the Stone Age primitive beings—savages still dominated by animal instincts—chipped stones into somewhat better shapes for crude tools. Obviously they eventually selected the harder stones such as flints, an impure variety of quartz. In the chipping process, sparks flew. Certainly it was observed that a rich enough spark would ignite certain dry powdered or shredded materials. This was largely a hit-or-miss method but it accomplished the result. It was far removed from the flint and steel of a century ago because the age of steel was still many thousands of years distant in the future.

Natural specimens of iron must have been found at times and treasured for their magic when struck with a flint. Certain Eskimo tribes have been found to make fire by striking a piece of quartz against a crystal of iron pyrites. This yellow sulphide of iron is most generally known as fool's gold owing to its yellow metallic luster. Alaskan and Aleutian tribes are known to have employed two pieces of quartz covered with native sulphur. When these are skillfully struck together, excellent sparks are obtained. Thus it is seen that materials are found abundantly in Nature for crude means of making fire. At first discoveries resulted from experience and later by the method of cut and try. These were the only means of gaining knowledge during early human history and are even now where modern scientific method is not in use. All the early methods of making fire used the unrefined raw materials of Nature, whether it was raw flint that made the spark or raw human energy which rubbed wood upon wood.

From these glimpses we gain some idea of the crudity of the early life of the human race. It bears few of the earmarks of our present ways of living but even these will appear crude when viewed from the distant future. Considering the enormous achievements of modern science, which has been in operation only a few centuries, human progress is bound to be overwhelmingly greater in the next thousand years than it has been in the past million years. Achievements in the next million years are inconceivable. They will only be limited by the laws of Nature and their applications. Viewed from either of those distant futures, our present civilization will appear barely removed from that of primitive beings which we have been discussing. Long before that time, science will have revealed how far we may depart from natural environment without paying severe penalties. Knowledge of what we have left outdoors will be fully known and its fundamental importance will be generally recognized.

MANKIND COMES INDOORS

In the production and use of artificial light, I have long advocated using Nature's textbook as a fundamental guide. And very slowly but irresistibly we are moving toward natural light and lighting in the production and use of artificial light. We are adding many refinements and many new uses because our artificial world makes these possible and desirable. But fundamentally as Nature's beings we cannot expect to be emancipated from the slavery of her basic environmental factors excepting through the slow processes of adaptation and evolution. A million years from now human beings will be more independent of Nature, but fundamental natural requirements in air, water, food, light and radiant energy are not likely to have changed appreciably.

We may now be prepared to appreciate the great changes indoors in the availability of light, lighting, ultraviolet and infrared energy to which human beings were exposed outdoors. Of course, until relatively recently mankind lived and worked outdoors much of the time and homes were largely shelters and places to sleep. But in the last century or two there has been an enormous trend toward the indoors in many civilized activities. As we go about our work or through our homes, flipping switches here and there to obtain light, most of us forget our great dependence upon artificial light. Even the sciences and professions dealing with health and hygiene have almost entirely ignored the great fundamental differences in the light, lighting and visual tasks of our artificial world compared with those of outdoors.

On those rare occasions when a mishap of wind, flood, man or machine temporarily shuts off the electricity from our homes, we may light a candle. How feeble the flickering flame is! Indeed, we have reverted to what seems to us a

TORCH OF CIVILIZATION

remote primitive period. We are more than inconvenienced. We are relatively helpless and are depressed at the thought of enforced inactivity. We dread the coming hours and try to think of some place to go—where there is lighting that we are used to. Our dependence upon modern artificial lighting is strikingly demonstrated to us, but few of us learn the important lessons. Few persons consciously realize how completely our artificial world and our civilized activities have been developed by and for seeing. From this experience let us learn some of the important lessons.

If the candle is an average one, about an inch in diameter, its light approximates that of the standard candle used as a basic unit for measurements of light and of lighting. The light from this candle flame, as from all sources, decreases as the distance increases, actually as the square of the distance. The maximum level of illumination on a surface at a horizontal distance of one foot from the flame is one *foot-candle*. This has been adopted as the unit of illumination. It is arbitrary, as all units of measurement are, such as the foot, quart or pound; but it is no more mysterious than these are. Through everyday usage we become familiar with such units of measurement and use them freely. This is just as true of the units used to measure light and lighting. And to understand light as the torch of civilization, we must master some of the simple units such as candlepower and footcandles.

In our home temporarily without electric service, how dingy the room appears in the light of the candle. Actually the surrounding walls and ceiling receive little light. At a distance of one foot, the illumination is one footcandle and at ten feet it has dropped to one hundredth of a footcandle, about the illumination measured under average moonlight conditions. The illumination varies inversely as the square of the distance from the candle flame or other light-source. If we should place a mirror on one side of the candle flame, we turn some of the light backward toward and past the source. We now see two candles, one being the image in the mirror. Now if we measure the illumination on a page of a book, held about a foot away from the burning candle on the side opposite the mirror, we may find two footcandles instead of one. It surprises most persons to learn that in this present age of electric light, most of the severe critical tasks of seeing in the indoor world are performed under a few footcandles of illumination. And besides light on the task we need light on the surroundings. In other words, lighting is also important. The modern room with the single burning candle demonstrates these important aspects of light and lighting.

Now, let us apply this unit of illumination to sunlight and skylight which primitive man, and the civilization which followed, left outdoors. On a clear day in midsummer the level of illumination at the earth's surface is commonly above 9000 footcandles. On average days about 80 percent of this comes directly from the sun and 20 percent from the sky. Skylight is merely sunlight scattered by the molecules of air and the particles of dust, water and other matter in the atmosphere. If there were no atmosphere or if it did not scatter light, the sun would shine in the midst of a black sky. The shadows would be black and harsh. We would have an abundance of light but not the natural lighting we are adapted to and used to. Thus the basic principle of natural lighting is direct light from the sun and diffused light from the sky.

This brings us to the distribution of brightness outdoors.

The areas of grass, woods, growing crops and barren earth reflect only a few percent of the light falling upon them. They are far less bright than the sky. In the distance toward the horizon the haze usually increases the brightness. As our eyes sweep from the foreground to the distant horizon, then upward to clouds and sky, the brightness is generally increasing. Rooms which appear natural indoors have bright ceilings, less bright walls and still darker furniture, floors and floor-coverings. Any general departure is novel because it is unnatural. Our fundamental desires and practices in decoration and furnishing rooms indoors have their roots in the natural landscapes outdoors. The condition is different outdoors in winter when the earth is covered with snow, but this is unusual over the earth's surface. It was unusual where life generally evolved on earth. It was unusual where the human race evolved. It is still unusual to us even in temperate zones, for we spend relatively little time outdoors in midwinter.

Now let us take some more intimate glimpses of the sky. This scattered light acts quite similarly to that of a piece of tissue paper held between our eyes and the sun. The paper scatters light toward us and also away from us, back toward the sun and out into space. The atmosphere does likewise. As we travel upward on a mountain or in an airplane, we are leaving more and more of the atmosphere below us. We are actually climbing through the sky and leaving more and more of it below us. At 25,000 feet I have measured nearly 10,000 footcandles on a clear day when there were only 9000 footcandles at the earth's surface. The difference represents the loss of light scattered outward, not earthward, by the large portion of the atmosphere below 25,000 feet. At that altitude the sky is a very dark blue and some stars may be visible. Only four percent of the total light which I measured at that altitude came from the sky. The shadows, which are illuminated by skylight, were nearly black. At high altitudes there is an appearance of harshness or rawness which is entirely due to light and lighting.

The blue of the sky is due to selective scattering of sunlight of different wavelengths. The blue component in sunlight is the sensation caused by visible energy of the shortest wavelengths. These wavelengths are comparable in size to the fine particles of air and other things in the atmosphere. These short wavelengths are obstructed more by the fine particles encountered in the atmosphere than the energy of longer wavelengths such as yellow, orange and red. The result is similar to that of a man and a small boy walking in a field of pumpkins. The long legs of the man have less difficulty than the short legs of the boy. The man walks in a fairly straight line but the boy zigzags, is "scattered" more. In photographing distant landscapes a yellow or orange filter is used to eliminate the bluish light of the haze. Thus much of the scattered light or haze is eliminated from the picture. In aerial photography, red filters are used for even better results. Infrared energy is of still longer wavelengths than red light and is scattered very little by the atmosphere. Our eyes are not sensitive to infrared energy, but photographic emulsions are made sensitive to this energy. With such films and filters, which transmit infrared energy and little or no light, mountains two hundred miles away appear in aerial photographs very clear-cut owing to the absence of haze.

If we cut a hole one inch square in a drawn window shade, a patch of blue sky seen through it emits about as much light as one or two candles. Thus we conclude correctly that the brightness of the sky is one or two candles per square inch. A hazy sky is brighter than a blue sky and has a brightness of several candles per square inch. A cloud reflects about as much light as snow. The sunlit surface of a cloud has a brightness of about 20 candles per square inch. These are brightnesses which we are accustomed to and under proper artificial lighting conditions, brightnesses within the range of sky brightnesses should not be harmful indoors in our artificial surroundings. These are fundamentals which, when properly considered, guide us in the production of light-sources, in the design of lighting fixtures and in the distribution of brightness in our indoor surroundings. Nature's textbook reveals what we are adapted to and indicates what is basically best for us. The difficulties arise in ascertaining these facts and particularly in applying them in our artificial world.

Skylight varies considerably in color from deep blue to a bluish white. Clouds reflect or transmit sunlight without appreciably altering its color. Therefore, the light from the sky may range from blue skylight on a cloudless day to a mixture of this with the white light from the sun on a cloudy day. Although skylight is quite variable in color and spectral character as it reaches the earth's surface, it does have a definite known range. This is taken into account in the production and use of modern artificial light.

Sunlight during several hours near the middle of the day is quite constant in color and spectral character. It is approximately colorless during this period. As the sun approaches the horizon it passes through greater and greater layers of atmosphere. Due to selective scattering of the light by the atmosphere and also to selective absorption of the dust and smoke, the sun appears yellow, orange and even red as it nears the horizon. Its color and spectral character are known and are also used as guides in the production and use of artificial light.

When the sky is covered by a cloud haze just thick enough to obscure the sun we have a thinly overcast sky. Sunlight and blue skylight fall upon the upper side of this diffusing haze which mixes them thoroughly. Obviously the resultant color of the light is that due to the combined sunlight and skylight above the overcast cloud haze. About as much light is diffused outward from the earth as arrives at the earth's surface. On such a day the level of illumination may be 4000 to 5000 footcandles. As the thin haze develops into a thick layer of clouds the overcast sky may begin to appear dark. Still there may be 1000 footcandles at the earth's surface. When the overcast sky thickens to the point of rain, the sky appears very dark. But one may be surprised to learn that the level of illumination is still likely to be ten times that under which most of the work of civilization is performed indoors under modern electric light.

To provide on a given surface a level of illumination equivalent to the maximum at the earth outdoors, about 10,000 burning candles would have to be concentrated into one source about a foot away from a surface. Thus the surface would have an illumination of 10,000 footcandles. About one-tenth of this level of illumination is obtained one foot from a 1000-watt tungsten-filament lamp. By utilizing the best principles of light-control in reflectors or lenses, wonders can be achieved. Even daylight levels of illumination can be obtained. These are indeed special cases at the present time when one considers that ordinary levels of artificial illumination are generally a few footcandles and very rarely fifty or a hundred footcandles. However, due to our

TORCH OF CIVILIZATION

recent revelations through the development of a science of seeing, these higher levels of illumination now promise to become quite common. But even these are very far below the levels of illumination outdoors in the daytime.

Inasmuch as illumination varies inversely as the square of the distance, it is possible to compute the candlepower of the sun. Taking into account the level of illumination at the earth's surface which is 93 million miles distant from the sun, we find the sun is a light-source equivalent to about 2.5 billion billion billion candles. This is only of passing interest, but it does aid in emphasizing the vast scale upon which Nature and the universe are built. It also aids in visualizing the great magnitude of natural light and lighting compared with which man's achievements so far are feeble indeed.

Let the great distance of the sun be eliminated from our computations and consider illuminating the earth from a reasonable earthly distance by means of lamps in reflectors. Suppose the population of the earth to be uniformly distributed over its entire surface. Each person would occupy a square about 500 feet on each side. If present-day 1000-watt tungsten-filament lamps were used and all the light were reflected toward the earth, each 500-foot square would require one million such lamps. In other words, each person on the average would have to manufacture one million 1000-watt lamps every 1000 hours, if this were the average life of the lamps. This would mean that each person on the average would have to manufacture about 25,000 1000-watt lamps every day to keep this artificial lighting installation competing with natural lighting on the earth's surface. Obviously the same people would have to mine the coal and do all the incidental things necessary to supply the electrical energy. There still remain the big jobs of feeding and operating civilization. Man's achievements are far from Nature's but, for specific purposes, artificial light and ingenious control of it can compete fairly well with Nature. But man can be proud of the many other ways in which artificial light is serving mankind beyond those services of natural light outdoors.

These are important glimpses of natural light and lighting outdoors. Primitive man admitted enough daylight, or provided enough artificial light to enable him to see. He supplied this demand of the visual sense just as he supplied other demands for obvious things. Our lungs demand air but they have a very limited ability to detect detrimental impurities. Our thirst is a demand for water, but germs are not obvious. Our hunger is a demand for food but we have no sense or organ with ability to distinguish unobvious vitamins in food or their far-reaching effects upon our health and life-processes. We have no sense which detects such benefits of ultraviolet energy as the killing of germs and the prevention of rickets.

Such refinements in our requirements are largely relatively recent discoveries of modern science. So it is with light and lighting. As long as human beings had to depend solely upon their unaided senses, only enough light was demanded for barely seeing. The kind of light and the character of the lighting were not obviously important. And more important still, the idea of providing adequate light and proper lighting for *easiest* seeing instead of for barely seeing could only be born through discoveries of unobvious deep-seated requirements and effects of seeing.

Indoors near the hole in the wall of a primitive hut, or near the window of a modern building, the daylight may range as high as a few hundred footcandles. A few feet away from the window it may be a few footcandles and often it is much less. By coming indoors mankind has reduced the general level of illumination from several thousand footcandles outdoors to only a few footcandles indoors. Daylight illumination indoors has been at about the same level as artificial illumination of the past. When the level of illumination outdoors drops to about 1500 footcandles outdoors, the meters in our central stations begin to record the turning on of artificial light very generally indoors. Recently much higher levels of artificial illumination indoors are beginning to reveal the futility of natural light in many places indoors.

This illustrates how severely the architecture of our artificial world restricts daylight indoors. In fact, at the present time daylight costs a great deal to obtain indoors. In many places it costs much more than artificial light. Generally it cannot be properly distributed indoors and, therefore, daylighting is not generally economical and in many places it is not satisfactory. In ascertaining these facts and pointing them out to architects and others for many years I have advocated the use of windows in many places primarily to let vision out. Letting light in is a secondary consideration. In considering the cost of windows and skylights and of window shades and Venetian blinds, and of the maintenance of all these, we must also add the cost of fuel which furnishes the heat lost through these glass areas. Finally, we must have artificial light standing by for the failure of daylight which comes once each day and may come at any time during the day. Thus in our congested cities, particularly, artificial light has already overshadowed daylight in importance.

In the entire artificial world from the smoky industrial district to the country home, the invisible radiant energy in sunlight has been left outdoors. Ultraviolet energy does not pass through ordinary window glass. Outdoors in the primitive state, human beings were naked or nearly so. Their skin received ultraviolet energy having some known benefits and probably possessing many others. Light and short-wave infrared penetrate deeply into flesh. We know from their specific applications that this kind of heating at a depth stimulates or augments circulatory processes in bodily tissue. Little is known of the benefits of daily exposure of large areas of the human body to ultraviolet, visible, and infrared energy. But these were ever-present, every day, in the environment under which human beings and their senses, organs, and life-processes evolved through eons of time.

During recent years we have revealed some of the hidden penalties of inadequate light and improper lighting. We have revealed the benefits of the abundant light as in Nature and something of the benefits of natural light and lighting. These revelations show in still another way that we human beings are the products of eons of adaptation to the outdoor environment. Our eyes and visual sense, and we as human seeing-machines, operate best and easiest when the brightness of our visual tasks is of the same order of magnitude as the brightnesses of the commonest areas with which we are intimate outdoors. Similar researches dealing with ultraviolet and infrared energy are also vastly important to civilized human beings sheltered in the indoor world. The most important knowledge we must have is that which tells us when we should fashion our practices after Nature, and when it is safe to depart on our own.

V. FLAMING SOURCES

BEFORE ME IS a little brass lamp. Only a year ago its single wick was feeding olive oil to its tiny flame. It was lighting the humble abode of a peasant family on the coast of Spain. For a century it shed its light upon family life, the foundation of modern civilization. It burned fuel that was readily available, oil from olives grown nearby. In another part of the world it might have burned whale oil or kerosene or other fuel characteristic of the land and of the times. This oil-burning lamp represents myriad oil-lamps and other flaming sources which have lighted civilization on its way. Now its work is done. It rests, belatedly relieved of its task by the advancing front of electrification. This is the history and the end of countless oil-lamps throughout an age which, beginning in antiquity, is gradually coming to a close.

One cannot contemplate this little brass lamp without being sensible of the romance, and being thrilled by the adventure, in the age-long search for better light-sources. With oil-lamps, as with all flaming sources of light, the search has been largely confined to material which would burn better and brighter. It began with the campfire and the crude hearth in the cave or hut. All woods burned, but some burned with better flames than others. The selected pine knot, heavy with resinous substance, replaced the unselected fagot. Grease from roasting meat dripping into the fire gave a flaming clue to better fuels for lamps. The vegetable kingdom was explored for oils and waxes. The animal kingdom was invaded for fats and oils. There was romance along all horizons of knowledge. Thrilling adventure met whalers along the horizons of the seven seas. Oils from vegetables, wax from bees, fats from animals and eventually oils from the earth were wrested from a bountiful Nature. Thrilling writings record courage and high adventure which supplied the oil for the lamps of civilization. But we must depend largely upon our imagination to sense the patience and ingenuity which improved these lamps throughout the centuries.

The fire on the hearth doubtless was the first source of light in the primitive home. It still serves on the fringes of civilization. After Lincoln's studies by the light from the fireplace this, for a time, became a part of the mythical formula for becoming President. Now the formula often includes promising the sun or at least the moon. In the crude beginnings of light-production when wood was the only fuel in use, a logical step was to place the fire on a shelf or in a niche in the wall. Later when metal became available, gratings or baskets were suspended from the ceiling or from brackets on the walls. Glowing embers or flaming chips were placed upon them. Some of these were equipped with crude chimneys to carry away the smoke and perhaps to increase the draft. Outdoors in cities and towns it was the duty of the watchman to keep the baskets supplied with wood. In our imagination we may see him toss in a pine knot as he made his round. There seem to have been no serious attempts at street-lighting until the early part of last century. With flaming torches escorts took pedestrians to their homes on dark nights. In England such service was rendered by link-boys until about 1840.

When it was too warm to have a roaring fire upon the

TORCH OF CIVILIZATION

hearth, man was forced to exercise his ingenuity. Glowing embers on shelves or gratings supplied little light and much heat. Selecting suitable wood of straight grain, he cut long thin splinters. These were stuck in the wall or otherwise held slanting downward. The flame burned slowly up the slanting splinter. These were improvements of considerable merit when we consider that human beings were just a few rungs higher on the ladder of intelligence than their immediate animal ancestors who did not even use fire or tools.

The rushlight was the child of the wood splinter and a forerunner, if not the father, of the candle. Long freshly-cut rushes, after being soaked in water for a time were carefully peeled. The lengths of pith thus obtained were dried and then soaked in hot grease. Many of these could be made at one time and stored for future use. The rancidity of the grease was probably not conspicuous among the other odors. These rushlights, two or three feet long, could be held in a splinter-holder where they would burn for about an hour. Pliny in his writings mentioned the burning of reeds soaked in oil as a feature of funeral ceremonies. Rushlights are mentioned in stories of Scotland and other countries dealing with events of rather recent times. The rushlight is relatively refined among most of the forerunners of the candle which were used in various parts of the world. For example, Malays made a torch by wrapping resinous gum in palm leaves. This is a sort of candle but with the fuel inside and the wick outside.

Eventually fats and oils began to replace wood as the fuel for light-sources. Doubtless natural dish-shaped stones were treasured as receptacles for animal grease. Moss served as wicks. As human beings acquired sufficient skill with their hands, receptacles were molded of wet clay. Experience

This shop-lamp of 1800, burning lard oil or whale oil, would be a poor partner of sight in the present era of streamlined mass-production.

FLAMING SOURCES

around the campfire must have demonstrated that clays harden when heated to high temperatures. Such experience probably revealed that some materials produced an impervious glaze when melted in the fire. As a consequence there was a continuous evolution of clay oil-lamps beginning long before history began to be recorded in writing. In fact, such things as oil-lamps are in themselves a record of the life and skill of early civilizations. Some of these lamps now in existence in extensive collections appear to have been made 5000 years before the Christian era. It is likely that primitive uses of receptacles for burning oil and grease antedate these by thousands of years.

As civilization advanced, metals came into use. Bronze, brass and pewter were readily melted. Oil-lamps of these materials were in extensive use at the height of ancient civilization along the eastern shores of the Mediterranean Sea. Large stone and metal vases filled with hundreds of pounds of liquid fat were a part of the festivals of ancient nations of Asia and Northern Africa. Egypt contributed many beautiful oil-lamps made of all these materials. Iron eventually came into the arts and many lamps of this cheaper metal were still widely used during the last century. Although the single open wick was most prevalent, as civilization developed more leisure and luxury, multiple wicks were used. Even metal pans were placed under these lamps to catch the drippings. In Scotland a shallow iron lamp, called a crusie, was one of the chief products of blacksmiths until the middle of last century. It was commonly suspended by an iron hood and the flow of oil was regulated by the tilt of the receptacle. This type of lamp was used throughout civilization for many centuries and was found in the catacombs of Rome.

TORCH OF CIVILIZATION

The wicks in the Scottish lamps consisted of the pith of rushes and also of twisted threads and strips of cloth. The early oil-lamps were generally shallow and most of the short wick dipped into the fat or oil. The material of the wick merely had to lift oil above the level of the liquid supply so that it would receive oxygen readily from the air and burn satisfactorily. From the raw natural materials such as moss and pith, it is a great stride to the cloth wicks of recent times. The changes in wicks and in the shape and the depth of the receptacles were due to, and made possible by, the refinement of animal and vegetable oils and particularly the discovery of mineral oil, petroleum.

After the first discoveries that certain resinous materials of the vegetable kingdom and the common fats of animals could be burned, the long search for unobvious materials began. Along the Mediterranean coast olives grew abundantly and olive oil supplied fuel for lamps as well as fuel for human beings. The Japanese and Chinese extracted oil from various nuts. Colza-oil came from coleseed or rapeseed. Coconuts and many other vegetable fruits yielded oil. We eat peanut butter today but we might be burning its oil in lamps if the age of gas, petroleum and electricity had not arrived.

The animal kingdom eventually supplied more material than the vegetable kingdom. Lard from swine supplied the lard-oil lamp. The head cavities of the sperm-whale yielded sperm-oil and other whales also supplied the whale-oil lamp. And eventually the discovery of vast sources of mineral oil deep in the earth gave a variety of products for the far more scientific oil-lamps of the past hundred years. It is impossible to apply even approximate dates to the introduction of the various fuels in early use. Only approximate dates can

FLAMING SOURCES

be given to the periods in which later fuels came into use. The candle is at least as old as the pyramids and oil-lamps are much older. Oil- and grease-lamps using various fuels were in use throughout all the centuries preceding the present one. A chimney of transparent material was not placed around the flame until 1784. This great event in civilized progress is readily fixed in mind by great events in this country. The Revolutionary War had just ended and the United States of America was definitely an independent nation. The lard-oil lamp was in use in New England in 1820. Whale-oil and sperm-oil lamps, commonly with two wicks, were widely in use in 1830. All these lamps and all oil-lamps throughout the preceding centuries had open flames unprotected by transparent chimneys. With the first production of petroleum from a well drilled by Drake in 1859, kerosene was distilled and the socalled coal-oil lamp with its glass chimney came into general use about 1870. It still serves admirably beyond the reach of electrical supply.

Long before the Christian era the candle was born. Considering simplicity and portability, it is the most remarkable light-source that was ever invented until the modern age of science. It is more than a light-source. It is a complete lighting-plant with no waste parts. All of it is consumed in the process of producing light. It can be carried in the pocket and can be stored indefinitely almost anywhere. It can be transported in boxes. No tanks are necessary as in the transportation of oil. The fuel is solid until melted by the flame. Only then does it become oil. It is not surprising that it has endured for thousands of years. It has been improved in materials, but its basic principle remains unchanged. It is not surprising that it became the universal ceremonial light

TORCH OF CIVILIZATION

for religious rituals. It still remains a festive light-source and in usefulness it is still unequaled in many places beyond and even within the boundaries of civilization. It is still the emergency lighting-plant throughout civilized activities.

The oldest materials used in making candles are beeswax and tallow. Owing to the more pleasant odor of burning beeswax and perhaps to the greater cost of this material, wax candles took precedence over tallow candles in the church and other places of refinement. Even in early centuries the wax was bleached before used. Persons still living have poured tallow in the familiar metal molds. Others have used the earlier method of dipping. Small ropes of twisted cotton or flax fibers were repeatedly dipped in the melted tallow until the desired thickness was obtained. Metal molds produce a more uniform diameter and length. Through the axis of each metal cylinder a twisted wick is strung tautly before pouring in the melted material.

Tallow is now used only as a source of stearine. Spermaceti, a fatty substance obtained from the sperm-whale, was introduced into candles in about 1750. Thus the hunt for sperm-whales was greatly stimulated. After the discovery of petroleum, a mineral wax, commercially known as paraffin, was a by-product of refining plants. It is a mixture of solid hydrocarbons. Stearine was used with paraffin and practically all candles excepting those of wax are now made of this product from the depths of the earth. Some vegetable oils are still used as well as large quantities of beeswax and other waxes. Wicks are now made by machinery and may be specially treated to cause practically complete combustion. Wax candles are made by pouring into molds. Dipping is not practiced excepting, possibly, in primitive circumstances. Candles may be drawn, which is a process similar in principle to dipping, but is a continuous one accomplished by machinery.

Besides our festive and ceremonial use of candles, we also treasure the candlesticks. They are universal ornaments, either the original antiques or modern replicas or designs. The original candlestick was nothing more than a simple holder to maintain the candle upright. This was either a sharp spike or a small cylinder. Later a shallow cup or pan was attached to the holder to catch the drippings. As civilization and human skill progressed, candlesticks became works of art and all the means of embellishment were applied to them. Much of their religious significance still clings to them. The candlestick even without the candle is not totally devoid of the symbolisms of goodness and knowledge. The two combined are widely used symbolically as the torch of civilization. When we consider its simplicity and portability, and the great part it has played throughout thousands of years of civilized ceremonies and other activities, we of the electric age may still view it with reverence and with pride in the ingenuity of our ancestors who preceded us a long time ago. Notwithstanding the advances in other means of light-production, the candle remains very useful and possibly the most ingenious light-source of all time.

The brightness of the flame determines the amount of light emitted by a given area. The Bunsen flame such as that of a gas-range in the kitchen is not bright. It is bluish until something rich in carbon is dropped into it. Then it brightens to a yellowish white and is quite luminous. These are facts now well known through scientific studies, but during most of the era of oil-lamps they were mere facts of observation. All the animal and vegetable products which were used as fuels in oil-lamps and candles are rich in carbon which accounts for the luminosity of the flames. The brightness of the flame is actually due to carbon particles heated to incandescence by the flame. Oils, fats and waxes are composed by weight of about 75 to 80 percent carbon, 10 to 15 percent hydrogen, and 5 to 10 percent oxygen. When the combustion is not perfect, free carbon escapes as smoke. A Bunsen flame represents fairly perfect combustion, which is achieved by mixing air with the gas instead of merely having the air feed the flame at its surface. Its day lay ahead in the era of gas-mantles.

After centuries of minor refinements in fuels, wicks and vessels, a great improvement was made by Argand, a French chemist, in 1784. He placed a glass chimney upon the lamp. Glass was made by the ancient Egyptians and Venetian glass-blowing was celebrated for many centuries. Still flame-sources of light remained unprotected from drafts until 150 years ago. Argand had been experimenting with tubular wicks. His burner consisted of two concentric metal tubes between which the tubular wick was held. The inner tube was open so that air could reach the inner surface of the wick as well as the outer surface. Argand set a cylinder of clear glass on the burner and the flame steadied and noticeably brightened.

The lamp chimney not only protected the flame from gusts of air but produced an updraft which drew more air to the flame. This socalled chimney-effect improved combustion which decreased the smoke. It also increased the temperature of the flame which made the carbon particles brighter and the flame more luminous. The advantages of the lamp chimney are obvious now but Argand for his achievement is entitled to a place among the great inventors of all time. He took the first step toward adequate artificial light and opened a new era in lighting. Uncounted millions of lamps since Argand's time have utilized the basic principles of his invention. Millions are still being manufactured.

After Argand produced a steady flame and a fairly smokeless lamp, many developments followed. Reservoirs which feed the oil by gravity were designed to maintain the oil at a constant level. This was an improvement owing to the viscosity of the oil which resisted the capillary pull of the wick. Later when mineral oil became available, this gravity feed was found unnecessary. The less viscous oil favored the capillary action of the wick which also had been improved. However, even in modern kerosene lamps the distance of the flame above the level of oil in the receptacle below it does make some difference in the amount of oil burned and of the light emitted by the flame.

In 1800 the Carcel lamp was introduced with a double piston operated by clockwork. This device forced oil through a tube to the burner. In 1836 Franchot invented a lamp in which a spring forced the oil upward to the burner through a vertical tube. Various other mechanical devices were tried and some came into use. All these lamps burned animal and vegetable oils, but the eventual introduction of mineral oil was destined to discard these complex mechanisms. Oil-lamps became simpler and better.

Long ago it had been observed that when coal is heated to moderate temperatures certain volatile liquids escape as vapors. If these vapors are trapped and cooled in a condenser, these liquids can be retained. This is the process of distillation. In distilling coal, liquid hydrocarbons are obtained such as gasoline and kerosene. Such liquids were suggested for use in lamps as early as 1781. However, there was no source of supply of such mineral oils until about 1820 when the coal-gas industry was getting under way. Coal-tar is a by-product of the production of artificial gas from coal. On distilling this tar some light oils are obtained.

The Holliday lamp was designed to use these mineral oils, similar to our modern kerosene which, it is interesting to note, is commonly called coal-oil although now it does not come from coal. In this lamp the oil was contained in a reservoir above the burner. It was carried by gravity down to the rose-burner, a metal part containing several orifices. The oil was heated by the flame and vaporized. The vapor or gas escaped from the orifices where it burned. This type of lamp has undergone many changes but its principle survives in the gasoline and kerosene burners hanging on a pole at the peddler's stand or in ranges in many kitchens. It may appear that the Holliday lamp departed from other oil-lamps because by design it converted the liquid oil into vapor by heating the oil with the flame. As a matter of fact, all oil-lamps burn vapor rather than liquid oil. Even the flame of the candle after melting the solid fuel vaporizes the liquid fuel before it actually burns.

While mankind was scouring land and sea for thousands of years for oils for the lamps of civilization, hidden deeply in the earth was another kind of oil in undreamed-of abundance. Trickles or puddles of thick dark liquid must have been observed here and there over the earth. Herodotus and other early writers mention something that must have been mineral oil, but no one seemed to suspect large underground pools of petroleum until a century ago. The Pharaohs of Egypt, the ancient Greeks and the Roman conquerors in celebrating their festivals had to be content with the feeble flames of vegetable and animal fats while in eastern Europe and western Asia great riches in "black gold" reposed in the ground. In 1847 petroleum was discovered in a coal-mine in England. James Young investigated the source and also the properties of the oil. Finding that it was good for lubricating purposes, he began distilling the oil from shale found among the coal deposits. This was the beginning of an industry which has ever since obtained oil from shale, particularly in Scotland. However, the oil was not seriously considered or used for lighting purposes.

Colonel E. L. Drake studied the possible relation of geological formations in Pennsylvania to pools of underground oil. He decided petroleum could be obtained by drilling and in 1859 he backed his conviction by drilling the first well in all history. His venture was not only a success for him but a great event in civilized progress. His oil-well opened the way to enormous underground supplies of petroleum with discoveries of new pools still exceeding the drain of old ones. Petroleum has made one of the great changes in civilized activities. Its products now supply light, heat and power throughout civilized activities. The crude petroleum is separated into a variety of products by fractional distillation. The lighter products generally vaporize at lower temperatures than the heavier ones. The densities or weights per gallon compared with water, 1.00, are approximately as follows: gasoline, 0.65; kerosene, 0.80; lubricating oils, 0.85 to 0.95. There are various solid or near-solid by-products such as paraffin and vaseline.

Before electric lighting came into existence in arc lamps in 1877, and in filament lamps in 1879, refined products of petroleum were ushering in a new era in lighting progress. When kerosene came into wide usage in lamps, gasoline was almost a waste product. The tables have turned since the gasoline engine has put civilization—and anti-civilization—on wheels and electricity has largely replaced the kerosene lamp. However, mineral oil was a great boon to lighting for the feeble flames of about one candlepower which flickered for centuries in their battle against darkness, were superseded by kerosene flames of ten to twenty candlepower. An increase of ten times in the light output of sources was such a great advance at the time that it cannot be completely obscured by the electric light-sources of the present time, some of which are thousands of times greater in candlepower.

Flame-sources possessed very great inherent handicaps which limited their usage. There was the ever-present danger of fire as demonstrated emphatically by Mrs. O'Leary's cow which, according to legend, kicked over a kerosene lantern and started the fire which destroyed most of Chicago in 1871. An inherent inconvenience of all oil-lamps was that they had to be lighted by some means of making fire. Before the advent of modern oil-lamps which burned mineral oil, the primitive means of making fire by rubbing two sticks together, by focusing a "burning glass" or by striking flint and steel had given way to improved means. Matches were at first cumbersome, dangerous and expensive. Early ones, such as wax-tapers and hemp treated with niter, were not self-igniting. They merely transferred fire from one source to another.

Phosphorus has played a dominant role in the preparation of matches for a long time. As early as 1680 small pieces of phosphorus were used in connection with small splints of wood which had been coated with sulphur. Owing to cost and danger this type of match did not come into appreciable use until about 1800. Many ingenious but cumbersome devices using sulphur and phosphorus and various chemical compounds had been invented previously but did not come into general use. The lucifer or friction match appeared in 1827 but really successful phosphorus matches were first made in about 1833. White and yellow phosphorus are very poisonous, which was a great drawback to their use. In about 1850 the discovery of the relatively harmless red phosphorus provided a great impetus to the development of the modern match. The original of the socalled safety match of the present time was invented in 1855.

Today the total daily output of matches reaches staggering figures. Needless to say they are so inexpensive that the careless pipe smoker smokes them one after another. They are manufactured at tremendous speed by automatic machinery which splits wood or cardboard into splints or strips, dips them into molten paraffin wax to make them burn well, and finally into the igniting compound which comprises the heads. They are so common that those thoughtlessly wasted every minute would have comprised great treasure for kings of yestercentury. Relatively few of them are used to ignite light-sources but where flame-sources are still in use, the modern match is indeed a boon.

Naturally with the advent of electricity, electric sparks came into use for lighting gas-jets and gas-mantles. Since these sources which burned gas have generally disappeared, perhaps many are not familiar with the old parlor stunt of igniting a gas-jet with the discharge of static electricity from the finger-tips accumulated by shuffling the feet across the carpet. An alcohol lamp or the wick of a cigarette lighter will do, but it is best to try the stunt in a dry climate or in the dryness of our interiors in winter.

TORCH OF CIVILIZATION

In passing it may be interesting to note that the principle of the old tinder-box has been revived, not primarily for lighting fires, candles and oil-lamps as in earlier times but for lighting cigarettes. Sparks are produced by rubbing certain minerals against steel. A common one known as cerite is a compound of the socalled rare-earth, cerium, and allied metals. The sparks ignite a highly inflammable liquid such as alcohol or, better still, a suitable hydrocarbon. Thus this cigarette lighter in the vest pocket, in a handbag or on a living room table is a reminder that modern science has made a sure-fire device out of the old cumbersome hit-or-miss flint and steel.

As we look backward in our imagination along the rough and tortuous pathway along which civilization struggled for uncounted centuries, we see it illuminated by the flames of oil-lamps and candles. Looking ahead to an eventual realization of the ideal brightnesses of daylight outdoors by means of artificial light, our present age is still dimly lighted. Looking backward we seem to be brilliantly illuminated and, in a relative sense, we are. We may be justly proud of modern electric light-sources—bottled light relatively unlimited in applications. But there is room both for our pride in today's achievements and respect for those of all the yesterdays. Accomplishments must be measured in the light of the knowledge of the time, and of the activities and desires of human beings.

As we look backward down that vista of time, the lights grow dimmer and dimmer. If we gaze knowingly enough, our respect for those achievements is transformed into a kind of reverence. Those flaming torches are not really behind us. They have always been ahead of us, leading the way. They are torches of civilization, first lighted in the actual darkness of little or no human knowledge. And we owe all that we know and all that we enjoy to that long line of torch-bearers of light and of knowledge. Black-outs there have been, but never a black-out of the light of knowledge. It burns brighter with each passing year.

VI. MODERN SCIENCE EVOLVES

TWO PERSONS ARE gazing at the night sky studded with stars. One is familiar with the facts of astronomy; the other is not. To the one, there is order in that apparent disorder. To the other, the starry sky appears as a chaos. One knows that only a few thousand stars are visible to his unaided sight. The other, in the absence of knowledge, multiplies them into an uncounted myriad. Painstaking measurements by many observers of many generations have brought order out of that confusion of stars. Through the invention of better instruments and methods, modern science has extended the boundary of the known universe millions of times further than the limit of unaided vision. And in that inconceivably great space are millions of heavenly bodies. This is happening in countless unknowns encompassed by all-inclusive Nature. Knowledge garnered by invading the unknown is turned back in the form of new instruments and methods to continue the invasion. For example, in astronomy knowledge gained here and there in the control and analysis of light has been put to work in such tools as telescopes, spectroscopes, and photographic processes to invade the unknown universe still further.

In the glimpses we have already had of the production and use of light we have seen new knowledge being acquired and put into use. The human race was born in ignorance. The darkness of the unknown crowded close from all sides. At first primitive beings could only learn by acci-

MODERN SCIENCE EVOLVES

dental experience. Doubtless a long time elapsed before their crude minds and knowledge developed sufficiently for them to create the method of trial and error or cut and try. This was a great improvement, but at best is a very crude method of obtaining knowledge compared with systematic scientific method of the present time. In our fancy we see knowledge as a slender thread of light brightening very slowly but steadily as the uncounted centuries passed. But until modern science was born, knowledge consisted largely of that which could be acquired by the unaided human senses. This was still true at the height of Grecian civilization about 2000 years ago, notwithstanding the fact that the ability to think, to observe, and to apply logic was highly developed in those ancient philosophers.

The deficiency was not in mind but in method. There is little evidence that the great minds of the Greeks of 2400 years ago suspected the existence of an unknown of enormous magnitude beyond the reach of their unaided senses. And certainly there was little enthusiasm for invading and exploring that unknown. They believed to be true that which seemed to be true. They philosophized rather generally without obtaining the facts, or proving them by experimenting. We have many classic examples of dogmatic opinions. Aristotle philosophized that two balls of equal size and smoothness, but differing in weight, would not fall at the same speed. He insisted that if dropped from the same height, the heavier would reach the ground first. This seemed reasonable to Aristotle as doubtless it seems to many persons today who are unfamiliar with physical laws. But now we know of thousands of facts that are contrary to what our senses, and even our unsupported reasonings, conclude. Apparently Aristotle did not see the need for testing his

TORCH OF CIVILIZATION

conclusion, or worse still, did not recognize the folly of reaching a conclusion at all before trying the experiment.

There are still many persons who use the method of Aristotle—reasoning without the facts or at least before obtaining the facts. And throughout civilization we still find the crude methods of cut and try and even of accidental experience being relied upon. Opinions, misconceptions, illusions and delusions still rule many persons in everyday life and in many realms such as politics, government and sociology. Compare the social inventions in those fields with the great inventions based upon the incontestable knowledge of modern science. Aristotle had such prestige, and human beings were so satisfied that reasoning was sufficient, that nearly 2000 years elapsed before someone decided to test his conclusions about falling bodies.

Galileo, the first outstanding exponent of modern scientific method, took two balls, equal in size but unequal in weight, to the top of the Leaning Tower of Pisa. He dropped them and behold! They reached the ground at the same time. Of course the experimental approach by actual tests had been developing slowly. No one can say when it was born but we know that it came decisively into use during the late Renaissance, in about the seventeenth century. And Galileo did more than anyone else to prove the great advantage of systematic experiments. He did not believe the sun revolved around the earth merely because it seemed to do so. He watched the swinging of a great chandelier as he sat in church and noted that the time elapsed during each complete swing to or fro did not vary with the amplitude or length of the arc through which it swung. He experimented methodically and revealed the laws involved and many others. He made a telescope and revealed celestial bodies

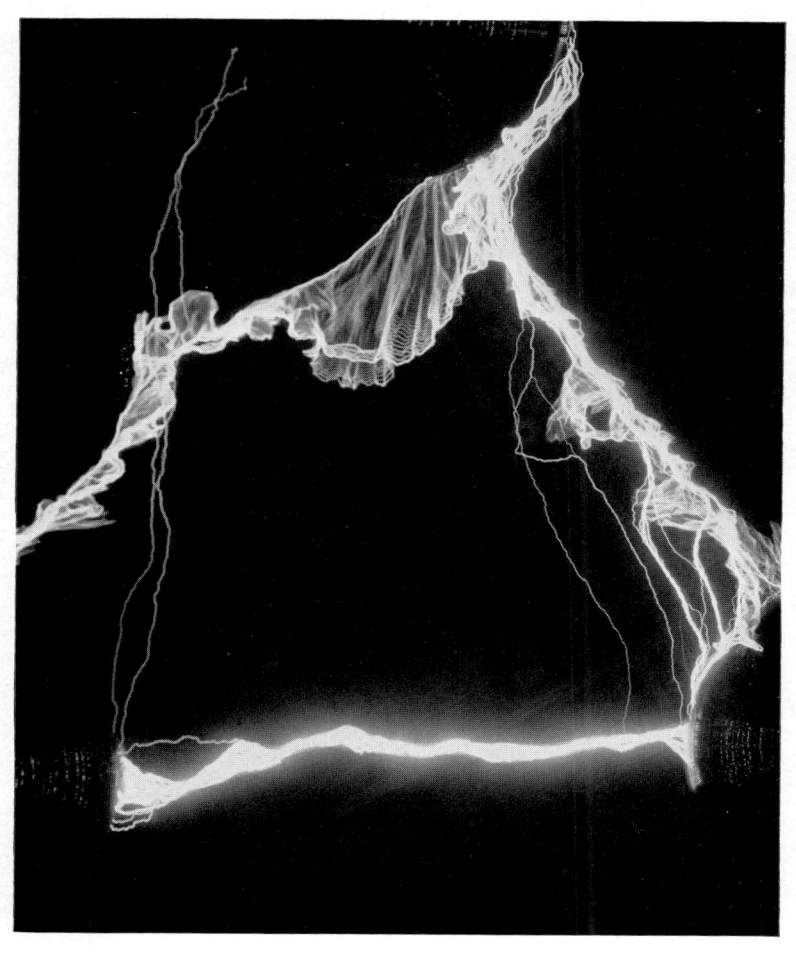

Nature's electricity is rampant and destructive, but man-made electricity, subjugated by modern science, has become the staff of civilized life.

MODERN SCIENCE EVOLVES

which had never before been seen by human beings. He possessed the spirit of modern science, experimenting in many fields, and producing the tested, testable and, therefore, incontestable knowledge of modern science. He suffered severe persecution by ruling powers with whose opinions his proved facts disagreed. He died at 78 years of age, disappointed that dogmatic opinion still prevailed over proved facts. But his contributions eventually prevailed because they revealed the truth. He had breathed much life into the awakened scientific spirit and was the first great demonstrator of Scientific Method.

From a vague beginning in the misty past, modern science took definite form and strength during the centuries of the Renaissance. In the last century it developed into a great movement. Everyone is familiar with some of the facts of science for these are taught in schools and colleges and ladled into books. But these are merely the products of modern science. To understand this new movement in the search for knowledge, we may take a fire as an analogy. The fire burns and our knowledge of chemistry now reveals the chemical reactions which are taking place. But there is more to that fire than the facts of chemistry. That fire radiates light and heat. The light is analogous to scientific method which produces tested facts. The warmth is analogous to scientific spirit which is devoid of prejudices of our senses, of our opinions or of anything else. Thus the irresistible forces which make modern science a powerful movement are the forces which eliminate ignorance and prejudice. These twin evils are the cause of all ills. Modern science has proved its power and possibilities wherever it has been applied. Every avenue of the social world should be opened to it. It is the hope of civilization.

TORCH OF CIVILIZATION

In order to understand and to weigh progress in any realm, such as the production, control and use of artificial light, it is helpful to glimpse the growth of knowledge and particularly the aids and hindrances to its growth. The setting into which Galileo was born should be viewed against the back-drop of the centuries beginning with the height of Grecian civilization a few centuries before the Christian era. The Greeks had progressed far with their thoughts and feelings. They had perfected the fine art of architecture, and more generally of form, to a very high degree. But they did not progress far beyond the realm of the obvious. Mathematics, the language of science, was developed considerably. Euclid, who was born in 330 B. C., is still a familiar name. He laid the foundation for elementary geometry by means of the logic of his propositions. His treatise probably holds the record of duration in influence.

Democritus, born in 460 B. C., was the first to develop the idea of atoms. He believed that every substance was made of its particular variety of atoms and that the size, number and arrangement of the atoms differed with the substance. He had no experimental evidence to support his theory but deserves to be remembered at least for proposing it. Now an atomic theory of matter has been adequately proved. Today the development of materials used in light-production is based upon knowledge of atoms, of their components and of their combination into molecules and substances.

Archimedes was a Greek mathematician, physicist and engineer and well deserves to be ranked one of the greatest men in scientific history. He laid the foundation for the branch of knowledge known as mechanics. He developed geometry and almost invented calculus, one of the most important mathematical tools of modern science. He made many contributions to physics. When Syracuse fell before the assaults of the Romans in 212 B. C., he was killed by a Roman soldier. There were other great minds at that time, including the notable philosophers, who could have turned their logic into profitable scientific channels if they had had the facts upon which to direct their minds. Their ideas of the unknown were crude and limited as indicated by Aristotle's belief that there were only four fundamental elements —earth, water, air and fire. This was a natural philosophic conclusion but a long way from the basic truth. However, if war had not descended upon ancient Greece, it is probable that modern science would have become a great movement early in the Christian era instead of many centuries later.

War did interfere with the development of basic knowledge as it still does. The Romans conquered the civilized world of the time and the Roman Empire rose to great power. But its viewpoint was that of the executive and militarist; and contributions to basic scientific knowledge, such as the Greeks had been making, came almost to a standstill. Desire to understand Nature and thirst for basic knowledge are not nourished amid the overwhelming clash of arms or of political ambitions. The Roman Empire became rich, with the evanescent riches gained by executive and military power, not with the permanent treasure of scientific knowledge. Softened by luxury, Rome fell and civilization went into a tailspin.

For nearly a thousand years the lights of civilization burned low during the Dark Ages. Torches of warriors lighted the primitive practices of war, pillage, and destruction. There were only two prominent occupations—war throughout the lands and religion in the cases of religious institutions. To the everlasting credit of the Church, and balancing to some degree the crimes of religious dogmatism, the lamps of knowledge were kept lighted in the monasteries. The Dark Ages finally ended in a burst of religious fervor which built the great cathedrals. The lights of civilization began to burn more and more brilliantly and the Renaissance surged into being about the thirteenth century.

The Great Awakening was a new and widespread declaration of independence in thought and action. Creeping science rose to its knees in the early dawn of this new era. At the request of Pope Clement IV, Roger Bacon, a Franciscan monk and brilliant scientist who was born in 1214, prepared treatises on physics and mathematics. He contributed something to optics. The sphericity of the ocean surface convinced him that the distance between the known continents could not be very great, and that Asia would be reached by sailing west from Europe. His facts and reasoning inspired Columbus two centuries later to set out on his westerly voyage which led to America because it lay between Europe and Asia. Bacon's works were condemned by the next Pope. Thus the struggle of science against dogmatism waxed and waned during the dawn of this new era.

At the sunrise of the Renaissance, science rose weakly and stood upright. Great names soon began to appear. Gutenberg in the fifteenth century invented movable type and laid the foundation for modern printing. Without such means of recording and broadcasting scientific knowledge, the growth of science as we know it would have suffered greatly. Today the necessary interchange of the voluminous production of scientific knowledge would be hopelessly impossible without the art of printing or something akin to it. Copernicus, Brahe and Kepler laid sound foundations for new astronomy.

MODERN SCIENCE EVOLVES

Gilbert began elementary studies of electricity and magnetism. He originated the term, *vis electrico*, from which arose our modern word, electricity. Francis Bacon still treated mathematics with the dogmatic approach of philosophy, but did much for science notwithstanding. Descartes, another contributor of the times, invented the coordinate or analytic geometry and dabbled somewhat in physics. Torricelli, through studies of vacua and hydrostatics developed the mercury barometer. Thus various specific unknowns were being invaded.

Among all the great men connected with science, Galileo (1564-1642) in the late Renaissance stands out preeminently as the right man in the right place at the right time. The greatest idea of all time became definitely crystallized—Nature could be understood and was worth understanding. And the greatest invention for ascertaining hidden truths, for invading unknowns beyond the reach of the unaided senses, and for producing incontestable knowledge, was being perfected and demonstrated. It was modern scientific method, including systematic experiments and the appraisal of the results without the prejudices of preconceptions and mere opinions. In this setting Galileo found and grasped great opportunity. He became the first outstanding exponent and demonstrator of scientific spirit and method. The impetus which he gave established modern science as a new and powerful movement in a world shot through with ignorance and prejudice and their evil products. He opened wide the door for many workers in science and for the geniuses in the centuries which have followed. More than anyone he deserves to be known as the father of modern science.

This brings us to the middle of the seventeenth century. As yet there is little evidence of the effect of science upon the story of light. Lamps still burned with feeble flames, flickering in the absence of chimneys, and smoking from poor combustion. But a growing army of scientific workers was paving the way in physics and chemistry. Newton (1642-1727) was born the year that Galileo died. He was a genius worthy to grasp the torch which fell from the hand of old Galileo. He contributed much basic knowledge in the realms of light and of optics. In the eighteenth century Priestley discovered oxygen and found that air was only partly oxygen. Scientific progress in the production of light by burning materials was necessarily slow when so little was known of the chemistry and physics of combustion.

Many workers began to lay the foundation of our knowledge of heat, of radiant energy, and of electricity. Young put the finishing touches upon explanations which established the wave theory of light, expounded by Huygens a century before and ably opposed by Newton because of the meager facts at the time. Fresnel discovered that light was diffracted around an object and that the fringes at the edge of the shadow were due to the fact that light traveled in a series of waves of definite wavelengths. This gave powerful support to the wave theory and left little to be criticized. Davy invented the miner's safety lamp consisting essentially of a metal gauze outside the flame. This reduced the temperature of explosive gases as they neared the flame with the result that they could not ignite and cause a catastrophe in the mine.

These gains in knowledge are representative of the vast offensive which was being waged against the unknown along a broad scientific front in the closing years of the eighteenth century. About the year 1800 modern science was beginning to make contributions to everyday living which were destined to bring about great changes. For a long time something like an aristocracy of knowledge had existed. Most scientists and others who had the leisure to follow science were so intent on the knowledge that they did not concern themselves with the applications of it to the service of mankind. Some looked disdainfully upon such use. The idea of pure science and pure scientists arose and has long persisted. But long ago that aristocracy became threadbare and was swamped by the tide of recognition that the ultimate purpose of knowledge is to serve human beings by easing their burdens and promoting their welfare and happiness.

During the early decades of last century, names began to appear which live in present-day practices. Among these are Ampère, Gauss, Volta, and Oersted. They developed some of the rudiments of electrical science. As is common in many fields of science and technology, their names were given to units of measurement which have to be invented in order to develop scientific knowledge. Most of us are familiar with amperes and volts which, working together, supply watts—electric power. Watt was a Scottish inventor who contributed much toward the early development of the steam-engine and properly his name has been given to the unit of power.

Until the epochal work of Faraday on electromagnetism, the only sources of electrical energy were meager batteries. Two plates of different elements—zinc, carbon, copper, etc. —immersed in an acid developed a voltage between them. If connected by means of a conductor, an electric current flowed. By connecting the plates to a frog's leg, the muscles twitched. They were galvanized into action, hence, the term galvanic current or battery. Many pairs of plates had to be connected in series to obtain a large current. Volta's pile consists of plates of two different elements stacked alternately into a pile and separated by cloths soaked in a salt or acid solution. Such "wet" cells were the only sources of continuously flowing electric current at the time. However, by building large batteries of them, Davy and others experimented in the production of electric light by heating platinum filaments electrically and by producing arcs which in effect are prolonged or continuous sparks. These and others were little more than electrical stunts at the time. Such experiments developed knowledge of electricity but would have remained largely laboratory playthings if a better source of electrical energy could not have been developed.

This gave Faraday an opportunity and is a good example of the creation of applications of knowledge by the growth of knowledge. We may consider knowledge as analogous to a clearing in the midst of a wilderness. As this clearing increases, the horizon of the unknown increases. And this horizon of the unknown is also the horizon of new opportunities, not only for acquiring more knowledge, but also for applying that which may have been available for a long time. Faraday was progressively a pupil of Davy, his secretary and assistant. He took up the study of electric batteries and discovered the fundamental law of electrochemistry. Upon the death of Davy in 1829, Faraday devoted himself to a serious study of magnetic fields and their effects. He started cutting magnetic fields with a conductor such as a copper wire. He found that electric currents were induced in these conductors. As he was thus working in Cavendish laboratory outside of London, not far away in Germany the great Goethe—poet, philosopher, scientist—lay dying. For him light was failing. He asked his attendant to raise the

MODERN SCIENCE EVOLVES

shades, murmuring *"Mehr Licht,"* more light—and passed away.

As if in answer, the young Faraday in that decade just one hundred years ago, laid the foundation for abundant light for civilization. In cutting a magnetic field with a conductor, mechanical energy is converted into electrical energy. The conductors may be arranged systematically on a revolving drum which may be driven by any kind of power. Our supply of mechanical energy is enormous. Whether it comes from engines feeding upon the energy stored in coal or oil or from the turbines turned by waterpower, it is incomparably greater than civilization has as yet put to use. Electricity born in the electrochemical reactions of batteries is a feeble infant compared with the incomprehensible giant arising from the conversion of mechanical energy whose supply is relatively inexhaustible.

Not long after Faraday's revelations of the laws relating electricity and magnetism, crude generators of electricity—dynamos—were developed. Advances in the generation of electricity continued, but until electric lighting was well under way few applications were made of electrical power to save man-power. Steam-engines were doing some of the work and mankind was still satisfied to use its muscles as it had always done. Not until the appearance of practical electric arcs and filament lamps in the decade beginning with 1870 did electrical energy begin to serve civilization seriously. With the advent of these electric sources of light, Brush, Edison and others developed complete systems, including the generation and distribution of electricity, with electric light as the end-product. Thus the debut of electricity in the service of mankind was made in the light from electricity.

TORCH OF CIVILIZATION

The acceleration of the growth and use of scientific knowledge during the past century is obvious and it is also apparent that the rate of acceleration is rapidly increasing. Only one hundred years after Faraday revealed the laws relating electricity and magnetism, and mechanical and electrical energy, civilization is immersed in an Electric Age, solely a creation of modern science. In the United States alone the electrical utility industry represents an investment of fourteen billion dollars. Twenty-three million homes in this country are enjoying electric service and there are about seven million other customers. The irresistible progress in electrifying our civilization is well illustrated by the growth of the electrical utility industry during the depression, and political thunder and legislative lightning, of the decade which has just passed. During that decade of disturbance four million new customers were added to the electric lines and the electrical utility industry grew about twenty-five percent while general business declined about that amount.

The kilowatt-hour of electricity, equivalent to a 100-watt lamp burning for ten hours, has become the most universally consumed commodity. In this country last year 125 billion kilowatt-hours served 125 million persons—an average of 1000 kilowatt-hours per person. Thus electricity supplied to each family, on the average, an amount of work equivalent to a team of horses working seven hours a day every day in the year. Already within the life-span of a human being, electrical kilowatt-hours, starting from scratch have attained a consumption in this country twice that of potatoes and five times that of loaves of bread—the staff of life! This man-made electrical kilowatt-hour has become the staff of civilized life! And this new kind of energy and power first came into practical use to supply electric light. Since then it has gone far into other fields such as heating, power, and communication. But electric lighting is still the chief and most essential service. It still accounts for a greater use of electrical energy than any other field of use. Electric light, as the torch of electrical development, is another incident of the major role of artificial light as the torch of civilization.

This hasty journey from ancient Greece to the present time reveals much that is encouraging for the future. It reveals the very slow growth of scientific attitude and purpose. It reveals the recency of modern science as an accepted method and movement. But of most importance, it reveals that we have entered an era of rapid expansion of science in the service of mankind. No one can look through this doorway without seeing ahead incomparably greater developments and services. Defeatism recedes into the darkness whence it came for it is merely a creation of selfish politicians or of those ignorant of the movement of modern science. It is a creed unworthy of anyone already so immersed in the beneficence of scientific knowledge. Everywhere modern science touches the efficiency, safety, comfort, welfare and happiness of human beings. Everywhere it is refining civilization—and aiming at perfection—where it is properly used for the benefit of mankind. It holds high the torch of knowledge which, nourished for centuries as a feeble flame, has become a powerful lighthouse. No longer do we fear the darkness of the unknown. Science reveals it as an inexhaustible mine of facts to be brought to light by systematic research.

In writing this book I have chosen this chapter as an appropriate place to pause in the story of light to give the reader a glimpse of modern science as it enters the story. Now let us both pause and pay our respects to modern science. In our imagination let us transport ourselves to Florence, Italy. There among the tombs and statues, the palaces and galleries, our imagination pictures the human struggles for freedom in all its senses—freedom to live, to think, to explore—freedom to hope for escape from the darkness of ignorance and prejudice. The way to such freedom was opened by the victory of humanism. It was the Great Awakening which we know as the Renaissance. We cannot pay our respects to every pioneer who helped to nourish the spirit of science and to demonstrate its method. But through one eminently deserving we can pay homage to all.

We seek out a modest church—San Croce—and enter its dim interior. The shadows are peopled with the spirits of those who created the Renaissance. We advance a few paces and find ourselves before the tomb of Galileo, the father of Modern Science—an appropriate shrine for all modern civilization. We look around to see in what company he lies; and we find ourselves standing between the tombs of Michelangelo and Galileo. Indeed, we find ourselves on a spot that preeminently deserves the glorification of modern civilization.

As we stand there with deepening reverence, we note that Michelangelo died the year that Galileo was born. In our imagination we see the failing hand of that superb creator of the beautiful, passing the Scepter from Art to Science; and we hear old Michelangelo saying to young Galileo:

"The Renaissance artists also questioned the old and created the new. They have shown that the world may be beautified superficially. But *Knowledge* alone can supply the understanding which will reveal the third dimension as well. And only perfect and complete understanding can beautify the world through and through."

The substance of that imaginary statement is a guiding creed and the ultimate objective of modern science. Only a relatively few acquire the knowledge of science which is perfecting—beautifying—our artificial world. But the humblest person can acquire the spirit of science and help drive out prejudice—the companion of ignorance.

VII. GAS FLAMES AND MANTLES

WE SIT BEFORE the fireplace. The light and heat radiating from it had their origin in bygone sunlight. Once wood and coal were living plants. The wood was alive recently; the coal lived eons ago. Living things live by a transference of energy and, when the transference ceases, they die. Sunlight enters directly into the life-processes of plants and at least indirectly into the life-processes of animals. Therefore, as we sit before the fireplace we are basking in sunlight, stored by chemical processes in chemical compounds and released by the chemical processes which we recognize as fire. Thus the radiant energy which we see and feel as we sit by the fire has completed a long cycle in an endless life. Similarly light from gas-jets fed by gases distilled from wood and coal came from the sun of bygone years or ages. The torch of civilization is a resurrection of the torch of Creation.

If we observe a wood-fire closely, we may see jets of flame here and there issuing from the wood. Many of these are gas-jets fed by tiny gas-plants. The charring of the wood by the heat of the fire is producing inflammable gases. If, from the cool end of a hollow stick smoke arises, this may be an outlet for gas generated at the other end of the stick which is burning. We may gather this by means of an inverted funnel and ignite it with a lighted match applied to the orifice. We may duplicate the hollow stick by rolling a newspaper into a tube. If we hold it somewhat inclined to the horizontal and light the lower end, inflammable gas will issue from the higher end. We may prove this by applying a lighted match. Thus we have a crude gas-plant. The crackling, hissing and explosions of a wood-fire may be largely due to the pressure of vapors produced by heating liquids or solids confined in the wood. But in that wood-fire artificial gas is being made and burned, and some of the jets are heard as well as seen. A smoldering coal-fire is even more definitely a gas-plant, for inflammable gases are being generated and burned.

These are crude demonstrations of the artificial gas-plants which ushered in the era of gas-lighting in about 1800. It is interesting that gas-lighting was born to use artificial gas, manufactured largely from coal. More than a half century was to elapse before natural gas came into use. Enormous quantities of natural gas lay hidden in the earth along with unsuspected pools of petroleum. Surely human beings long before had seen flaming natural gases near volcanoes and coal-mines, but writings are silent on the matter. Of course, the spirit of systematic inquiry and experimentation had been rare and, at best, feeble in earlier centuries. Even now few persons would stop to inquire the cause and character of the bubbles arising from the muddy bottom of a stagnant pool as it is disturbed by pushing an oar into it. These bubbles of gas may be readily caught in an inverted funnel and burned at the upper end. It is methane gas, a combination of hydrogen and carbon, which is commonly one of the gases in both artificial and natural gas.

In the Transactions of the Royal Society of London in 1667, a paper was published by a Mr. Shirley under the clumsy title, "A Well and Earth in Lancashire taking Fire at a Candle." This illustrates very well the meager knowledge of the time. It also reveals the spread of the spirit of inquiry by the method of modern science. From this account we see a group of persons contemplating a bubbling spring of water in rural England in 1659. Nearby inhabitants had spread the rumor "that the Water of this Spring did burn like Oil." Shirley journeyed there to investigate and excerpts from his account are as follows:

> When we came to the said Spring and applied a lighted Candle to the Surface of the Water; there was 'tis true, a large Flame suddenly produced.... I applied the lighted Candle to divers parts of the Water ... and found, as I expected, that upon the Touch of the Candle and the Water the Flame was extinct.... This Boiling I conceived to proceed from the Eruption of some bituminous or sulphureous Fumes.

The water was then drained away and an inflammable gas was found to be escaping from a hole in the ground, thus accounting for the bubbling. Shirley noted that a coalpit was not far away and that the ground was underlaid with coal. This is readily recognized as a discovery of natural gas now commonly associated with underground deposits of coal and oil in many parts of the world. There is no record of this or of any other natural supply of gas being used to furnish light and heat until nearly two centuries later. Artificial gas distilled from coal came into use long before natural gas did. Amply supplied with coal deposits, England became the birthplace of gas-lighting by means of coal-gas.

Although Murdock did not originate the idea of producing artificial gas from coal and of using it for lighting, he was the outstanding developer of early gas-lighting. In 1808 he published an account of his first industrial gas-lighting installation in which he begins with a description of his experiments in 1792 in distilling gases from certain vegetable

The lighting art as a new specialized practice was born when gas lighting inaugurated the era of permanent locations for light-sources.

and mineral substances. The results induced him "to try the combustible property of the gases produced from coal." He found that these gases burned satisfactorily so he piped the gas into his home and burned it at the open end of the pipe. Finding this method wasteful, he closed the ends of the pipes and bored small holes from which the gas-flames diverged. It is said that he first placed his wife's well-worn thimble over the open end of a pipe. Gas emerged from several small holes in the thimble and the lighting was more satisfactory and less wasteful of gas. This incident is said to have been the forerunner of later burners with small holes. He piped gas to a street-lamp in front of his house and thus inaugurated street-lighting by gas. He filled bladders with his coal-gas "to carry at night, with which, and his little steam carriage running on the road, he used to astonish the people."

Long before this Clayton described some observations on coal-gas which he described as "the spirit of coals." He filled bladders with the gas in order to store it until he wished to use it. By accident he pricked one of the bladders with a pin and, being an experimenter, it was natural to apply a candle to the orifice. The gas burned and Clayton apparently had thereby produced the first portable gas-light. A summary of Clayton's experiments did not appear in print until 1739 but, according to the evidence, Clayton had written the original notes at least a century before Murdock began his work. Therefore, he provided some of the foundation for gas-lighting by means of coal-gas, although Murdock supplied most of the early technical development and practice. Clayton in describing his early laboratory work deals with heating coal in a retort placed over an open fire. He stated that first "there came over only phlegm, afterwards a black oil, and then likewise a spirit arose... the spirit which issued out caught fire... and continued burning with violence." He then decided to save some of the gas in bladders. He was surprised at the amount of gas obtained from a small amount of coal for "the spirit continued to rise for several hours, and filled the bladders almost as fast as a man could have blown them with his mouth."

In its early years, gas-lighting was chiefly a matter of making suitable gas and piping it where it was to be used. The best first-hand accounts available are those of Murdock who pioneered and persevered through many early difficulties. The process of making gas from coal consists essentially of baking coal in a closed vessel and piping off the gas. The familiar retort of the chemist is a suitable vessel in principle. Apparently Murdock actually used glass retorts at first. Next he placed about fifteen pounds of coal in cast-iron cylinders which were heated in a furnace. By 1804 he had constructed larger cylinders with doors for feeding the coal and for extracting the coke which is left after the coal is baked to distill the gas. Eventually he perfected the mechanical details to the point where a solid foundation was laid for producing coal-gas for lighting purposes. For the first time in the history of lighting, fuel was piped to light-sources fixed in position. Thus the important practice of modern lighting was born.

At first the burners were merely flattened ends of small pipes or caps perforated with small holes. The cockspur burner is named from its shape. It was merely a small jet of flame which was more or less bent somewhat by drafts because the pressure of the gas was low. Murdock standardized a three-flame burner of this type suggesting the *fleur de lis*. Argand, who had put the glass chimney on the oil-lamp and developed ventilated wick-holders, also bequeathed his experience to gas-burners. The first extensive installation of gas-lighting in a large industrial plant was described by Murdock as consisting of 271 Argand burners and 636 cockspurs. Each of the former "gave a light equal to that of four candles; and each of the latter, a light equal to two and a quarter of the same candles; making therefore a total of 2500 candles." He standardized for his measurements a molded candle weighing six to the pound and consuming tallow at the rate of 0.4 ounce per hour. Thus we see the candle becoming a standard light-source for measurements so necessary in science and in placing any practice upon a sound foundation. It became so thoroughly established for the purpose that all later sources, including electric lamps, are measured in terms of it. Candles are not actually used for measurements of light but our present standard lamps are carefully specified modern light-sources rated in terms of candlepower and lumens. From the simple geometry of a sphere a light-source which has an intensity of one candlepower in all directions emits 12.57 lumens.

The gas-lighting installation which Murdock described in 1808 provided about five times as much light for the same cost as candle-light. Thus he reduced the cost of lighting to one-fifth of that obtained by means of candles. The cost of present-day light is now far less than a hundredth of the cost of candle-light. Murdock had installed gas-lighting in the principal shops at Soho foundry during several years previous while he was developing his gas-making equipment. Others were experimenting in France and Germany at the time. Le Bon was granted a patent in Paris in 1799 for making illuminating gas from wood and gave a gas-lighting exhibition in 1802.

There was more or less controversy over various claims, patents and processes in those early years of gas-lighting. Investigations were made by the House of Commons at which Sir Humphrey Davy, leading English scientist at the time, testified that Murdock was the first person to apply coal-gas in actual lighting practice. This testimony, and the Count Rumford Medal of the Royal Society bestowed upon Murdock for "his economical application of the gas-light," established Murdock as the father of gas-lighting.

In 1812 a company was organized and granted a franchise for supplying gas-lighting in London. Probably this was the predecessor of all modern public utility companies. As such, an excerpt from its charter is of interest.

The power and authorities granted to this corporate body are very restricted and moderate. The individuals composing it have no exclusive privilege; their charter does not prevent other persons from entering into competition with them. Their operations are confined to the metropolis, where they are bound to furnish not only a stronger and better light to such streets and parishes as chuse to be lighted with gas, but also at a cheaper price than shall be paid for lighting the said streets with oil in the usual manner. The corporation is not permitted to traffic in machinery for manufacturing or conveying the gas into private houses, their capital or joint stock is limited to 200,000 pounds sterling and his Majesty has the power of declaring the gas-light charter void if the company fail to fulfil the terms of it.

It will be noted that the company was not permitted to pipe gas into private houses and that it did not have a monopoly. Gradually since that time it has been found that a monopoly properly regulated can provide gas, electric or telephone service at the lowest cost to the consumer. Duplication of equipment by competing companies in the same locality inevitably increases the cost and is a needless waste.

GAS FLAMES AND MANTLES

This is the sound basis for regulated monopolies for these kinds of service and is almost the universal practice in this country. The exceptions are few and most of these are dominated by politics instead of economics.

With gas-lighting being supplied on the streets of London, crimes greatly diminished according to publications of the period. Even now street-lamps aid policemen and replace some of them. Citizens in London were no longer reminded in official mandates "on pains and penalties to hang out their lanthorns at the appointed time." Watchmen as they made their rounds no longer had to note who was disobeying the law passed in 1668 whereby the inhabitants were ordered "for the safety and peace of the city to hang out candles duly to the accustomed hour." Apparently this divided responsibility for street-lighting was not entirely successful. In 1679 the Lord Mayor complained that the result of the failure of the inhabitants to hang out their light was "when nights darkened the streets then wandered forth the sons of Belial, flown with insolence and wine."

A notable event in the early years of gas-lighting, as well as street-lighting, was the installation of gas-burners on Westminster Bridge and in the next few years gas-lighting spread throughout London. In 1817 it is reported that 300,000 cubic feet of coal-gas were being manufactured daily in London, "enough to supply 76,500 Argand burners yielding 6 candle-power each." This probably required 50 or 100 tons of coal daily. Gas-lighting expanded first outdoors along the streets and indoors in industrial places. Owing to lack of purification of the gas which resulted in smoky flames and sooty burners, its adoption was slow indoors excepting in industrial plants. It was particularly slow in entering houses owing to fears that it was dangerous. Not until about 1850 was it generally used in residences.

Naturally after gas-lighting became definitely established, attention was turned to refinements. Gas was purified to obtain better light and cleaner burners. Gas-meters were developed so that the gas used by each customer could be measured. Many experiments were made from which all phases of gas-lighting profited in improvements, but developments of the burner now became of considerable interest from the viewpoint of light-production. The output of light from a single cockspur burner was about equal to that from a candle for each cubic foot of gas burned per hour. Obviously these cockspurs could be grouped so that the multiple burner could equal a number of candles. A natural step was to flatten the welded end of a pipe and bore a series of holes in a line. When pointing upward, as they did, this series of flames had somewhat the shape of the comb of a rooster. Naturally it was called the cockscomb burner. By slitting the welded and flattened end of a pipe along its edge by means of a fine saw, the batswing burner was produced. All these were simple orifices and had merely the obvious advantage of producing a number of tiny flames or a thin wide flame. These expedients resulted in more light from a given amount of gas burned by exposing a large light-emitting surface for a given flow of gas.

From the viewpoint of light-production, the most important law of radiation is that relating the temperature of a source of light with its brightness or light-output. In general, sources that emit light solely by virtue of their temperature, rapidly increase in brightness as the temperature is increased. Therefore, for such light-sources, whether flames or electric filaments, the primary object is to increase the temperature of the source as much as is practicable. When gas-flames first came into use, the laws of radiation were not thoroughly established, but these aspects of physics were far more developed than their interpretation into everyday use. There still remained a wide gulf between the aristocrats of knowledge and the inventors and socalled practical men. However it was becoming obvious that a primary means of increasing the luminous efficiency of gas-flames was to increase their temperature. Cold air coming to the flame cools it. Also metal parts in contact with, or close to, the flame reduce its temperature. Recognition of these facts was slowly dawning.

The first real improvement was made by Nielson in 1820 when he arranged two orifices so that the jets of flame collided in the air and spread out into a flat flame. This fish-tail burner was somewhat higher in efficiency than the earlier ones and its flame was steadier in drafts of air. Eventually the orifices were made in durable non-metallic materials which were poor conductors of heat. The fish-tail burner was so satisfactory that it was used widely throughout a half-century until the gas-mantle greatly improved gas-lighting.

All this time the Argand burner was being improved. Murdock originally adapted it from oil to gas and used a lamp chimney to improve combustion as well as to steady the flame. He and others knew that the light-output was considerably influenced by the temperature of the flame. Therefore, the metal part which conducted heat rapidly away from the flame, thereby lowering its temperature, was replaced by materials such as steatite which conduct heat much more slowly. However, it was not until 1853 that Frankland, by an arrangement of two chimneys, made an

Argand burner in which the air was intentionally heated before it reached the flame. These and other improvements, which conserved the heat and increased the temperature of the flame, led to regenerative gas-burners.

Bowditch brought out a lamp with the socalled regenerative burner in 1854 and is generally credited with its creation. However, the principles were known and burners had been progressing in that direction for a long time. Others brought out similar lamps and all were based upon the principle of heating both the air and the gas before they reached the burner. Bowditch's burner was like an Argand oil-burner excepting that the circular flame projected downward with a central cusp. The air and gas passages were directly above the flame so as to be heated by it. Many patents were issued to various persons for variations of the same general principle.

The basic test of progress in light-production is the advance in luminous efficiency—light-output per unit of energy supplied. This is true whether the energy is supplied by oil, gas, electricity or anything else. The luminous efficiencies of the various burners, in candlepower per cubic foot of gas consumed per hour, vary with size and various improvements. In candlepower for equal rates of consumption of gas they were approximately as follows: cockspur, 1; fish-tail, 0.6 to 2.5; Argand, 3 to 3.5; regenerative, 7 to 10. Thus it is seen that the efficiency of regenerative gas-burners was as much as ten times that of the original cockspur burner. This increase was achieved in about the first half-century of gas-lighting and represents creditable progress.

Gas-lighting spread out into countries which had the necessary materials for making gas. Naturally it came to this country where large supplies of coal had been discovered.

GAS FLAMES AND MANTLES

The first attempt to organize a gas-lighting company here was made in Philadelphia in 1815 but progress was so slow that New York and Baltimore led the way. There was much opposition to piping gas indoors and even outdoors. Sir Walter Scott, who had branded gas-lighting as a pestilential innovation projected by a madman, is representative of some of the severe opposition. But anything which deserves to survive usually does and gas-lighting grew into a mighty industry. In 1800 Philadelphia was a city of 50,000 inhabitants dependent for its lighting entirely upon oil-lamps and candles. An old account of a grand ball on Washington's birthday in 1817 states that the ballroom was lighted by 2000 wax-candles. This would be a fascinating sight today but the danger and inconvenience would now be considered rather overwhelming. Philadelphia had its first gas-plant in 1835. Today it has more electric street-lamps, each equivalent to many candles, than it had inhabitants in the early years of gas-lighting.

The modern method of making gas from coal is essentially destructive distillation. The principles are the same as Murdock used but with great refinements in technique and knowledge. The coal is placed in a retort and when heated to about 700°F by an outside fire the coal fuses and the hydrocarbon vapors begin to be freed from the coal. As the temperature is increased these vapors are broken up into various chemical combinations. They are caught and some condense into liquids. Among these is tar which is used in many ways. It even yields dyes of many colors for textiles. Fairly pure carbon is deposited upon the upper part of the retort and coke remains in the place occupied originally by the coal.

The coke found many uses, one of them being in the production of socalled water-gas. If through a mass of red-hot coke, steam is passed, hydrogen and carbon monoxide are produced. Both of these gases are inflammable. Their flames are hot but not bright, but for lighting purposes they could be enriched by hydrocarbons. This was accomplished by mixing oil with the steam.

Eventually much attention was given to purifying the gases used in gas-lighting and in enriching them for illuminating purposes. For example, coal-gas contained compounds of sulphur which were removed by washing the gas with water and ammonia. It contained some carbon dioxide which is not inflammable and, therefore, just went along for the ride. It merely diluted the gas. On distilling a ton of coal a typical yield was about 10,000 cubic feet of coal-gas which was about 17 percent, by weight, of the original ton of coal. About 70 percent of the end-product was coke; 5 percent was tar; the remainder was largely a solution of ammonia. The coal-gas consisted approximately of 40 percent hydrocarbons and 50 percent hydrogen.

Just as increases in knowledge of physics improved gasburners, increases in knowledge of chemistry improved the fuels used in gas-lighting. The heating value of a gas is important but the illuminating value depends upon the amount of carbon particles in the flame and upon their temperature. Hydrocarbons, combinations of hydrogen and carbon, are the important providers of carbon in the flame. Among the various liquid and gaseous hydrocarbons are acetylene, C_2H_2; benzene, C_6H_6; and methane, CH_4. It is seen that acetylene is richer in carbon than methane. It has one carbon atom for each hydrogen atom while methane has only one carbon atom for four hydrogen atoms. As the chemistry of gas-lighting advanced much attention was given to enriching gases for illuminating purposes. This was accomplished in various ways. Coal-tar was chemically broken up and the gases high in carbon content were added to coal-gas. Water-gas was carbureted. This consisted of introducing more carbon by passing it through benzene, by adding oil-gas, and by any process which added the hydrocarbons rich in carbon.

It was inevitable that gas-lighting would not remain confined to the areas reached only by gas-mains connected to the central plant and storage tank. Small plants and portable lamps were bound to be developed. Pintsch gas, made of oil and rich in illuminating value, was widely used in isolated places such as light-buoys for navigation and on steamships. It is associated with the era of red plush in passenger railway cars. Gas suffers in illuminating value when compressed but oil-gas depreciates less in this respect than coal-gas does. Pintsch compressed his gas to a pressure of 150 pounds per square inch but through a reducer it came to the burner at a pressure of one pound per square inch. About 1880 the Pintsch system began to be adopted for isolated lighting plants and for many years it served well.

Although the Pintsch system represented a long step from the fixed gas-lighting systems which were tied to the gas-mains in the streets, there was still a great field for small portable plants. With the development of the electric furnace through the availability of cheaper electrical energy from such a hydro-electric plant as that at Niagara Falls, electricity gave birth to a new form of gas-lighting. Many chemical compounds can be conquered by the high temperatures of the electric furnace. Limestone is cheap but the calcium in it clings tenaciously to other elements in the chemical compounds of which limestone consists. However, the electric furnace produced a rare combination of calcium and carbon called calcium carbide. It is said that this was a waste product of a furnace process and that by accidentally throwing water on it acetylene gas was found to be produced. At any rate calcium carbide is a solid readily stored and transported. All that is necessary to produce this rich hydrocarbon gas, C_2H_2, is to add water to the solid calcium carbide. Here was a new method of producing illuminating gas in plants as small as a tin can. As a consequence acetylene lighting came into wide usage on automobiles, trains, ships, buoys, lighthouses, and in many other isolated places.

Notwithstanding the great achievements in gas-lighting it was doomed by electricity. It served well throughout most of the nineteenth century. It spanned the period from the advent of the Argand oil-lamp to the early decades of electric lighting. Oil-lamps were greatly improved during that period and were given a longer lease on life by the discovery of mineral oil in underground pools. They also served throughout the regions to which gas was piped but gas-lighting gave to civilization fixed lighting on streets and in interiors which eliminated some of the inconvenience of the individual oil-lamps. And it greatly increased the luminous efficiency of light-sources, a perpetual objective in light-production. With the discovery of petroleum, natural gas came into use and was destined to supply fuel for heating after electricity supplanted gas for lighting. With the advent of electric lighting, gas-lighting continued for several decades and this lease on life was largely due to the advent of a new principle in light-production introduced in the gas-mantle.

The brightness of the mantle is far in excess of what it would be if it were due solely to its temperature. Some things glow much more than others when heated. In other words, some radiate more visible energy than others in proportion to the invisible energy radiated. This is termed selectivity. It can be demonstrated by burning a piece of magnesium ribbon and holding the ash in the Bunsen flame of a gas-range. The ash glows much more brightly than one expects. This is the principle of the old lime-light, developed by Drummond in 1825, in which a button of lime was heated by a Bunsen flame. It was used for searchlights, for lantern slide projectors, and also for spotlights in theaters, hence the term "in the lime-light." The Bunsen burner provides a hot flame by mixing the air with the gas before it reaches the flame. At first coal-gas was used and later hydrogen and oxygen gases were combined. Eventually the button of lime was replaced by zirconia, an oxide of zirconium. The lime-light used in practice was generally of several hundred candlepower. It was the most powerful single light-source available for a long time. It was the first searchlight to be used in warfare and played a part in the attack of Charleston in 1863.

A group of elements called rare-earths possess the useful property of glowing unusually brilliantly when heated to a given temperature. Their oxides are zirconia, thoria, ceria, erbia and yttria. If a bit of one of these oxides is placed on a strip of glass or metal and heated to a high temperature, it will glow very brightly in comparison with the glass or metal. Naturally this property attracted the attention of those interested in light-production and many ways of using these rare-earths were experimented with. Welsbach was the most successful by making a mantle of woven cotton which he immersed in solutions of salts of some of these rare-earths. After burning the fabric, the ash glowed brilliantly when left in a hot gas-flame. His mantle came into use in 1885, a few years after electric lighting was introduced into practice. Soon he introduced thoria, an oxide of thorium, into his solution of rare-earth oxides. This made a stronger mantle which also glowed more brightly.

Many improvements in mantles followed. The oxides were purified and by adding a slight amount of ceria, a still better mantle was produced. Much improvement was made in the textiles. The mantle shrinks when burned to ash, but it must not shrink too much. By experiment it was found that the best proportions for the rare-earth content are one part of ceria and ninety-nine parts of thoria. The actual percentage of the rare-earths in the ash of the mantle is about ten percent. Thus it is seen that the actual content of the ceria is only one part in a thousand; but it has a very great effect. The mantles consist of knitted cotton or other fiber tied together at one end with an asbestos string. This fabric is soaked in nitrates of cerium and thorium. After the organic matter of the mantle is burned away, these nitrates are converted into oxides which are very durable under the high temperature of the Bunsen flame. All the gas-burners used for mantles were of this Bunsen type because of its high temperature. Many other details were worked out but the general principles remained the same.

Thus it is seen that the illuminating value of the gas became less important than the heating value. In the limelight and particularly in the gas-mantle an entirely new principle entered into light-production. This property of selectivity continues to be important at the present time throughout the still greater advances in light-production by means of electricity. Mantles greatly increased the candlepower above that of the gas-flame. Thus a gas-burner which supplied a flame of one or two candlepower could now supply the same gas to a mantle which in turn yielded several times more light than the flame. Natural gas of high heat value was quite satisfactory. In other words, before the entrance of the gas-mantle, the fuel was overwhelmingly important but the gas-mantle assumed the major role when it appeared.

I well recall the last years of gas-lighting when great ingenuity was combined with scientific knowledge to keep gas-lighting in successful competition with electric lighting which was on the rise. All kinds of lamps, burners, and mantles, higher gas-pressure, electric ignition and portable study lamps came into use to stem the rapidly rising tide of electric lighting. But to no avail. Gas-lighting was doomed but it went down not in defeat but to a glorious end of a great service. It greatly increased the luminous efficiency and the candlepower of light-sources. It advanced lighting wherever it was in use. It steadied and brightened the torch of civilization through a great period of growth of the new world as well as the old. It still remains the torch of civilization in many places beyond the reach of electricity.

VIII. ELECTRIC ARCS

SPECTACULAR FIREWORKS burst from brilliant electric arcs as the welders work their magic in the industrial plant. But the light and lighting effects are incidental to the arc's present purpose. Electric arcs had their day in lighting —a half century long. They still serve well in special lighting applications but the old types of electric arcs have passed from the stage of general lighting progress. The epilogue of their drama is now being played but it may evolve into a prologue of a new drama in which new kinds of electric arcs may be featured. Much that was learned of arcs during their sojourn in general lighting applications has been passed on to new fields such as welding. Thus the growth of knowledge extends the opportunities.

Sparks fly from the blinding acetylene torch as it cuts through a steel rail. Even though the light is merely incidental to this new service it outshines Drummond's limelight. Great searchlights sweep the sky in search of aircraft. Their beams flow from extremely brilliant electric arcs which have no close competitors among other electric sources where beams of very high candlepower are needed. The projection of motion-pictures to the distant screen in the large theaters is another of these special services. Such special lighting applications of electric arcs comprise the epilogue of their story in general lighting service. From their debut in electric lighting in about 1875 they served on streets, in stores, in industrial plants and various large inte-

ELECTRIC ARCS

riors. Filament-lamps very generally replaced them and now certain vapor-lamps are beginning to appear. If these are classed as electric arcs the prologue of a new story is beginning, but electric arcs as we have known them in the past are making their last stand in specialized services.

The electric arc was definitely born as a scientific fact in 1800. It came into practical use in about 1875 and served throughout extensive applications for about a half century. The delay between its birth and its practical use was primarily due to absence of adequate sources and distribution of electrical energy. These had to await the fundamental work of Faraday on electricity and magnetism in the decade following 1830. In following decades inventors worked to apply this knowledge in successful mechanical generation of electricity. The Gramme dynamo in 1870 provided the necessary practicable source of electrical energy. Naturally from then on electric light-sources were rapidly developed. The electric arc preceded the filament-lamp by a few years. It almost appears that because human beings had always burned something to make light they still insisted upon burning carbon by electricity. The electric filament-lamp embodied the opposite principle. The light was completely bottled in a vacuum so that the heated carbon filament could not burn. It glowed more or less permanently in the absence of oxygen.

In 1800 Volta greatly excited the scientists of his day by announcing a source from which a continuous flow of electrical energy could be obtained. Until that time about the only kind of electricity available was static electricity obtained by friction. Intermittent sparks could be obtained but they were so feeble that they gave no promise as light-sources. The ultimate source of Volta's electrical energy was in certain chemical processes not at all understood by him or anyone else at that time. He arranged zinc and copper disks alternately in a pile. This source of electricity was eventually called the voltaic pile. At first he placed wet cloths between the disks. Later when it became evident that chemical action was involved the cloths were soaked in a dilute acid. Volta was showered with honors which he well deserved, for he had supplied the first source of continually-flowing electricity. The voltage depended upon the number of cells that were placed in series and the current depended upon the area of the disks. Thus by Volta's discovery a new door was opened for exploring the great unknown of electricity. The source was adequate for much research but impractical for much practical use.

Sir Humphrey Davy was quick to sense the possibilities of Volta's discovery for researches in electricity and immediately constructed voltaic cells in his laboratory. Late in 1800 Davy began to use charcoal for electrodes of his crude miniature arcs. He quickly discovered that the arc between the two charcoal points was larger and brighter than between two brass spheres which were commonly used for the spark-gap of the machines for generating static electricity by friction. Through the habit of dealing with sparks from static electricity Davy continued to call his new continuous arcs, electric sparks. By 1808 scientific progress in this electrical unknown had become so great and promising that by subscription among the members of the Royal Society of London—a scientific body—Davy obtained a voltaic battery of 2000 cells. Now he could study arcs on an extensive scale. In 1809 he demonstrated a carbon arc publicly which is described in his notes as "a most brilliant flame, of from half an inch to one and a quarter inches in length."

This incidental light from arc-welding is reminiscent of the years when electric arcs illuminated much of the work-world.

ELECTRIC ARCS

Davy's notes made during those years in which he did so much pioneering work on the electric arc and other phenomena of continuous or direct current, were systematically arranged by his assistant, Michael Faraday. They are available in two volumes. In these notes the word, spark, was used at first. Later he describes a horizontal arc between two charcoal electrodes as "a most brilliant ascending arch of light, broad and conical in form in the middle." A horizontal electric arc naturally curves upward because it consists of heated air, carbon particles and various products of the electrical and combustion processes. From the appearance of this arch, or curved arc, Davy in 1820 definitely named this electric flame, the electric arc. The name has continued in use even though the arc between vertical electrodes is not arched or bent as it is between horizontal electrodes.

It was soon discovered that the arc could be attracted or repelled by a magnet. A current flows through the arc between the two electrodes and, therefore, the arc-flame is affected by a magnet just as a wire carrying a direct current is attracted or repelled. These are well-known facts which are taken advantage of in countless ways in electrical devices. It was taken advantage of in modern arc-lamps in which inclined carbons were used. In such arcs the magnet kept the arc in place, for without such control the arc would climb up the inclined carbons and would break. Much ingenuity was exercised to keep arcs steady and in position in the variety of electric arcs which played their parts as torches of civilization.

In the early experimental arcs charcoal was used for the electrodes but this relatively soft and porous carbon burned away rapidly. Foucault in 1843 appears to have been the first to use carbon from the deposit on the crown of the

TORCH OF CIVILIZATION

retorts used to make gas from coal. This harder carbon does not waste away as rapidly as charcoal. However, charcoal, owing to its softer porous character, produced a longer arc and a fatter flame which are desirable characteristics of a carbon arc. In 1877 after the advent of dynamos made electric service possible, the advantages of hard and soft carbon were combined into carbon electrodes. Carbon rods were molded very hard and dense but with a small core of soft carbon running along the axis. Carbons for ordinary arc-lamps were made of retort-carbon, soot and coal-tar. This paste was forced through dies and the carbons were baked at a high temperature. The cores were made by inserting a rod in the center of the die. This hollow core was then filled with a powder of soft carbon. The soft carbon enriched the arc-flame and aided in keeping the arc centered.

For seventy years during which electric arcs were being studied in the laboratory, and later during their early introduction into lighting-practice, they were carbon arcs operating on direct current. Gassiot discovered in 1838 that the positive carbon wasted away more rapidly than the negative one. This is due to the much higher temperature of the tip of the positive carbon. As the direct-current carbon arc burns, a crater forms at the positive tip where the carbon appears to boil. However, the globules are not carbon but other ingredients of carbons. The temperature of this crater is 6000 to 7000 degrees Fahrenheit which was by far the highest man-made temperature used in light-production, or perhaps in any other art, up to the time the carbon arc appeared. By putting the electric arc under high pressure, brightnesses equivalent to that of the sun have been obtained. The electric furnace, which is so widely used at the present time to manufacture materials unheard of before the electric age, was born of the carbon arc. The crater on the tip of the positive carbon is about one-tenth of the brightness of the sun and at least 20,000 times brighter than a candle flame. Craters in present-day carbon arcs used in searchlights are even much brighter than the ordinary carbon arc.

The flame of the ordinary carbon arc emits only a small percentage of the total light. The negative tip shows a small bright spot where the arc-flame is attached but most of the light is emitted by the large brilliant crater on the positive carbon. For this reason in arc-lamps for general-lighting purposes the positive crater was placed above the negative one. In this position the brilliant crater radiated its light downward where it was generally needed and desired. In projectors for lantern slides and motion-pictures and in searchlights and other apparatus where the light is to be controlled optically by lenses and reflectors, the carbons are inclined, or even placed at right angles, in order to expose the brilliant crater.

All practical arc-lamps were provided with a mechanism for bringing the carbons together to strike the arc and then separating them the proper distance. As the arc burns the electrodes away, the gap between them lengthens. Eventually it gets too long and the arc goes out unless the electrodes are moved closer. The current flowing through the arc-flame varies with the arc-length. Therefore, with some ingenuity it was possible to design mechanisms involving electromagnets which maintained the arc at the proper length. The force of gravitation was also a factor which could be utilized to counterbalance the electromagnetic forces of the mechanism.

Knowledge of the chemistry of combustion was increasing during the practical development of gas-lighting which was the laboratory period of the carbon arc. Naturally, the carbon arcs had to burn in air but Staite in 1846 discovered that the carbons were consumed less freely if the arcs were confined to some extent. He enclosed the arc in a glass envelope which restricted the free access of air to the arc. This was the forerunner of the socalled enclosed arc of the practical era of arc-lighting. The first successful open arcs operated with about 65 volts across the arc. Enclosed arcs were not successful at this voltage but Jandus in 1893 produced a satisfactory one operating at about 80 volts. Later Marks made improvements by showing that a smaller current and a higher voltage, 80 to 85 volts, produced a very satisfactory enclosed arc. It was necessary to use an electrical ballast with all arcs. These were so designed that the entire lamp operated on standardized voltages in the neighborhood of 115 volts.

The carbons of an arc operating in free air are consumed rapidly by simple combustion. When the arc is enclosed in a small loosely-fitting glass envelope the oxygen is quickly consumed but the heated gases, which result from this combustion, are more or less retained in the enclosure. Thus the supply of fresh air—oxygen—to the arc is greatly restricted and the carbons are consumed only about one-tenth as rapidly as in the open arc. The luminous efficiency of the enclosed arc was less than that of the open arc chiefly because no brilliant crater is formed on the positive tip. As a consequence the arc wandered considerably. However, the enclosed arc came into favor, notwithstanding these handicaps, because it would operate a long time without "trimming"—renewing the carbons. Actually it would operate without attention for a hundred hours or more, equivalent to a week or even several weeks in actual lighting service, depending upon the hours burned daily or nightly. Before the enclosed arc was introduced, open arcs used for all-night burning had to be supplied with two sets of carbons. The second pair went into operation automatically during the night after the first pair had been consumed.

After the modern age of electric service got under way, certain advantages of alternating current over direct current became obvious. In general, important apparatus for generating and transmitting alternating current is much simpler. Transformers, without a moving part, can step up the voltage for transmitting electrical energy a long distance with less loss. The voltage can be stepped down as easily for the user. In many ways alternating current is so much more flexible and practicable that it began to enter into competition with direct current. Now it has almost entirely replaced direct current excepting in the downtown districts of large cities. Even in these places the area of direct current is continually growing smaller.

Mechanisms of electric arcs had to be quite different for alternating current but these were readily developed. The alternating arc has no positive or negative carbons, for the current and polarity are generally reversing 120 times per second. They pass through sixty complete cycles each second. As a consequence there are no marked craters on the tips of the carbons and both carbons are consumed at about the same rate. The average temperature and brightness of the tips of the carbons are lower than the crater on the tip of the positive carbon of the direct-current arc. The alternating-current arc hummed and the direct current hissed some of the time. The humming is characteristic of alternating current changing its direction 120 times a second in the arc-flame and controlling mechanism. The hissing of the direct-current arc took place during various changes in the size of the positive crater and of the deposit on the negative tip. Both open and enclosed carbon arcs were developed for alternating current and were widely used.

During the period when voltaic cells and other chemical batteries were the only sources of electricity, the electric arc was often demonstrated to the public. As early as 1848 carbon-arc lamps were used in Paris for general lighting but all such applications were impracticable until a more satistory source of electrical energy became available. With due respect for such early attempts, they were little more than spectacular stunts. Carbon arcs came into actual use in this country through the practical pioneering of Brush in 1877. The year before Jablochkov invented his "electric candle" consisting of two vertical rods of carbon placed side by side and separated by an insulating material. The arc played across the adjacent ends. However, electric lighting required a generating source of electricity and a distribution system. Progress had been made in the mechanical generation of electricity. Brush not only invented an arc-lamp but also an efficient dynamo. I have listened to his amusing accounts of making his first carbon rods of lampblack and pulverized high-grade coke. He descended upon the kitchen and borrowed molasses for a binder. He molded the carbons from this sticky mess and baked them himself in the kitchen oven. A year or so before Edison invented the carbon-filament lamp, Brush lighted the Public Square in Cleveland with his arc-lamps and electric generating and distributing system.

For the next score of years ordinary carbon arcs and carbon-filament lamps were the only practical sources of electric light. The carbon arc had been greatly improved in operation and life of the carbons, but little or no attention had been given to certain obvious expedients for altering the spectral character of the light and particularly for increasing the luminous efficiency. It had been known that different chemical compounds when heated in a Bunsen flame gave characteristic colors to the flame. The "fairy powders" that are sprinkled upon a wood-fire provide a colorful demonstration of this property. Salt spilled in the flame of the kitchen range gives the yellowish color characteristic of the element, sodium. This general fact is the basis of spectrum analysis which reveals the elements in a mixture with great certainty and sensitivity.

Almost a century passed since Davy's first demonstration of the carbon arc, and a score of years passed since its advent in lighting, before anyone introduced chemical compounds into carbons for a lighting purpose. In 1898 Bremer introduced fluorides of calcium, barium and strontium into the carbons. These salts deflagrate, or burn intensely and rapidly, and a fat luminous flame envelops the ordinary flame of the carbon arc. By selecting proper salts of metals, the luminous efficiency of the carbon arc was increased many times. Owing to the richness of the flame, these arcs, in which impregnated carbons were used, were called flame-arcs. Considerable control over color is possible. The reddish flame arc owes its color to strontium. Looking at this flame through a spectroscope one sees the signals from the strontium atoms, operating on certain wavelengths or frequencies. Characteristic of the spectrum of strontium are certain wavelengths which we see as yellow and red light. The spectrum of calcium is characterized by green, orange and red light. Barium produces a whitish flame-arc because its colors are so distributed in its spectrum as to produce almost colorless light.

TORCH OF CIVILIZATION

Many special carbons were made for a variety of purposes in industrial and photographic processes. The flame-arcs were such powerful sources of light that they were chiefly used outdoors and indoors only in large spaces such as industrial plants. Some rather poisonous fumes were emitted by them so that it was desirable to have adequate ventilation wherever they were used. One disadvantage was the rapid consumption of the carbon rods or electrodes. Therefore, these were made as long as practicable and the flame-arc lamps could be recognized by their excessive length compared with the ordinary carbon arcs. In one type of flame-arc, both carbons were fed downward in a long slender V and the arc-flame played across the lower tips. Naturally the arc tended to travel upward and if permitted to do so it would stretch itself beyond the breaking point. By means of a magnet the arc was readily kept where it belonged.

Objection to the rapid consumption of the carbons of the open arc led to the enclosed arc. It did the same for the flame-arc but the procedure was not as simple in this case. Solid products were deposited from the electrodes of the flame-arc in much greater quantity than from ordinary carbons. This is due to the impregnating salts themselves and to the various compounds formed in the high-temperature combustion. A simple enclosure of glass as used for the enclosed carbon arc would get coated with these vaporized solids and greatly absorb the light. The Jandus regenerative flame-arc lamp is representative of the development of an enclosed flame-arc. In addition to the inner glass enclosure, two cooling chambers of metal were provided. These operated as the condenser of an ordinary still. Air entered at the bottom and the fumes from the arc passed upward and into the cooling chambers where the solid matter was deposited.

ELECTRIC ARCS

The gases on returning to the bottom were relieved of the solid matter and the glass envelope remained fairly clean. The life of the electrode was about seventy-five hours. The lower carbon contained the metallic salts and the upper carbon had a core of soft carbon.

With the inspiration of the flame-arcs many materials were tried out for impregnating carbon and for actually replacing carbon. The magnetite arc was a flame-arc of a radically different kind. One disadvantage in an era of rapidly expanding use of alternating current was that it was essentially a direct-current arc. The positive electrode consisted of a solid cylinder of copper which was consumed very slowly because it rapidly conducts heat and keeps relatively cool. It was usually the upper electrode. The negative electrode consisted of an iron tube in which was packed a mixture of three parts of iron oxide, known as magnetite, and one part of titanium oxide. The magnetite is a good conductor of electricity and was readily vaporized in the arc. This made the flame large and the titanium made it very luminous. It actually became known as the "luminous arc."

Many factors make a light-source successful but a primary objective in light-production is to increase the luminous efficiency. With electric sources this is readily expressed in lumens per watt. The lumens per watt of the arc-lamps as used in practice were approximately as follows: open carbon arc, 4 to 8; enclosed carbon arc, 3 to 7; enclosed flame-arcs, 15 to 25; magnetite arc, 10 to 25. It is interesting to compare these luminous efficiencies with the early carbon-filament lamps of 3 to 4 lumens per watt and present-day tungsten-filament lamps of 10 to 30 lumens per watt. Although luminous efficiency is always a most important fundamental factor in light-production, it is not always the basis of practical and commercial success. For example, the enclosed carbon arc was generally accepted over the open arc because of less nuisance in trimming notwithstanding its lesser light-output per watt of electric power supplied. Furthermore, filament-lamps were used in homes and many other places rather than the flame-arc regardless of the luminous efficiency. This is true today and always will be. In actual use many factors of convenience and adaptability are more important than luminous efficiency or cost of light.

The relatively small and extremely brilliant crater of the direct-current carbon arc immediately attracted attention to its use in searchlights and in other devices for controlling the light by optical means. A light-source, such as the concentrated filament of the lamp used in automobile headlamps, radiates light in all directions. It may have a candle-power equal to 30 candles in any direction. But if the light radiated in many directions is intercepted by an efficient reflector of proper shape and most of it is turned in one direction, the intensity in that direction may be a thousand candlepower. In the automobile headlamp, the light is gathered by a parabolic mirror and sent out in a beam where it is desired. A searchlight is merely a much larger device of the same optical principle.

The principle of a parabolic reflector is that if a small light-source is placed at the focal point all the light intercepted by the reflector is re-directed in a parallel beam of light. However, the source must be small physically in comparison with the parabolic reflector because only that part of the source which lies in or close to the focus is reflected into a narrow beam. This is one way that light is multiplied in any desired direction. It is taken from where it is not wanted and sent where it is wanted. Optical control transforms into useful light that which otherwise would be useless or wasted. Lenses and other optical devices operate to place light where it is desired.

The brightness of carbon arcs used for searchlights eventually became 100,000 times brighter than a candle flame and about as large. The struggle to increase the brightness of even as brilliant a source as the crater of the carbon arc is well illustrated by the intensive flame-arc developed by Beck during the World War. His chief aim was to send a much greater current through the arc than had previously been accomplished without increasing the size of the carbons or the size and unsteadiness of the arc. In the ordinary carbon arc, excessive current causes a rapid consumption of the carbons, unless they are correspondingly increased in size. Beck greatly reduced the oxidation of the carbons by directing a stream of alcohol vapor on the arc. He used cored carbons and impregnated them with certain salts to obtain a flame of high brightness. The positive carbon was rotated so that its crater was maintained in a constant position. These and other expedients resulted in searchlight beams several times more powerful than those from ordinary carbon arcs.

It is obvious that the surface of the reflector is important as well as its size and shape. The optical principles involved had been known for a long time, but as is usually the case, the difficulties lay in putting them into practice. Mangin in 1874 coated a glass reflector of proper shape with silver and through considerable ingenuity laid the foundation for practicable reflectors. Since that time heat-resisting glasses have been developed and various metallic surfaces have been developed which do not tarnish quickly as silver does. In the present socalled sealed-beam headlamp for automobiles the reflecting surface is made by exploding aluminum by passing excessive electric current through it. This sprays quite pure aluminum very suddenly upon the molded glass making an efficient accurate parabolic reflector.

During the World War, reflectors five feet in diameter were developed for the latest and most powerful electric arcs. They weighed only one-fifth as much as the previous standard carbon arc searchlights and were much more powerful. They were operated by remote control so that the operator does not have to look through the fog of light near the searchlight. Mobile power-units supplied the electrical energy and towed the searchlight which was on wheels. For the first time in history the sun was being challenged in brightness and in the level of illumination of nearby objects in the beams which had candlepowers running into the hundreds of millions.

Developments in filament-lamps entirely enclosed in glass bulbs requiring little or no attention throughout their relatively long life, began to press electric arcs on all fronts in the early part of the present century. Gradually the electric arc retired from the general-lighting stage. However, certain characteristics left it fairly well entrenched in special fields as illustrated by the searchlight. Great beacons in lighthouses still guide the mariner along shores and into harbors and an intense beam of light brushes the ground as the pilot lands his transport plane. The high-powered arcs in projectors are still hard-pressed to supply enough light on the motion-picture screen and as yet have no competitor in large theaters. In motion-picture studios arc-lamps gave way to filament-lamps of unusually high wattage when the talkies displaced the silent picture. The humming and static of the arc-lamp temporarily ruled it out, but with improvements in

ELECTRIC ARCS

both the arc-lamp and in sound-recording, they are again competing in the motion-picture studios.

Electric arcs emit ultraviolet energy which is useful in many industrial processes. From the bare arc, ultraviolet energy of wavelengths far shorter than the short-wave limit of sunlight can be obtained in great quantities. The spectral character of the ultraviolet energy may be controlled within wide limits by the materials of the electrodes and a variety of glass filters. This short-wave ultraviolet energy, which causes inflammation of the outer membranes of the eyes, is readily excluded by glass and for lighting purposes glass globes had to be used on arc-lamps to prevent this conjunctivitis. Short-wave ultraviolet energy is emitted by the sun, but much of it does not reach the earth. It disappears in the upper atmosphere not only by absorption but largely in the process of producing ozone. Much ultraviolet energy is absorbed by the earth but snow reflects it. Therefore, long exposure to sunlit snow causes snow-blindness.

The magnetite arc radiates ultraviolet energy throughout an extensive range of wavelengths far beyond the short-wave limit of the solar spectrum. This is a characteristic of iron and the iron arc is used for many laboratory purposes. Special carbons and other electrodes are used in photo-engraving and in testing paints and other materials for their durability under sunlight. Wherever powerful ultraviolet energy was desired, the arc-lamp has been generally useful. It has been widely used in therapy for treatment of skin diseases, tuberculosis, rickets and many other ailments. But in most of these applications, and particularly where convenience and simplicity are important, another kind of arc—the mercury arc—has been steadily invading.

The mercury arc is a new kind of arc which is as completely confined in glass or quartz as the glowing filament is confined to its bulb. This arc appeared early in the era of electric lighting and at the present time exists in a variety of sources of light and of ultraviolet energy. But that is another story, one which promises to be important in the history of civilization. Evolution from the early mercury arcs into a variety of mercury vapor lamps already has presented an prologue of a new drama of light-production and service. These new actors on the stage of lighting may not be properly called arc-lamps. However, they are closely akin to the arc and are not even distantly related to the filament-lamp which, in a battle of a half century, eventually was left almost complete master of artificial lighting.

Thus we see the overwhelming principle of Nature—survival of the fittest—operating among man-made things in a man-made civilization. There is no escape from this inexorable law of Nature and of artificial products. It operates in all civilized activities, sometimes slowly, but always inexorably. The electric arc always had a competitor—the filament-lamp. Gas-lighting always had a competitor—the oil-lamp. Competition, the life of trade, is equally the life of technical development.

IX. GLOWING FILAMENTS

THE BIRTH OF the electric arc took place when a source of electrical energy became available. It was nourished in the cradle of enthusiasm over Volta's gift of electricity to experimental science in 1800. This chemical source of electricity was not powerful, but it was adequate for starting a great invasion of the electrical unknown. That was only 140 years ago. One cannot contemplate the recency of that event without, at the same time, realizing the recency of most scientific knowledge which has transformed civilized activities and enormously extended them. The year, 1800, might well mark the dawn of a technical renaissance in the artificial material world of civilization. The recency of that event, just two lifetimes ago, emphasizes the opportunity that still confronts every human being. Progress in obtaining scientific knowledge, and in applying it, is still so near the beginning that one in his lifetime can be a great factor in the progress of the material world. By looking back 140 years we cannot help looking ahead with great expectations. Politicians, through stone-age methods, may discourage and terrorize but they cannot close or monopolize that great storehouse—the unknown.

Throughout the seventy years between the electric battery and the electric dynamo, the fundamental principles of the electric arc had become established. No such period was necessary for understanding the fundamental principles of the filament-lamp. It soon became obvious to Davy and others that if a wire were heated by an electric current it would glow and emit light. When better electric batteries became available after Faraday had established the underlying laws of electrochemistry, some serious efforts were made to make light by heating metals by passing an electric current through them. Naturally such glowing metals rapidly deteriorated in air. They oxidized or slowly burned.

It was early recognized that the wires should be thin and of high melting-point. Platinum was tried with some success. Carbon had a high melting-point but burned rapidly at temperatures which made it glow. There was little to be learned of the fundamental principle of producing light by heating a filament. The difficulties lay in finding the proper combination of filament and its environment. But there was little incentive to work along these practical lines when there was no adequate source of electrical energy to supply such filament-lamps. Therefore, the prologue of the story of filament-lamps was a scanty one. The great drama began rather suddenly with the advent of the electric dynamo and is still being enacted on an ever-widening front.

Edison is deserving of much of the credit for the development of the carbon-filament lamp but others also pioneered. Among these were Sawyer and Man in England who obtained a patent in 1877 involving platinum wire as a filament. Swan in that country particularly paralleled the work of Edison in this country. As early as 1860 he carbonized strips of paper which he operated in poorly-evacuated glass vessels. He resumed this work in 1877 and in 1878 exhibited a lamp containing a thin carbon rod. In an exhibit in the great Kaiser Wilhelm Museum in Munich, Germany takes credit for the first carbon-filament lamp several years before 1879, the year Edison announced a lamp containing a carbonized

This greatly magnified coiled filament of a tungsten lamp is inspected by the highly controllable light from similar filaments.

GLOWING FILAMENTS

filament of paper. However, Edison's contribution was very great. He exhibited a lamp which burned at 100 volts for 40 hours. He scoured the world for filament material, persevered in experiments with filaments, and developed the necessary complete electric service to supply his lamps with electrical energy. In confining the story of the first carbon-filament lamps largely to Edison's contribution, we are dealing with lighting progress in this country which led the way for the world and whose torch-bearers still comprise most of the vanguard in the production and use of artificial light. Late in 1879 Edison gave a practical demonstration of his lamps, operating on his own lighting system in his laboratory, in the street and in adjacent houses. In 1880 the steamship Columbia was lighted by him.

Among the metals, platinum was the most promising known at the time. However, it is quite volatile at high temperatures and its melting-point, 3200 degrees Fahrenheit, is far below that of carbon. From experiences with carbon arcs and from other knowledge, carbon quickly became the center of attention as material for filaments. Edison had coated platinum wire with carbon and had made thin rods of mixtures of finely divided metals, such as platinum and iridium, and of such oxides as magnesia, zirconia and lime. Here we detect the avenue of thought leading directly back to the gas-mantle and even further back to the lime-light. Edison even wrapped a platinum wire around a rod of rare-earth oxides.

The results of these experiments were of no immediate practical value excepting to point to the inherent superiority of carbon for filaments and to the necessity of mounting the filament in an evacuated glass bulb. Such negative results are not spectacular; only the positive ones are. But they are valuable in revealing that which fails, and in forcing attention toward that which may be successful. The highway of research is chiefly paved with negative results. Positive results are as rare as cross-roads, and often lead into a cross-road.

The characteristics and desirability of carbon were unquestioned but these early workers had difficulty in making fine filaments of it. Years later these difficulties fade into unreality as automatic machinery makes filament material by the mile. Very narrow strips of paper, threads of cotton and twisted strands of silk were charred or carbonized. Edison and also Swan became convinced that success lay in carbonizing thin fibers or filaments of organic matter. Edison tried such things as fibrous grass and in 1880 tested 6000 vegetable growths from various parts of the world. The basic requirements of the filament were known, so it became a matter of cut and try. Today the same problem would be approached by pressing through very small orifices the variety of man-made organic compounds and carbonizing them. Edison found that carbonized Japanese bamboo was the best material for filaments in those early years of the filament-lamp. Bamboo was still used in some special carbon-filament lamps in 1910 long after science had perfected processes of making carbon filaments from man-made material.

In 1904, only twenty-five years after his first invention of a carbon-filament lamp, Edison described his early experiences which were still vivid memories. He said:

> It occurred to me that perhaps a filament of carbon could be made to stand in sealed glass vessels, or bulbs, which we were using, exhausted to a high vacuum. Separate lamps were made in this way independent of the air-pump, and, in October, 1879, we made lamps of paper carbon, and with carbons of common

sewing thread, placed in a receiver or bulb made entirely of glass, with the leading-in wires sealed in by fusion. The whole thing was exhausted by the Sprengel pump to nearly one-millionth of an atmosphere. The filaments of carbon, although naturally quite fragile owing to their length and small mass, had a smaller radiating surface and higher resistance than we had dared hope. We had virtually reached the position and condition where the carbons were stable. In other words, the incandescent lamp as we still know it to-day [1904] in essentially all its particulars unchanged, had been born.[1]

After Edison's success with carbonized bamboo filaments, Swan was more than ever convinced that organic matter was the most promising source of carbon filaments. Soon he was turning out material which, when dried, appeared like the cat-gut strings on a violin. These could be cut into proper lengths, bent into desired shapes and carbonized by baking at high temperature in the absence of air or oxygen. He invented a process of squirting filaments of nitrocellulose into a liquid which coagulated the material. Very thin uniform filaments were made by this method, which was improved from time to time but remained essentially the same for many years. In later years cotton was dissolved in a suitable solvent, such as a solution of zinc chloride. This material was forced through very fine dies consisting of circular orifices in diamonds. After cutting into suitable lengths the filaments of organic matter were bent upon a suitable form. They were then immersed in plumbago and heated to a high temperature to destroy the organic matter and leave the reasonably pure carbon.

After the carbon filament was ready, it had to be sealed in a bulb. Naturally some means had to be provided for passing current through the filament from an outside source.

[1] *Electrical World and Engineer,* March 5, 1904.

Therefore, two conductors of electricity had to be sealed in the glass in a manner which did not let air leak into the evacuated glass bulb. Here platinum, which failed as a filament, returned in another but successful role. It expands and shrinks with increasing and decreasing temperature, respectively, about the same amount as the glass used at that time. Many great improvements in filament-lamps were made in the next thirty years, but throughout this period platinum was used for the socalled lead-in wires. However, the cost of platinum continually increased and, as the number of filament-lamps increased to hundreds of millions annually, a substitute was desired. Eventually, a wire was made with a nickel-iron alloy core and a copper sleeve which combined had the same expansion as platinum and as glass.

For forty years continual improvements were made in carbon-filament lamps. Bases and sockets eventually were standardized. Better pumps were developed for exhausting the air from the bulbs. Still some air remained not only in the bulb but in the filament and other parts. This caused some disintegration of the carbon filament and was eventually reduced by chemical means. But a conspicuous shortcoming of the filament was the actual evaporation of carbon from the filament which was evident from the blackening of the bulb. No direct improvement in this direction was made until Whitney in 1906 developed a way of treating the carbon filament so that its surface was harder and less carbon was evaporated.

By this time research laboratories were beginning to be established in private industry. The research laboratories of the General Electric Company were among the first of these and Whitney directed the scientific work. His treatment of

GLOWING FILAMENTS

carbon filaments consisted of heating them in an atmosphere of hydrocarbons such as coal-gas. The hot filament broke down the hydrocarbons with the result that a coating of hard carbon was deposited on the filament which increased its electrical resistance and decreased the evaporation of carbon during its life. From the appearance of this graphitized surface it was called a "metallized" filament. This new carbon-filament lamp became known as the "gem" lamp, the word being coined from the initials of General Electric and of the word, metallized. The luminous efficiency of the gem lamp was 4.5 lumens per watt compared with 3 lumens per watt of the ordinary carbon-filament lamp.

This improved carbon lamp was introduced widely into practice, but its reign was short-lived. Metal filaments were destined to replace carbon-filaments. About a century before, actually in 1803, a new element had been discovered. It was a metal which was named tantalum. This dark metal is harder than steel and has a high melting-point, about 5160 degrees F. Eventually it was found that it could be drawn into fine wire but somehow it had escaped attention as a possibility for filaments of electric lamps. Inasmuch as the luminous efficiency of filament-lamps increases rapidly with increases in temperature, the high melting-point and other properties made it attractive as filament material. The first tantalum lamps were made by von Bolton and they appeared on the market in 1905.

The efficiency of the tantalum lamp was 6.5 lumens per watt, which was more than twice that of the untreated carbon-filament lamp and about fifty percent greater than the gem lamp for the same useful life. Thus a great advance in light-production was achieved by this first metal filament. However, there were drawbacks. The filament had to be long and thin owing to the low electrical resistance of tantalum. Therefore, a considerable length of filament had to be draped on many supports in a lamp in order to operate it on circuits which were being supplied with the standardized voltage of 110 to 120 volts. After the tantalum lamp was operated a few hundred hours, the filament became brittle and faults developed. Doubtless modern metallurgy would have decreased or even eliminated some of the deficiencies of tantalum as filaments, but other more promising metals came into use.

Welsbach, who had invented the gas-mantle which was still resisting the invasion of electric lamps, introduced the osmium filament in 1905. This metal is extremely brittle and could not be drawn into wire. Welsbach powdered the metal very fine and made a paste, using organic matter as a binder. These filaments were squirted through dies, cut into lengths, formed and dried. They were then heated to a high temperature, driving off the organic matter and sintering the fine particles of osmium. Obviously the filaments were very brittle and the lamps had to be handled carefully in use. However, their higher efficiency, 7.5 lumens per watt, gave the osmium lamp a place in lighting progress. Its existence was cut quite short by the appearance of tungsten-filament lamps in 1906. Thus we see that the element of risk and of luck exists in technical developments as in other enterprises. Creditable and costly achievements may be replaced at any time by new ones.

In 1870 Scheele discovered the element, tungsten, which was destined to revolutionize artificial lighting. This metal is known as wolfram in Germany and to some extent in other countries. It is a very heavy metal, being twice as heavy as lead, fifty percent heavier than mercury, and having a spe-

GLOWING FILAMENTS

cific gravity of 19.1. It has a high melting-point, about 6100 degrees F, which is a necessary property for use as filaments for electric lamps. However, it is naturally brittle, as osmium is, and the first filaments had to be made of powdered tungsten contained in an organic binder. This paste was squirted through a die, and after cutting this product into proper lengths and forming these into the shape of hairpins, they were heated to a high temperature in the presence of steam and hydrogen. The sintered hairpins were then fastened systematically on supports and welded together to form a continuous filament of the proper length.

The first lamps were introduced in 1906 and were very fragile and costly. Tungsten unites readily with oxygen so that the bulbs were evacuated as all the previous filament-lamps were. The luminous efficiency of the vacuum tungsten lamps was 8 lumens per watt. This increase in efficiency over previous filament lamps and certain promising properties of tungsten led to a great metallurgical attack to overcome the brittleness. Coolidge of the research laboratories of the General Electric Company led this attack and after years of organized effort succeeded in making ductile tungsten which could be drawn into fine wires for filaments. Many workers and the facilities of great laboratories were involved, and the results obtained have been of inestimable value to civilization. Coolidge entered the growing ranks of the torch-bearers with an achievement which brightened the torch of civilization and created many new opportunities for artificial light to serve mankind.

The tungsten evaporates from the heated filament in a vacuum and blackens the bulb. It had long been known that this evaporation was diminished if the bulb were not evacuated. However, an inert gas such as nitrogen, argon, krypton or helium would have to be used in order to prevent chemical action on the hot filament. Obviously, the hot tungsten would oxidize or burn rapidly in air. But on placing an inert gas in the bulb, heat was found to be conducted so rapidly from the filament that the luminous efficiency of the lamp greatly decreased. The filament could be operated at a higher temperature than in a vacuum for a given life, but the heat-losses through the gas were greater than the gain. Langmuir, in the same laboratory as Whitney and Coolidge, made a systematic study of the relation of heat-losses of filaments in nitrogen gas to the diameter of the filaments. When the latter were large enough, the heat-losses through the gas were more than compensated for by the increased brightness of the filament.

A filament of a certain diameter must have a certain length in order to be of a certain brightness when the standard voltage, say 115 volts, is applied. Therefore, to give the long filament the effect of a large diameter, Langmuir coiled it into a helix. This made the filament short and fat, simplified construction and, of greatest importance, it increased the luminous efficiency considerably. The first gas-filled tungsten lamps with coiled filaments appeared in 1914. In general their efficiency was about 50 percent greater than the vacuum tungsten lamps. Now they vary, depending upon the wattage and purpose, from 10 to 30 lumens per watt. At first only lamps of the higher wattages had coiled filaments in nitrogen gas. As the many details of lamps were studied and perfected, the principle of the gas-filled lamp was adopted for smaller and smaller wattages. Argon was eventually added in addition to nitrogen. Coiled filaments were also introduced into lamps of smaller and smaller wattage. In lamps of the smaller sizes, the tungsten wire is so

GLOWING FILAMENTS

small that it must be coiled on another wire such as copper which is later eaten away by acid. Now some of these small coils are coiled again so that the coiled-coil filament has been put into use in certain lamps with another gain in luminous efficiency.

The coiling must be done very accurately, for the pitch and diameter affect the temperature of the filament and the life and efficiency of the lamp. The coiled-coil filament of the 60-watt, 115-volt tungsten lamp consists of a tungsten wire 0.0019 inch in diameter and about twenty inches long. After the first coiling, it is reduced to a fine coil 3.4 inches long consisting of about 1200 turns. This coil is again coiled into a coiled-coil a little more than a half inch long. This high concentration of filament material, providing in effect a short fat filament, increases the luminous efficiency about ten percent over that of the single coil. At the present time this country's lighting bill is a billion dollars per year. A ten percent increase in lumens per watt is equivalent to a bonus in additional light worth ten million dollars to light-users as a whole.

Throughout the entire progress of light-production, a primary object has been to increase the temperature of the light-source, whether it is a flame, arc, or filament. Carbon came into use in electric lamps because of its high melting-point, but the evaporation of carbon was a drawback which eventually opened the door for metal filaments. The temperature at which these filaments can be operated is only limited by their melting-point, but to be practicable the lamp must have a satisfactory life and its candlepower or light-output must be reasonably maintained throughout its life. These practical considerations have limited the filament temperatures of the various kinds of lamps. From the carbon

TORCH OF CIVILIZATION

filament operating at about 3300 degrees F, temperatures have increased to 3800 degrees F for the early vacuum tungsten lamps, and up to 5300 degrees F for gas-filled tungsten lamps. This is close to the melting-point of tungsten, 6120 degrees F. At these temperatures, twice that of molten steel, asbestos and fire-brick melt into uselessness. Considering that the filament of a 6-watt, 115-volt tungsten lamp is only 0.00047 inch in diameter, and is only discernible to unaided eyes under good seeing conditions, it is obvious that it must be very uniform in diameter and composition in order to operate dependably at those high temperatures and live a designed lifetime.

Naturally one may wonder why all tungsten filaments are not operated at the same temperature and why this is not just short of the melting-point. This could be done if no one cared what the life of any lamp would be. The number of hours any given tungsten lamp will burn before unduly blackening or failure of the filament, depends primarily upon the operating temperature of the filament and secondarily upon many other factors. A reasonable life is desired because the user does not wish to change lamps too often. But what is a reasonable life depends upon the usage. A photoflood lamp used in photography can have a very short life because it is used for short periods and burned-out lamps are easy to replace. Besides, the photographic power increases rapidly with increasing temperature. On the other hand, a quarter of a million lamps on a huge electric sign on top of a skyscraping building present a different problem. A reasonably long life, and particularly a uniform one, are desirable so that all the lamps could be changed at definite intervals.

The cost of light is determined by the cost of electrical energy, the cost of the lamp, and the amount of light emitted

GLOWING FILAMENTS

by the lamp. The light-output increases as the temperature of the filament increases, but the life of the lamp decreases. Thus there is a conflict among the various factors and the proper relationship is determined by complex mathematics. As a result, lamps for various purposes are designed for different useful lives which vary from an instant to more than 1000 hours. The photoflash lamp, which consists of metals in the form of thin foil, fine wire or shreddings, lives only an instant. A filament, so fine and short that even the low voltage of a dry cell sends through enough current to melt it, ignites the metallic charge. The old smoky flashlight powder has been replaced by bottled light-sources just as the old flames were. The tungsten lamps in ordinary use in homes have lives from 500 to 1000 hours, depending upon the design. The voltage is important because the lamp is designed for a specific one at which it delivers as much light as possible for the energy consumed. The voltage designated on each lamp is the proper one for the most economical relationship of light, energy and life.

This evolution of filament-lamps has been presented without digressions, but in the progress of light-production there were many. A notable one was the Nernst lamp first introduced in 1897. This lamp radiated ingenuity as well as light. The peculiar property of rare-earth oxides, glowing far more brilliantly than their temperature warranted, was effectively used in the lime-light and the gas-mantle. Nernst first used a slender rod of magnesia. It does not conduct electricity at ordinary temperatures but does when heated. A tiny auxiliary heater, consisting of coiled platinum wire, received electric current when the lamp was turned on. Soon the glower was heated enough to conduct electricity and in a few moments it glowed brilliantly. Then a tiny electromagnet cut out the heater. Obviously, the resistance of the glower decreased as its temperature increased; therefore, a ballasting resistance had to be provided in series with the glower.

The entire housing of the Nernst lamp was small so that the lamp could be screwed into any suitable socket. In later lamps the glowers, which were about an inch long, were made of a mixture of the rare-earth oxides, zirconia and yttria. Eventually a mixture of ceria, thoria and zirconia was used. The Nernst lamp was a marvel of ingenuity. Its light was considerably whiter than that of carbon-filament lamps and this had some advantage in stores where the appearance of the colors of merchandise is important. Arc-lamps were in use in many stores and could not be replaced by the yellower light of the filament-lamps. In such places, and elsewhere, Nernst lamps made inroads. For a few years this ingenious lamp played a role on the lighting stage but metal-filament lamps forced it to withdraw. Even though Nernst was a great scientist with many achievements to his credit, he must have been disappointed; but this is just another example of love's labor lost. There are many similar examples along the highway of technical progress. But the knowledge is not wasted, for it is continually resurrected in many other applications—generally by someone else.

At the end of the exclusive reign of the untreated carbon-filament lamp, its luminous efficiency was three lumens per watt. With the advent of each marked improvement in filaments, luminous efficiency jumped to a distinctly higher value until today tungsten lamps used in the home supply 10 to 15 lumens per watt. Lamps of higher wattages used in the work-world supply as many as 20 lumens per watt.

GLOWING FILAMENTS

Other special tungsten lamps yield as many as 35 lumens per watt. This glimpse of luminous efficiency of filament lamps reveals, in less than four decades, the great achievement of a ten-fold increase in light-output for a given consumption of electrical energy.

There has been a continual increase in luminous efficiency due to continual improvements in the hundred details of tungsten lamps. Many factors conspire to affect the operation of the lamp. Extreme purity of the gas and of other materials in the lamp, and extreme cleanliness of the parts, are essential. In addition, minute quantities of special chemicals are introduced to clean up any undesirable substances which may be exuded by the interior parts. A single drop of moisture divided among a half million lamps would cause a noticeable early blackening of the bulbs of all of them. Great laboratories and hundreds of scientific and technical men hunt for troubles and for improvements in the lamps and others help to find or to perfect their applications in the service of mankind. And all lamps are designed to give as much light as possible throughout their lifetime, which is determined by the service they are to render.

With ductile tungsten available, fine wires can be drawn and filaments can be wound into various forms. They may be concentrated into small brilliant sources so that accurate optical control is possible. They may be long and straight to provide lines of light. Thus it has become possible for artificial light to expand into many applications beyond general lighting. The wire can be drawn so fine that it is scarcely visible. Lamps are as small as a grain of wheat and as large as a bushel basket. They range from a small fraction of a watt to 50,000 watts. This largest lamp emits 1,500,000 lumens and has a maximum candlepower equivalent to

166,000 candles. Its filament consists of 1.6 pounds of tungsten, enough to make filaments for 56,000 60-watt lamps or 21,000,000 of the smallest tungsten lamps.

The tungsten-filament lamp has not merely remained a source of light. The inside frosting was developed to diffuse the light without appreciable absorption or loss of light, to protect eyes from brilliant sources, and to leave a smooth surface outside so that the lamps remain clean longer and may be easily washed. An enormous amount of research has been directed toward making the lamps physically smaller so as to be usable in smaller equipment of all kinds and to reduce costs all along the line. The lamps have not merely remained bulbs with filaments. Bulbs are now made in the shape of reflectors and projectors, metallized on the inside by new processes. This eliminates the need of auxiliary equipment for controlling the light. The bowls of some lamps are silvered with the result that additional equipment necessary for good lighting is minimized.

The new sealed-beam headlamp for automobiles is a complete headlamp. It only requires an inexpensive protective housing or a recess in a fender. It consists of a concentrated filament at the focus of an accurate paraboloid of glass which is surfaced inside with a highly reflecting metal. A glass lens containing proper prisms for further control of the light-beam is sealed to the mirrored glass reflector by actually melting together the two contacting glass surfaces. All that is known about tungsten lamps is combined with technical skill to produce this complete product to supply the light and lighting, revealed by research to be desirable on the highway at night.

Long ago our knowledge of the spectral character of daylight led to developing a blue-green bulb which altered the

GLOWING FILAMENTS

yellowish light so that the emitted light was white, simulating average daylight. This bulb reduced the excess yellow, orange and red rays so that colors could be judged more accurately. In other words this bluish bulb made a whitish light out of yellowish light. Other colored bulbs make many technical and decorative applications possible. Even a black bulb transmits infrared energy, without appreciable light, for therapeutic and other purposes.

For the dry-heat bath, tungsten lamps of the higher wattages are most suitable. The visible and short-wave infrared energy penetrates deeply into flesh and heats at a depth without discomfort to the user of the light-bath. Special bulbs also transmit mild ultraviolet energy which can make the light-bath a sunbath as well. Rickets in babies have been actually prevented and cured by the mild ultraviolet energy from these tungsten lamps with special bulbs. They are used in brooders for baby chicks and for poultry houses. Other lamps of the mercury type provide more potent sunlamps for those in a hurry and for the professional treatment of superficial skin affections and other disorders.

Tungsten lamps are now used for drying purposes. The visible and infrared energy do many jobs of this sort quickly and more conveniently in many cases than the common methods of heat conduction. Freshly painted automobile bodies now run through tunnels lined with tungsten drying lamps. This new application of radiant energy is spreading rapidly. Countless uses of this sort are to be found. In our artificial world where speed and continuous production cannot rely upon sunlight and where heating by steam or gas is less satisfactory, the tungsten lamp promises to be an ever-increasing factor in the independence of mankind from Nature in many ways as it has been in lighting. Already it has revolutionized lighting for seeing and, although its primary function is to supply light in countless applications, it has invaded such realms as heating, drying, health, therapy and photography.

The torch-makers of the present time may look backward with great satisfaction and forward to far-off goals. The theoretical maximum luminous efficiency attainable would be reached if yellow-green light, to which the visual sense is most sensitive, were produced without being accompanied by any other visible or invisible energy and if none of the energy supplied to the lamp were lost in other ways. The luminous efficiency of this theoretical lamp would be about 620 lumens per watt. However, this illuminant would be very unsatisfactory for lighting because colors would disappear and we would live in a monochrome world of shades of yellow-green. A theoretical light-source that radiated all the energy entirely as visible energy and distributed throughout the spectrum so that the light was white, would have a luminous efficiency of about 200 lumens per watt. Obviously this is a more suitable goal. If we had a filament which was a perfect radiator and would withstand any temperature, we could demonstrate the temperature which would yield the highest luminous efficiency. Not having this, we can compute it from the well-known laws of radiation. This temperature would be about 10,000 degrees F, but it would radiate ultraviolet and infrared energy as well as light. Its luminous efficiency would be about 80 lumens per watt.

With the foregoing theoretical goals of 620, 200 and 80 lumens per watt, we may compare the progress which has been made. The approximate efficiencies of some of the past and present light-sources in lumens per watt are as follows: candle flame, 0.1; kerosene flame, 0.3; acetylene, 0.7; gas-

GLOWING FILAMENTS

mantle, 1.2; carbon arcs, 3 to 8; flame-arcs, 10 to 25; carbon filament, 3 to 4.5; tungsten filament, 8 to 35. Thus it is seen that luminous efficiency from the candle flame to the tungsten lamps used at present in homes has increased 100 times and compared with the most efficient tungsten lamps at present has increased more than 300 times.

On the other hand, it is seen that the practical limit of luminous efficiency of tungsten filaments is far short of the ideal goal of about 200 lumens per watt. No one can safely predict that other forms of carbon, or even of tungsten, and other operating conditions may not increase the limit of possibilities. However, at the present time the more promising avenue toward the ideal goals of luminous efficiency points in the direction of vapor lamps, gaseous discharge lamps, and fluorescent lamps. Efficiencies as high as 100 lumens per watt have been obtained under laboratory conditions. Of course, there always remain the factors of simplicity, divisibility and convenience which, for example, kept the carbon-filament lamp in the lead of arc lamps for most interior lighting applications. In these respects tungsten lamps rank near the top of possibilities. They are likely to serve throughout many of their present fields and in many new ones for many years, notwithstanding the recent advent of other kinds of electric light-sources of greater luminous efficiency.

About one billion tungsten-filament lamps are being manufactured annually in this country. Through continuous research and technical development the convenience and dependability of artificial light have enormously increased. At the same time the cost of light has greatly decreased. The beginning of the present century will go down in history as the dawn of the Light Age. With the aid of feeble flames civilization emerged from literal and figurative darkness. Its activities extend and expand as the lights grow brighter and more efficient. It has now emerged into artificial twilight. The annual lighting bill in this country is about a billion dollars. If progress in light-production had stood still since the beginning of this century, even the present artificial twilight would now cost several billion dollars annually. The same amount of light from candles would cost more than a hundred billion dollars each year.

X. LUMINOUS VAPORS

TONIGHT ON THE treeless tundras of Siberia and on the arctic shores of North America primitive beings watch the play of northern lights with the same awe and ignorance as their ancestors did for ages. For centuries thoughtful persons have pondered that restless display to the north. The faint glow of the corona embellished with shifting streamers and trembling curtains—the aurora borealis—was completely a mystery until recently. Its causes had remained hidden in the electrical unknown. Now we know that northern lights have something in common with neon lights. Both are due to electric discharges in rarefied gases. Something emitted by the sun crosses the 93 million miles of space and excites the atoms of the tenuous atmosphere, 50 to 500 miles above us, so that it glows with auroral light. There is still some doubt as to the primary cause. It may be ultraviolet energy or electrons. However, there remains little doubt that the ultimate effect is due to electrically-charged particles of electricity and matter.

A group of modern light-sources utilizes the principle of electric discharge through gases or vapors. At the present time three elements—sodium, mercury and neon—are most prominent in the production of light by gaseous conduction. Oddly enough all three states of matter are represented. At ordinary temperatures sodium is a solid so it must be vaporized in the lamp. Mercury, being a liquid, possesses obvious advantages but it also must be vaporized. Neon, being a gas, is ready for use as a gaseous conductor of electricity.

It is not surprising that mercury, a very versatile element, extended its repertoire by appearing in a lighting role. This peculiar element was already playing many roles from villain to benefactor. In a dark brown crystalline compound, mercury fulminate supplies the initial explosive which discharges cartridges and bombs. Other compounds of it are antiseptic and safeguard the wounds of victims from infection. In the capillary tube of a thermometer it measures temperature. It amalgamates with gold and silver and gathers the fine bits of these metals in the milling of ores. Its sulfide is the rich scarlet pigment, vermilion. In many other ways it serves throughout civilized activities but its most unique achievement has been in lighting.

When artificial light was being made entirely by heating things, materials possessing high melting-points were sought far and wide. Carbon met this requirement quite well, as tungsten did later, but in the midst of its reign mercury defied the trend of light-production. This metal, 13.6 times heavier than water, melts at 38 degrees F below zero. Indeed, this was defiance. In 1902 Cooper-Hewitt exhibited the first mercury arc that met with success. Notwithstanding this radical departure from the common method of light-production, he followed the trend at least to the extent of enclosing the arc in glass as tightly and as completely as carbon filaments were at that time. This was the practical beginning of a long series of developments of mercury arcs which serve better, and are more promising, today than ever before.

As is usually true, other workers had experimented with vapors and gases. In 1860 Way permitted a fine jet of mercury to fall from one vessel into a lower one. Both vessels

The ingenuity of modern science tames the vicious metallic solid, sodium, and it joins the ranks of light-sources.

LUMINOUS VAPORS

were connected in series with an electric battery. The electric current scattered the falling thread of mercury into fine drops between which tiny arcs were formed. He actually exhibited this light-source but it was little more than a novelty. At any rate it was merely a combination of the principle of filaments and arcs and did not solve any of the various problems of the mercury arc. Other investigators worked along various lines and the first laboratory arcs were generally in the form of inverted U-tubes with lead-in wires at the ends with some mercury covering them.

Cooper-Hewitt mercury arcs were long straight tubes of glass with enlarged ends to facilitate cooling of the electrodes. The tubes were hung slightly inclined to the horizontal so that as the mercury condensed it would run back to the pool of mercury which acted as the negative electrode. The lamp was started by tilting the tube until the flowing mercury formed a continuous thread connecting the positive electrode of iron. After the current was passing through, the tube was tilted back to its slightly inclined position. Thus the thread of mercury broke and an arc formed at the break. The heat of this arc vaporized enough mercury to fill the entire tube with mercury vapor. Electric current continued to pass through this vapor, making it luminous.

This light-source required a ballast just as the carbon arc did, and for the same reason. Its resistance decreases as the current through the mercury vapor increases. Therefore, a ballast is obviously necessary in order to prevent the current from increasing indefinitely and destroying the lamp. This is not true of filament-lamps because solids, such as carbon and tungsten, increase their resistance as their temperature increases. And, of course, their temperature increases with the current or energy input. All the modern light-sources consisting of luminous vapors or gases are arcs, if judged by the electrical characteristics such as the requirement of ballast to prevent a destructive increase in current. This applies to gaseous light-sources such as neon tubes, to sodium-vapor lamps and to all the interesting modern mercury arcs. Therefore, all light-sources of this character must have auxiliary devices designed specifically for each light-source. Obviously, by contrast the simplicity of filament-lamps is emphatically apparent. However, one advantage of the auxiliary device is that it can provide any fitting voltage for the lamp, and the entire equipment can be operated directly on the electric service of standard voltages.

Improvements were soon made in mercury arcs so that they need not be tilted for starting. Heating coils were supplied for vaporizing the mercury on starting. Electric sparks were also used. With continual improvement the long tubular mercury arcs competed successfully in certain fields with the rapid advances made in tungsten-filament lamps. Owing to its high output of blue, violet and long-wave ultraviolet energy, the mercury arc early invaded commercial photography. However, the absence of red light from its total light was a handicap in many fields. Many colors disappeared or were badly distorted in appearance and, therefore, mercury arcs did not come into general use in lighting-practice.

Mercury arcs in quartz tubes were developed for various purposes. The quartz withstands a high temperature and considerable current could safely be sent through a small tube. In this sense these were forerunners of the high-pressure mercury arcs to come. The quartz transmits ultraviolet energy and the quartz arc became widely used in therapy, for sterilizing swimming pools and in many industrial proc-

LUMINOUS VAPORS

esses requiring ultraviolet energy. The light from the quartz arc is whiter than that of the long low-pressure Cooper-Hewitt mercury arc. It was used in lighting to some extent by enclosing it in a glass globe which did not transmit the ultraviolet energy harmful to the eyes. A variety of quartz mercury arcs is still available for many purposes.

During last century when carbon and flame arcs were studied and developed, and even in the early part of the present century when Cooper-Hewitt invented the mercury arc, the nature of electric current was still almost unknown. It was considered vaguely as a flow of electricity from the socalled positive (anode) to the socalled negative (cathode) terminals of a battery or other source of direct current. But scientists were just beginning to peek into the atom and were on the verge of epochal discoveries. J. J. Thomson had already developed the idea that mass is of electrical origin. Roentgen had discovered X-rays. The Curies had isolated radium in 1898 and its emission of energy and particles of electricity was being studied. Planck enunciated the quantum theory in 1900. A new entity—the electron—was being discovered. The atom ceased to be considered the smallest thing known.

In 1904 J. J. Thomson introduced a model of the atom. This was a miniature universe or planetary system, an orderly arrangement of electrons revolving in orbits around a nucleus of positive electricity. Great advances in knowledge have been made since the discovery of electrons as definite entities of negative electricity. The idea of electric current being an actual flow of negative electrons became well defined. Instead of current flowing from the positive to the negative terminals it became a flow of negative electrons from the negative (cathode) to the positive (anode) terminals. As a consequence the cathode became important as the source of electrons.

The ultimate source of light was now conceived to be within the atom. Swiftly-moving electrons are driven through vapors and gases from the cathode toward the anode. Their velocities depend upon the voltage. During this journey these electrons strike mercury atoms and jar revolving electrons from their natural orbits. Such displacements result in the emission of quanta of radiant energy of wavelengths characteristic of the particular atom or element. This is a mere glimpse into the new electronic concepts of electricity and of matter. Applied to luminous vapors and gases these concepts provide a basis for understanding such light-sources which was absent when the carbon, flame and mercury arcs were first practically developed and extensively introduced into lighting-practice.

The first mercury arcs were started by making a connection of liquid mercury between the two electrodes. When this connection was broken the arc formed at the break vaporized mercury which filled the entire tube. Current then passed through that vapor. The Cooper-Hewitt mercury arc operated at a low pressure. This was not a complete vacuum but was only about one-thousandth of normal atmospheric pressure. With the discovery of electrons which led to a better understanding of the electrical phenomena of the mercury arc, new developments began to take place. Socalled high-pressure arcs were developed which operated at pressures about equal or slightly above one atmosphere. New starting methods were based upon supplying electrons more freely by the cathodes. This is accomplished by heating the cathodes electrically and by coating them with substances which emit electrons freely. Extremely high-pressure

LUMINOUS VAPORS

mercury arcs have been developed which operate at pressures of many atmospheres. Others of extremely low pressure are also available which produce short-wave ultraviolet very efficiently.

Many years ago Geissler, Crookes, and others, studied the spectra of the light emitted by gases through which an electric discharge took place. If the pressure of the gas is rather low and the voltage is high enough, each gas will glow with its own particular color due to its own characteristic spectrum. In each case, the atoms send out energy of various wavelengths characteristic of that specific element. These Geissler tubes were useful in spectrum analyses but as light-sources they were mere novelties. For many years they were standard equipment for the lecturer on physics who often demonstrated these luminous gases in glass tubing of fancy shapes. Unknowingly he was demonstrating stunts which were to become commonplace in lighting-practice, particularly in signs.

In about 1892 D. McFarlan Moore developed this simple principle into practical light-sources. In a gaseous conductor there is a large drop in voltage at the cathode, which results in such a loss of electrical energy, that these light-sources had to be long in order to be efficient. Furthermore they operated only at rather high voltages. Moore first used nitrogen gas in tubes of great length which emitted a pinkish white light. As a tube of this sort is operated for a long period the gas gradually disappears but Moore devised a valve for introducing gas automatically. He also used carbon dioxide which yields a white light with a spectrum so close to that of average daylight that this illuminant was used for accurate discrimination of colors. Moore also used other gases but confined himself chiefly to the common gases,

157

nitrogen for general lighting and carbon dioxide for color-discrimination. Moore was the outstanding pioneer in the practical development of gaseous conductors as light-sources and made many practical installations in the early part of the present century. This method of lighting did not take hold commercially and actually declined into dormancy. To add to Moore's disappointment, toward the end of his life, his gaseous conductors were revived and improved by others, and became quite successful in certain fields of lighting.

About twenty years after Moore's first introduction of gaseous conductors, Claude in France made various practical light-sources in which he used various gases. After mediocre success for several years socalled neon light-sources came into extensive use. The distinctive orange-red color of neon makes this illuminant unsuitable for general lighting but quite satisfactory for signs and certain spectacular effects. Other gases and glass tubing of various colors produce a variety of colored lights. However, the monotony of the characteristic color of neon is rather obvious on many streets. These light-sources operate on relatively high voltages which are dangerous indoors. By certain expedients, fairly efficient sources of moderate lengths have been developed with the result that these gaseous light-sources may find further uses in decorative lighting and some uses in general lighting-practice.

The sodium lamp is a relatively recent arrival on the lighting stage. Inasmuch as sodium combines freely with water or oxygen it is difficult and dangerous to handle. It attacks ordinary glass and, therefore, a very special glass must be used for the bulbs of sodium lamps. In the simplest form this lamp consists of a suitable glass bulb into which

LUMINOUS VAPORS

a cathode and an anode are sealed. Some neon gas is admitted to the bulb and the pressure, when the lamp is cold, is about one five-hundredth of an atmosphere. Means are provided for heating the cathode electrically. This and the neon are relied upon for starting the lamp. At first the electric discharge is confined to the neon gas because the sodium is entirely in the solid state. Gradually the bulb is heated by this discharge to about 425 degrees F at which point there is enough sodium vaporized to carry the electric discharge. When the sodium lamp is in full operation the light is characteristic of sodium notwithstanding the fact that the number of neon atoms is thousands of times greater than the number of sodium atoms.

The production of a practical light-source is not merely a matter of producing light. Many problems must be solved which lead into various realms of science and technology. Hot sodium vapor attacks ordinary glasses and discolors them. It actually causes chemical disintegration in some of them. Some special glasses which resist the action of sodium fairly well offer difficulty in forming them into bulbs. Therefore, this problem was solved by coating a common glass with a glaze resistant to hot sodium vapor. Owing to the necessity of having the bulb operate at a temperature of about 400 degrees F or more, the lamp is enclosed in a vacuum glass jacket. In other words, the primary bulb containing the luminous vapor operates in a double-walled thermos bottle of clear glass.

The luminous efficiencies of sodium lamps at the present time are 45 to 55 lumens per watt. These are more than twice the luminous efficiencies of the tungsten lamps with which they compete. However, the sodium light-source is quite large so that the light from it cannot be controlled as efficiently as from a more brilliant concentrated source such as a tungsten filament. Therefore when the light is measured where it is used on the highway, for example, tungsten lamps overcame their initial handicap of lower luminous efficiency.

The light from sodium lamps is typical of the sodium atom and is confined to two wavelengths close together in the deep yellow portion of the spectrum. The spectrum of neon, or any other starting gas, is present but this is insignificant in contributing to the output of light. All colors disappear under sodium light excepting yellow, and the world becomes a monochrome of shades of yellow. This spectral deficiency precludes any general use of sodium lamps. They must be confined to places where their suppression of colors is not objectionable.

A tungsten arc operating between tungsten electrodes in an evacuated bulb has been in existence for quite a few years but it has not been used in general lighting-practice. The arc-flame consists of tungsten vapor but, as in the case of the ordinary carbon arc, the hot tungsten electrodes emit most of the light. The temperature of the hottest spot on the positive electrode of the tungsten arc has been increased by experimental high pressures to 8700 degrees F. This reveals future possibilities in this direction.

A direct outcome of work on the tungsten arc was the first of a long line of new mercury-vapor lamps. There are so many of these that no practicable descriptive names, each sufficiently distinctive, can be given to them. Therefore, we shall have to resort to the uninspiring technical designations such as Type H and Type S. The S-1 and S-2 lamps are distinctly sources of artificial sunlight with emphasis upon the ultraviolet energy which, for example, prevents and cures

LUMINOUS VAPORS

rickets. H-1 and H-2 are essentially light-sources for lighting purposes. Other Type H lamps are efficient light-sources but may be adapted to the production of ultraviolet energy for various purposes.

The mercury arc which directly descended from the tungsten arc is the 400-watt S-1 lamp. In this lamp a mercury arc is maintained between two very hot tungsten electrodes. The radiant energy from the arc-flame is the typical discontinuous spectrum of mercury consisting of violet, blue, green and yellow light. It is deficient in red light as is characteristic of mercury light obtained from arcs operating at low pressures. The hot tungsten electrodes emit light of a continuous spectrum; that is, of all visible wavelengths. Therefore, the light from the S-1 lamp is a satisfactory illuminant from the viewpoint of the appearance of colors. However, it came into use in socalled sunlamps to supply artificial sunlight. It supplies ultraviolet which cures and prevents rickets and has other therapeutic applications. The bulb of special glass does not transmit any appreciable ultraviolet energy of wavelengths shorter than the short-wave limit of the solar spectrum. The 130-watt S-2 lamp is a smaller edition of the S-1 lamp.

The original Cooper-Hewitt mercury arc operated at a low pressure. Therefore, when mercury arcs were made to operate at approximately one atmosphere they were called high-pressure arcs. Later this designation became misleading when practical mercury arcs were developed to operate under pressures as high as 80 atmospheres.

The 400-watt H-1 mercury lamp consists of a glass tube nearly eight inches long in which a discharge takes place in mercury vapor between two electrodes, one in each end. The electrodes are coils of tungsten wire coated with barium-

TORCH OF CIVILIZATION

strontium oxide which supplies the essential electrons freely. The tube contains argon gas for starting purposes before the mercury is vaporized. The quantity of mercury in the arc-tube is carefully measured so that the lamp operates at the proper pressure which in this case is about one atmosphere. Another tube of glass encloses the arc-tube in order to minimize the effects of great variations in the outside air. The space between the two tubes contains about a half atmosphere of nitrogen. The luminous efficiency of the lamp alone is about 40 lumens per watt and including the necessary auxiliary is about 37 lumens per watt. The H-2 lamp is a smaller simplified edition operating at luminous efficiencies of 25 to 30 lumens per watt.

As knowledge and experience were gained with higher pressures of mercury vapor their advantages in certain directions became evident. As the pressure increases, light of a continuous spectrum becomes a larger fraction of the total light. This helps to fill the gaps in the spectrum of mercury light. The output of ultraviolet energy is also affected. Thus the possibilities of new sources of light and of ultraviolet energy were extended. At this point a new principle was introduced. Mercury was contained in a small capsule or capillary tube of quartz. The short length and small diameter of the space containing the mercury vapor promotes high pressures and temperatures. This quartz capsule transmits ultraviolet energy as well as light. The 100-watt H-4 lamp, embodying this principle, operates at a mercury-vapor pressure of eight atmospheres. A protective outer bulb of glass is used. When this consists of a special ultraviolet-transmitting glass the lamp becomes the S-4 lamp used in sunlamps. The H-4 has a luminous efficiency of 35 lumens

LUMINOUS VAPORS

per watt and, including the necessary auxiliary, about 30 lumens per watt. The 250-watt H-5 lamp is of similar construction but operates at four atmospheres of pressure. It is designed principally to supply more long-wave ultraviolet energy for special purposes such as fluorescent effects. Its luminous efficiencies are 35 to 40 lumens per watt.

Now there appears on the scene an astonishing light-source. It is at present the acme of capillary mercury arcs but points to even greater possibilities. Therefore, this is the proper place to credit Bol with the first mercury arc of this type a few years ago and with much development work along this line in succeeding years. His first practical light-source consisted of a capillary tube one inch long with an inner bore about an eighth of an inch in diameter. With a carefully measured amount of mercury in it the electric current raised the temperature of the mercury vapor so that pressures of 8 to 30 atmospheres were attained. The higher pressure is about the limit of endurance of the quartz when operated in air. This led to water-cooling. This is not the first use of water-cooling for it was adopted long ago in connection with quartz mercury arcs of the earlier types.

The 1000-watt H-6 mercury lamp consists of a capillary quartz tube about 1.5 inches long with an inner bore of about one-twelfth inch and an outside diameter of about one-fourth inch. A tungsten wire is sealed through each end. The inner ends of these two terminals dip into a small pool of mercury in each end of the capillary tube. Thus it is seen that the light-source is extremely simple and very small. When unlighted and cold the pressure is only about one pound per square inch. Actually it is the pressure of the pure argon in the tube. When the lamp is turned on it reaches its full brilliancy in a second or two and the pressure quickly mounts to 80 atmospheres or about 1175 pounds per square inch. The water-jacket is carefully designed so that water passes rapidly over the quartz capsule even though the flow is less than a gallon per minute.

This 1000-watt source emits 65,000 lumens and, obviously, its luminous efficiency is 65 lumens per watt. The overall luminous efficiency, including the necessary auxiliary is about 55 lumens per watt. The maximum brightness of the actual source is about one-fifth that of the zenith sun. Its maximum intensity approaches that of 25,000 candles concentrated into a single small source. The water-cooling absorbs about 90 percent of the infrared energy. Therefore, we have been able to illuminate naked human beings without discomfort in a special enclosure to levels of illumination equivalent to that from five midday June suns. This lamp is a rich source of ultraviolet energy so that we have been able to deliver upon naked human beings without discomfort, tanning and sunburning energy equivalent to that from twenty-five midday June suns. Besides its possibilities in lighting for television, its service in photo-engraving and in other processes, it provides a new tool for much needed research in the life and health processes of human beings. It represents a torch of civilization transcending all others in certain directions. And the end is not in sight. The input of electrical energy into such small sources may eventually be greatly increased.

Let us turn from these spectacular high-pressure mercury arcs to equally recent arcs operating at very low pressures. These are just as spectacular but in unobvious ways. These arcs are contained in long tubes. They contain some argon gas through which starting takes place. Only a small amount of mercury is introduced into the tube. This is carefully measured in order that the vapor pressure when the lamp is in operation will be maintained at a proper low value. The low current density results in an inefficient source of light. However, it is a powerful source of short-wave ultraviolet energy far beyond the short-wave limit of the solar spectrum. This ultraviolet energy is readily absorbed by mercury vapor. Therefore, in order for it to be produced efficiently, the vapor density must be low and this is achieved by operating the lamp at a very low pressure.

This short-wave ultraviolet energy is a powerful germicide. It kills not only microscopic organisms but even larger living things. Of course, any powerful source of ultraviolet would kill human beings if they exposed most of their body long enough to produce a severe sunburn. By using a very special glass these low-pressure arcs become germicidal lamps. There are many uses for these in the destruction of germs, molds and other lowly forms of life. However, much research is needed to establish their efficacy and economic value.

The chief interest here is that these low-pressure arcs are the heart of the new Type F fluorescent lamps. In these the well-known principle of fluorescence is utilized. Many things emit light when illuminated by ultraviolet energy. This fluorescent light is "cold" for it is accompanied by little or no invisible energy. To make light without wasting energy either in the lamp or in invisible radiant energy has long been the romantic goal of the light-producer. By no means has this goal been reached nor is it in sight. However, in the newest light-sources for general use, the production of light by the fluorescence of substances excited by ultraviolet

TORCH OF CIVILIZATION

energy has been achieved for the first time on a large practical scale. The torch of civilization has advanced materially along this new avenue which may lead toward the ideal objective of light-production—light with no waste of energy in other by-products.

XI. FLUORESCENT SOURCES

IN THE JUNE twilight tiny living lights puncture the shadowy landscape. Fireflies are flashing their lights for reasons of their own. For ages human beings have wondered and some have pondered, for the secret of the firefly is not immune from the prying method of science. We catch one of the fireflies and hold it in our hand. The brilliance of the glow seems to be inconsistent with the absence of heat. We conclude that here we have "cold light"—the dream of light-producers. Measurements reveal that the firefly's light is unaccompanied by invisible radiant energy. It closely approaches the highest possible luminous efficiency of the most efficient radiant energy—that which produces yellow-green light. This is an inspiring fact which too often has obscured the underlying question.

What is the luminous efficiency of the firefly as a lamp or a lighting-plant? No one has answered that question as yet, but, from various considerations, it appears safe to assume that it is quite low. The energy radiated by the firefly produces light at 82 percent of the highest possible efficiency. But the energy used by the firefly in fuel—food, air and water—determines the firefly's efficiency as a lamp, which is probably low compared with modern man-made lamps. Nevertheless the firefly, and myriad other living lights, contain secrets which eventually may be of great help in the production of artificial light more efficiently.

Human beings have lived in a world of light produced

by incandescence—by hot bodies such as the sun, flames, arcs and filaments. But there is another world of light produced by luminescence—by relatively cold bodies. Usually luminescent things emit such feeble lights that they are concealed by the overwhelming daylight or artificial light. Only the more brilliant of the feeble luminescent lights, such as the firefly, are readily visible. Only when our eyes are adapted to darkness for a long period are we able to see most of myriad luminescent lights. But darkness is the period of sleep and inactivity for human beings, which accounts for the general lack of acquaintance with the extensive world of luminescent lights.

There are many living and non-living sources, and numerous natural and artificial causes. Suspended in the darkness of the depths of the ocean, Beebe saw a world of living lights—living things varying in size from small bacteria to large fishes. Harvey for a quarter of a century has investigated living producers of luminescent light in the controlled darkness of the laboratory. The luminescent wake of a ship on a tropical night has been noted for centuries. The ghostly glow of rotten wood has intrigued many persons. At best only a relatively few of the living lights are seen by accident. According to Harvey, the animal kingdom contains at least forty orders in which there are living lights and in the plant kingdom they are found in the great groups of bacteria and true fungi. Luminous bacteria are the smallest lamps known. The light from each is so feeble that many thousands must shine before the human eye can detect the combined light. Luminous fungi are commonly found in the woods growing on, or even throughout, molding wood. Luminous animals are very numerous and widespread throughout the animal kingdom.

With this flask of cold light, produced uneconomically at present, this scientist crystal-gazes into the future.

FLUORESCENT SOURCES

The secrets of these living lights are being wrested from them. Oxygen appears to be very generally essential to the production of light by living organisms. Through the chemistry of these processes, perhaps the production of light by luminescence may eventually be influenced. However, for the present we are more interested in luminescence which we can produce in non-living substances directly by electrical energy or indirectly through its products. This turns our attention to the world of luminescent light produced by non-living forces and matter. Of course, the distinction between living and non-living things is arbitrary and even vague. When one pictures the continual activity of orderly particles and motions inside the atom and the eternal life of atoms, non-living matter is not properly or adequately described as dead matter.

Luminescence is excited by transference of mechanical, radiant and electrical energy. With our eyes adapted to darkness, we may see the light of friction as we tear a piece of electrician's or surgeon's tape from its roll. Many substances when rubbed together exhibit this light. Splitting a sheet of mica, breaking a rubber band, fracturing a crystal and many other mechanical operations are accompanied by the production of momentary light. Cathode rays, radium rays and X-rays make many substances glow. In fact, it appears that most things are luminescent under such radiations of electric particles or of radiant energy. If the luminescence ceases when the excitant ceases, it is commonly termed, fluorescence. When it persists for some time after the exciting agency is removed, it is termed, phosphorescence. The latter term is a misnomer which has lingered from the time when the chemical luminescence of phosphorus—exhibited by wetting an old-fashioned match-head—was first noted.

TORCH OF CIVILIZATION

Ultraviolet energy is a most common and convenient means of exciting luminescence in a great variety of substances. It is invisible and for many years the most common method of detecting it was the use of fluorescent materials. On projecting the spectrum of a light-source upon a white surface, the rainbow colors are seen. Beyond the violet of this spectrum we see nothing, but if we place certain fluorescent substances in that region, they will glow. Such substances are frequency-changers in the realm of radiant energy. They absorb ultraviolet energy of certain wavelengths or frequencies and emit energy of longer wavelengths or lower frequencies. When the latter are in the wavelength range of visible radiation, they stimulate the sensations of brightness and color. In other words, invisible radiant energy is converted into visible energy by socalled fluorescent or luminescent materials.

Many ingenious demonstrations have been made of this phenomenon for many years, but these could not be conveniently produced until illuminants rich in ultraviolet energy became available. By equipping a mercury arc, for example, with a filter which transmits only the ultraviolet energy, one discovers in a dark room that some substances fluoresce brilliantly and many of them feebly. Many uses of this and other effects of ultraviolet energy have been developed such as the examination of jewels, old paintings, paper currency, and erasures on legal documents. Human skin, nails and teeth, certain buttons in clothing and many dyes in neckties and gowns fluoresce under ultraviolet energy.

Years ago I gave what might be described as a fluorescent party. The glassware was of uranium glass. China was decorated with fluorescent paints and on the tablecloth a pattern was drawn with colorless solutions of fluorescent materials.

FLUORESCENT SOURCES

These decorations were invisible under ordinary light but under ultraviolet energy they fluoresced in various colors. Into glasses of water and other liquids a tiny drop of a solution of esculin made them glow with a bluish white light. Fluorescein in the water of glass vases containing flowers produced a brilliant yellow-green glow. The flowers had been previously dipped in various fluorescent solutions. Paintings with certain fluorescent dyes glowed mysteriously on the walls. On the ceiling stars and various constellations were painted with a colorless solution of anthracene in alcohol. They literally shone in the darkness. The paper wrappers of cigarettes had been brushed lightly with fluorescent liquids and allowed to dry. Eosine in water fluoresces orange or red even when dried. An ultraviolet source emitting only "black light" rested in the center of the table and two projectors of this invisible excitant were appropriately located. Guests ate, drank and smoked by the fluorescent light from the things mentioned. And added to these effects were those of dyes in gowns, the glowing teeth and eyes and various accidental ones as in cosmetics, salad oil and other foods. To the novelty was added a weirdness due to the slight fog of fluorescent light in the eye-media. And the blackness of artificial teeth was amusing or embarrassing, depending upon the viewpoint.

With powerful ultraviolet sources available such as modern mercury arcs, uncounted applications of fluorescence can be made. They may run from strictly utilitarian to spectacular uses and may combine novelty and usefulness. The millions of persons who proceed falteringly down the aisle of the darkened motion-picture theater may walk on a carpet whose pattern of fluorescent dyes glows under ultraviolet energy. Programs may be printed with fluorescent inks or on fluorescent paper. The pilot of an airplane may read his instruments and instructions in fluorescent light excited by invisible ultraviolet energy. We may sleep semi-naked under invisible ultraviolet energy, getting tanned and at the same time receiving possible health benefits. A thousand practical applications come readily to mind. A dozen kinds of practical sources of ultraviolet energy are now available for producing fluorescent effects. Some are equipped with glass tubes or bulbs which transmit the ultraviolet energy with little or no light accompanying it. Appropriate heat-resisting glass is available as filters for use in housings for any of the powerful sources of ultraviolet energy.

Hundreds of minerals fluoresce, and it is obvious that ultraviolet energy has added a new tool of detection or analysis of ores. But our chief interest in these lies in the production of light by them or by the more refined inorganic chemical compounds produced for the purpose. It will be recalled that among the latest developments of mercury arcs are the low-pressure arcs which emit an abundance of short-wave ultraviolet energy. These are not efficient as light-sources, but their ultraviolet energy is a powerful excitant of fluorescence in certain inorganic substances. If the inside of the glass tube of such a mercury arc is coated with appropriate "phosphors" as they are called, the invisible ultraviolet energy is converted into light. In fact these new fluorescent lamps have luminous efficiencies considerably higher than any light-sources heretofore available for general lighting purposes.

Here again we witness the bringing together of well-known cause and effect to produce a radically new and efficient means of producing light. The excitation of fluorescence by ultraviolet radiation had been known for a century but the

FLUORESCENT SOURCES

practical development of the Type F fluorescent lamps had to wait until the evolution of mercury arcs reached the point where adequate ultraviolet energy could be produced efficiently and conveniently. These low-pressure mercury arcs are now relatively simple electric-discharge lamps. However, the relations of their electrical characteristics with the length and diameter of the glass-tube containers are extremely complicated. For various reasons these fluorescent lamps may well be considered to be the most outstanding development in light-production of all time.

Up to the present time not all possibilities in the development and use of phosphors, the fluorescent powders, have been exhausted. It is probable that many are still hidden in the chemical unknown. However, a few that are in use emphasize the fact that, for the first time in the entire history of light-production, great control over the quality or spectral character of the light is now available. Heretofore, complete control over the distribution of light had been developed. Considerable control over the candlepower or light-output from individual sources had been achieved. But relatively little direct control over the color or spectral character was possible. This had to be accomplished by the inefficient means of transmitting light of various wavelengths in the proportions desired. The remaining light was absorbed and wasted.

To produce colored light from tungsten-filament lamps by means of a colored bulb or accessory, the percentage of the total light which must be absorbed, and actually wasted, is approximately as follows: blue, 98 percent; green, 95 percent; yellow, 60 percent; and red, 90 percent. Starting with a tungsten lamp operating at 20 lumens per watt, it is seen that the luminous efficiencies of the resulting colored lights are reduced to a range from 0.4 to 8 lumens per watt. In producing colored light by exciting fluorescence in suitable materials, the luminous efficiencies already reach the surprising values of 25 to 75 lumens per watt, excepting for red fluorescent light. No phosphor has been discovered as yet to produce red fluorescent light efficiently so that the luminous efficiency of the present lamp which furnishes red light is only about 2.5 to 3.5 lumens per watt. Obviously, these truly enormous increases in the efficiency of production of colored lights greatly increase their applications and are outstanding achievements in light-production.

All the chemical compounds now employed as phosphors, with which the inner surface of the glass bulbs (tubes) of fluorescent lamps are coated, are sensitive to ultraviolet energy of wavelengths to which ordinary glass is generally opaque. Most of them are most sensitive to ultraviolet energy of rather short wavelengths and close to the wavelengths of energy produced abundantly by the low-pressure mercury arc. The energy emitted by this particular mercury arc is very effective in killing germs. In fact, the 15-watt germicidal lamp is a fluorescent lamp without the inner coating of fluorescent powders and with a tube of special glass which transmits the germicidal energy. As a matter of interest, phosphors in use at present and the color of their fluorescent light are as follows: calcium tungstate, blue; magnesium tungstate, blue-white; zinc silicate, green; zinc beryllium silicate, yellow-white; cadmium silicate, yellow-pink; and cadmium borate, pink.

Obviously, the powdered phosphors may be mixed together in any desired proportions. The results are the same as mixing colored lights together. In fact it is rather inspiring to visualize the modern torch-maker mixing lights in the

FLUORESCENT SOURCES

form of powders. This is the simplest conceivable way of controlling the spectral character of light emitted by a source. Certainly it represents a radically new, simple and efficient way of exercising control over the spectral quality of light incomparably superior to any other means available heretofore. As a consequence, our dream of reproducing efficient artificial daylight has come true. And at the same time mankind forges far ahead of Nature by efficiently producing controllable colored light of various degrees of tint or saturation. By carefully choosing the phosphors and determining the proper proportions, any variety of natural daylight can be produced from the warmer white near the end of the day, to white light of average daylight during midday, to the cold bluish white light from the clear north sky.

Fluorescent daylight lamps produce light closely approximating the spectral character of average daylight during midday at luminous efficiencies of 33 to 45 lumens per watt at the present time. Including the necessary auxiliaries these luminous efficiencies are somewhat reduced. However, they are far above 5 lumens per watt, the approximate luminous efficiency at which average daylight can be produced by means of tungsten lamps and colored glass filters. These fluorescent daylight lamps are quite generally satisfactory for color-discrimination. Their light mixes perfectly with daylight and thus the annoyance of yellowish artificial light in the daytime is eliminated from offices, factories, stores and other places.

Since the first fire on the floor of the primitive cave or hut, artificial light has been yellowish in color. Thus yellowish light has become associated with many interiors and with artificial lighting. In the home, excepting perhaps in work-places, there is a deeply-rooted prejudice in favor of yellowish artificial light and against white artificial light. This is also true to some extent in stores. Recognizing this, a fluorescent lamp emitting a "warm-white" light has been made available. The tint of this light is about the same as that from a tungsten filament operating very close to the melting-point of tungsten. From years of experience with socalled daylight tungsten lamps, this prejudice or attitude had long been apparent. Everyone is generally satisfied with the whiteness and even blue-whiteness of daylight entering a window in the daytime. However, this same whiteness of light produced by an artificial source is often considered to be too cold by the esthetic sense. Probably with white and warm-white light available from efficient fluorescent lamps, the prejudices of habit may be altered gradually. However, the almost perfect control of spectral character of light by phosphors makes it a simple matter to supply whatever general demand may arise. It is as easy to simulate the warm yellowish light from the candle flame, if this should be generally desired in homes, as to reproduce the whiteness of average daylight.

The coolness of the light from fluorescent daylight lamps is not only psychological but actual and this becomes a very important factor in high levels of artificial illumination. The science of seeing has shown that we see most easily, with the least strain, fatigue and waste of human resources, under levels of brightness under which we evolved outdoors. This means that, for example, for reading and clerical work in general, a level of illumination of at least 100 footcandles, and probably several hundred footcandles, is ideal. Under such levels of illumination from tungsten lamps by good lighting methods, human beings may be conscious of the

FLUORESCENT SOURCES

heat and even be uncomfortable under certain conditions. We are not conscious of any heat or heating effect attending hundreds of footcandles of light coming from the sky through a window or in the shade outdoors.

Daylight footcandles are relatively cool because much less invisible radiant energy accompanies each lumen of light than in the case of artificial illuminants of the past. This advantage of daylight arises from two causes. Primarily owing to the high temperature of the sun, much of its radiant energy is visible energy. This is also true of skylight because it is scattered sunlight. Secondarily, owing to the water-vapor in the atmosphere, much of the invisible infrared energy is absorbed before it reaches the earth.

Actual measurements of energy, or the heating effect, per footcandle, reveal the actual coolness of the light from fluorescent lamps. The heating effect per footcandle obtained from tungsten-filament lamps, commonly used in lighting-practice, is in the neighborhood of 7 to 10 times that from natural skylight entering through a glass window. The average heating effect per footcandle obtained from fluorescent daylight lamps is less than twice that from natural skylight through a glass window and is about the same as that from direct sunlight. If ordinary glass is interposed between the fluorescent lamps and the work-place where the light is used, the footcandles from fluorescent lamps are actually cooler than those from natural skylight entering a window. This is a marvelous advance in light-production and reveals the latest step in mankind's progress toward independence from natural light.

Incidentally, we made some careful tests of the maximum level of illumination that produces a barely perceptible heating effect upon human skin. Subjects were blindfolded and a beam of light was directed upon the entire forehead. This beam was silently intercepted at a regular rate of four times per minute. There was a difference in sensitivity among the subjects but the average results are quite consistent with actual measurements of energy. Light from a 100-watt tungsten lamp produced a barely perceptible heating effect at about 125 footcandles as compared with about 600 footcandles from 15-watt fluorescent daylight lamps. It should be noted that the sensitive skin of the upper forehead was the receiver, that the subjects were blindfolded and that the beam of light was broken abruptly. Therefore, it is obvious that human beings can work under hundreds of footcandles from fluorescent lamps without noticeable heating effect and under much higher levels without discomfort. In fact, the science of light-production has made it possible to supply the high levels of illumination required for easiest seeing with artificial daylight as cool as natural daylight.

An explanation of the difference in the heating effect per footcandle from tungsten and fluorescent lamps is worth while for itself and for the glimpse it provides into new realms of production and use of light. In order to obtain a given level of illumination on the plane of the desk tops in a schoolroom, for example, it is necessary at present to use about twice the wattage of tungsten lamps as of fluorescent lamps in the same kind of lighting system. This is due to the fact that fluorescent lamps emit approximately twice the lumens per watt as do the larger tungsten lamps. But this is not all there is to the matter. The electrical energy used in a lamp does not all come out along with the light or lumens and for two radically different light-sources the energy is dissipated in different ways. Therefore, from two radically different kinds of light-sources, having identical luminous

FLUORESCENT SOURCES

efficiencies, the radiant energy accompanying each lumen of light may be far from the same for the two different illuminants. It will be recalled that a lumen per square foot of area produces a level of illumination of one footcandle.

Owing to the importance of cool footcandles, it may be worth while explaining the difference between the energy content of light from tungsten and fluorescent lamps, respectively. In producing artificial light by electrical energy, the latter disappears as such and appears in other forms such as radiant energy and heat. The heat is convected into the air or is conducted away by sockets, etc. Only *radiant* energy can accompany the lumens and, therefore, contribute to the heating effect of the footcandles.

About 60 percent of the total energy from the fluorescent daylight lamp is convected and conducted by the materials of the bulb, base and necessary auxiliary or ballast. About 15 percent of the total energy from a 200-watt tungsten lamp is convected and conducted by the bulb and base. This energy does not accompany the lumens. In other words, about 85 percent of the total energy used by a 200-watt tungsten lamp can accompany the lumens and only about 40 percent in the case of the fluorescent daylight lamp. Thus for this reason the heating effect of the footcandles from large tungsten lamps should be about twice that from this fluorescent daylight lamp. But we obtain about twice the lumens per watt from this fluorescent lamp as we do from this large tungsten lamp. Therefore, these two facts account for the footcandles from large tungsten lamps having a heating effect about four times that from this fluorescent daylight lamp.

The foregoing analysis applies to fluorescent lamps of the present time but this method of light-production is so new

TORCH OF CIVILIZATION

that we may expect rapid advances. At present fluorescent lamps are confined to the range of 15, 20, 30 and 40 watts. The corresponding lengths of these tubular lamps are 18, 24, 36 and 48 inches. Higher wattages and longer lengths are already on the horizon of probability. Theoretically the possibilities extend far beyond that horizon.

The import of fluorescent lamps in the future of lighting-practice is very great. The force of their immediate impact is not entirely a matter of obtaining two or three times as much light as from the same wattage of tungsten-filament lamps. Much of their revolutionary effect is found in their very low brightnesses compared with those of tungsten-filament lamps. Their brightnesses are found within the range of those of the sky outdoors. Measured in the usual units, these brightnesses vary from 1 to 5 candles per square inch. The brightness of a sunlit cloud is about 20 candles per square inch. The smaller inside-frosted tungsten lamps have a brightness of about 80 candles per square inch. Bare tungsten filaments have brightnesses of 1000 candles per square inch and more.

The high brightness of the filaments of tungsten lamps makes possible a high degree of control of light which is desirable in many uses of light. However, for general lighting, tungsten lamps have frosted bulbs to reduce the harshness. Good lighting-practice demands that even these be hidden behind shades or otherwise concealed from the eyes. The low brightness of fluorescent lamps permits a freer use of them in lighting-practice, although in cases where human beings work and live long hours under them, they should be concealed from normal view.

In general lighting-practice we now have two kinds of lamps which represent opposite and reasonable extremes.

FLUORESCENT SOURCES

One is of high brightness and relatively small; the other is of low brightness and reasonably large. These two lamps and illuminants can solve easily and conveniently most of the problems of lighting and of seeing. And with various other sources for special purposes, the present artificial world is fairly independent of Nature's light. During the past twenty-five years lighting practitioners have become rich indeed in available resources.

We have had glimpses of all the important torches of civilization as they evolved slowly through the centuries and very rapidly during the present one. Therefore, this is an appropriate place to summarize the achievements of the torchmakers. From the lowly flames of about one candlepower each (or 12.57 lumens) individual light-sources have increased in intensity to thousands of candlepower and in output to tens of thousands of lumens. The efficiency of light-production from the feeble flame of the ingenious candle, emitting one-tenth of a lumen per watt, has increased several hundred times. Since the dawn of electric lighting, the luminous efficiency of electric lamps has increased more than twenty times and practically all of that enormous increase has taken place in the present century.

The cost of artificial light is much less than a hundredth of its cost a hundred years ago. And in the meantime the cost and standard of living have greatly increased. All this is the product of private initiative and private enterprise. It is illuminating to compare these with costs of government and achievements of politicians. No enterprise can escape the measuring-stick of efficiency—the ultimate production of something per dollar expended. The record of light-production is outstanding and probably has no close second among the necessities of modern civilization.

TORCH OF CIVILIZATION

And as we glance backward and view with justifiable pride the enormous progress of the torch-makers, let us not forget that artificial light is more than the literal torch of civilization. No man-made product excels artificial light in the service of mankind. But the story of light transcends the material aspects of the artificial world of civilization. It is an epic of spiritual and intellectual progress as well as of material achievement. The dramas of light, from primitive ceremonies to uncounted symbolisms of the present, give us glimpses into the emotional hearts and spiritual minds of peoples. The continual brightening of the lamps of civilization reveals the progress of science which continually brightens the lamps of knowledge.

The epic of artificial light reveals the human race born in the darkness of ignorance, emerging into the twilight of knowledge, achieving some creditable independence from Nature, and eventually reproducing and even surpassing Nature's light and lighting. As we witness the birth of a new light-source in the laboratory, or an outstanding improvement in the service of artificial light to civilization, there is intermingled with the pride of accomplishment the inescapable feeling of reverence for the torch of civilization—a feeling which is a common heritage of all mankind.

XII. BEACONS OF LIGHT

THE NIGHT IS inky black as a transoceanic liner ploughs through the fog. Compasses have guided it across the ocean, within a hundred miles of the coast. But strong winds have persisted and they have been variable in direction. Now compasses alone cannot point the liner directly to its destination, for they make no allowance for wind-drift. Far beyond the horizon faithful beacons of light await to be picked up. But this is the age of radio and radio-beacons are also on duty. From a hundred miles over the curvature of the sea's surface, through blinding weather, the radio-beam reaches out to the craft. Far beyond the range of powerful lighthouses, the radio-beam is intercepted by officers on watch. Thus steamship or airship is guided straight into the range of the light-beacon. Then the partners, light and sight, take it safely to its destination.

Hundreds of radio-beacons throughout the world now extend the effectiveness of great seacoast lighthouses and lightships even in the densest fog or blinding rain or snow. About 150 radio-beacons operate along the shores of this country among 15,000 light-aids to navigation. There is no doubt that the radio-beacon is the most important recent development in lighthouse service. By means of a direction-finder the master of a craft at sea can determine the exact direction of the lighthouse or lightship from which the distinctive signals come. He may steer toward it—ride the beam —or he may pick up another radio-beacon and plot his exact

TORCH OF CIVILIZATION

position on the navigation chart. But radio-beacons only extend the range of the important seacoast lighthouses. They are not substitutes for light-beacons, for the master of a ship must depend upon light and sight to guide him around dangerous shoals and into harbors.

It is a far cry from our modern beacons of light, of millions of beam candlepower, to the wood-fires which served along the Mediterranean Sea when the Roman Empire encircled it. No application of artificial light more clearly reveals progress in the production and control of light than lighthouses. And besides their usefulness in saving lives and property, they have always been beacons of romance and of drama. For more than two thousand years they have pointed toward adventure beyond the horizon and have welcomed the adventurer to the snugness of harbor or of home. For many centuries prosperity and empires were built upon shipping. Transportation was largely by water in olden times and in new countries. And beacons of light early marked the waterways.

Although light-aids along waterways have been developed to a high degree, they are no longer confined to marine navigation. Transportation is no longer dependent upon the power of fickle winds or confined to natural waterways. With the development of man-made engines and the consequent control of power, highways of travel expanded from the sea to the land and thence to the air. And wherever traffic went, light-beacons accompanied it. Criss-crossing the continent are rows of lighthouses on the land to guide the airplane. The pilot may ride the radio-beam and may even land his craft blindfolded, but light and sight is the most important partnership in air-transport as in most other human activities. Everywhere along airways and at airports,

Everywhere, from city street to mountain-top, men keep the lifeblood flowing to faithful beacons of light throughout every artery of civilization.

controlled light does its work in beacons, signal-lights, approach-lights and landing-lights. On railways and highways, traffic is guided, protected and controlled by headlamps and signal-lights. The partnership of traffic and safety depends largely upon the partnership of light and sight and this, inevitably, upon the partnership of production, control and use of light.

Beacon-fires are mentioned in writings as early as the seventh century before the Christian era. These were merely fires of burning wood maintained by priests and others on the top of a hill or cliff. The first notable lighthouse was built on a small island near Alexandria by Ptolemy II in about 331 B.C. This tower was called Pharos and lighthouses for centuries afterward inherited this name. In fact, pharology is the term given to the general science of lighthouses, light-signals and other light-aids to navigation. Caesar, after a visit to Alexandria two centuries after the Pharos was built, described it as "a tower of great height, of wonderful construction." Pliny wrote of it, "During the night it appears as bright as a star, and during the day it is distinguished by its smoke." This first notable lighthouse was found in ruins in 1349 and it is known to have served mariners considerably more than a thousand years. Many other lighthouses were built in those early centuries. On a cliff at Boulogne, France, are the remains of an ancient pharos which is said to have been built by Caligula in about 40 B.C. At Dover, England, are the remains of another supposedly built by the ancient Romans.

For many early centuries the beacon-fires were little more than bonfires maintained only as the occasion or weather demanded. With the advent of towers built for the purpose, systematic maintenance of the fire began. In fact, at the top

TORCH OF CIVILIZATION

of the pharos towers was a compartment in which the fire was maintained. It had a roof and open sides. Provisions were made for protecting the fire from high winds and for supplying it with the proper draft of air. Eventually where coal was available, it was burned in grates at the top of lighthouses. Beacons of burning coal were still in use in the British Isles as late as 1820 and in northern Europe until about 1850. It is not clear when more refined fuels and reflectors came into use. Although the simple principles of light-control by reflection and refraction had been known in ancient Rome, they did not come into use until many centuries later. More refined fuels came into use in oil-lamps long before they entered service as light-beacons. Lighthouses which guided ships home from the four corners of the earth with cargoes of better fuels for oil-lamps did not share the fruits of those voyages until relatively recently.

The first lighthouse in the United States, and probably in the western hemisphere, was the famous Boston Light. This was completed and put into commission in 1716, about a century after the Pilgrims arrived. It was maintained by an impost upon ships of "one penny per ton inwards, and another penny outwards." Local craft were assessed a few shillings a year. Many of the lighthouses in England were privately owned at the time but the Boston Light was a public enterprise promoted by the merchants. Its tower of stone was erected at a cost of $10,000. It was blown up by British raiders in 1776 and was rebuilt in 1783. Since that time it has been increased in height. Now it sends forth a beam of 100,000 candlepower gathered from electric light-sources by modern lenses. This powerful beacon now beckons to great steamships from the same spot where two

BEACONS OF LIGHT

centuries ago the light from a few "oil blazes" braved darkness and storm to aid small sailing vessels.

During the first session of the Congress of the United States, a law was enacted which provided for the erection and maintenance of lighthouses. Thus this service is one of the oldest functions of our government. Up to that time about a dozen lighthouses had been built by the Colonies. These were the beginning of a service which at the present time involves 30,000 aids to marine navigation, about half of which are light-aids.

Although for thirty years the Boston Light was the only lighthouse on the coast of North America, several others played dramatic roles in Colonial times and in the Revolutionary War. The original masonry tower of Sandy Hook lighthouse still stands at the entrance of New York harbor, a dignified structure about 100 feet in height. Built in 1764 by the proceeds of two lotteries, it was the first in that locality which was destined to be one of the greatest ports in the world. It played its part in the Revolutionary War but escaped with only small damage. When it was lighted for the first time, a New York paper described it in detail, stating that "the lanthorn is 7 feet high; the circumference is 33 feet. The whole construction of the lanthorn is iron; the top covered with copper. There are 48 oil blazes."

Perhaps the most famous lighthouse in England is the Eddystone off Plymouth. The first tower, erected in 1698, was swept away a few years later. A successor was destroyed by fire but another was erected in 1759. In this one it is definitely recorded that 24 large candles were used, each flame being of 2.8 candlepower. Crude parabolic reflectors, consisting of flat pieces of mirrors set at different angles in cement, were introduced at this time in several lighthouses.

Even with such reflectors concentrating the light and sending it seaward, a source equivalent to 67 candles could not supply a very powerful beam. However, compared with the coal-fires, the Eddystone light was a creditable beacon at the time.

In the British Isles oil-lamps with flat wicks were first used in 1763. The Argand lamp with its cylindrical wick, better supply of air and its glass chimney, became extensively used in lighthouses after its invention in 1784. Lange improved the lamp chimney by constricting it somewhat near the top. The need for much more light in lighthouses led to the development of multiple-wick burners by Rumford, Fresnel and others. These light-sources were additionally protected by enclosing the top of the tower with glass. The principal chores of the keeper of the lighthouse were to trim the wicks, clean the glass and polish the reflectors, if any. And similar chores persist in the present age of electric light. Naturally the oil used depended upon the period because there was a continual improvement and refinement in fuels. Whale-oil, colza-oil and even lard-oil were burned in lighthouses until long after the middle of the nineteenth century.

After the discovery of petroleum and the tapping of great underground pools, mineral oil came into general use. However, it was not until about 1877 that it was introduced into lighthouses. Doty invented a successful multiple-wick mineral-oil lamp which, with inevitable modifications and improvements, was generally used for a score of years after the advent of electric light-sources into this service near the end of last century. These oil-lamps for lighthouses were of two general types. In one the oil was supplied to the burner under pressure. In the other the oil was automatically maintained at a constant level. Obviously both methods avoided any variation in the capillary force in the wick with the result that the candlepower of the flame was maintained constantly at its maximum.

About the middle of last century gas-lights began to enter the field of navigation-aids. Coal-gas requires a rather elaborate plant for its manufacture and, therefore, its use was confined to places where the gas could be piped conveniently from the local gas-mains. Gas-flames were arranged in concentric rings forming a stepped cone of light. Naturally gas-mantles eventually superseded these flames with the result that a radical increase in the brightness of the light-source was achieved in light-beacons for the first time in their long history. It will be recalled that beams of high candlepower can be efficiently obtained only by controlling the light by means of accurate reflectors or lenses. High control of light by such means requires a small brilliant source. Fortunately in lighthouses the controlling apparatus may be large and at an appreciable distance from the light-source. As a consequence even the relatively large size of a cluster of gas-mantles furnished beams of several hundred thousand candlepower in some instances. Later gas made from mineral oil in the regenerative burner could be used to heat special mantles to incandescence. The first incandescent oil-vapor lamp was installed in this country in 1904 in a lighthouse near Sandy Hook.

Fortunately other gases were developed such as Pintsch gas, which could be compressed into tanks, and acetylene which could be made readily from water and calcium carbide. These were convenient to use in isolated lighthouses and were quite suitable for the completely isolated light-buoys. The first lighted buoy went into service in 1881 in an eastern harbor. Great improvements were made in the operation of automatic gas-feed, and untended lights such as minor beacons and light-buoys eventually reached a high stage of development and usage. Untended lights burn for several months very dependably. Thousands of these are still in use where gas-flames behind efficient lenses are satisfactory for short-range signals. About 2000 light-buoys float along the waterways and many of the minor lights and beacons are untended. Electricity from dry cells is being introduced particularly in flashing minor lights. Where the filament is merely flashed at intervals the drain on the battery is not severe and it need not be charged or replaced for several weeks.

Although crude silvered reflectors were introduced as early as 1763 and spherical and parabolic reflectors a score of years later, accurate control of light into beams was not achieved until much later. Drummond in 1825 developed the lime-light and a fairly accurate reflector for use in surveying coastlines where long distances had to be sighted. Naturally he suggested the use of his system for lighthouses. His work shows that comparatively little had been accomplished toward the accurate control of light into powerful beams. Glass lenses had come into use to some extent but mere spherical lenses have their limitations.

The object of a reflector or lens is to gather light from a source throughout a large solid angle and to send this light out in a parallel beam. All the light outside the cone of gathered light is wasted. At large angles from the axis of the lens, the latter is inefficient. Fresnel, beginning in 1822, greatly increased the gathering power of a lens by extending the size of the glass lens with glass prisms, which refracted and reflected the light into a beam. This entire optical system could be made in the form of a solid of revolution.

BEACONS OF LIGHT

That is, the Fresnel lens could completely surround the light-source as a glass cylinder might. The result is a gathering of light from above and below the axis. This is sent out in a flat beam of light, if desired, like a ring of Saturn. The Fresnel lens was a great contribution toward the control of light. Cylindrical pencils of light pointing in one direction, sheets of light shining in all horizontal directions, and asymmetric beams of various kinds are in extensive use today. Fresnel lenses or modifications of his system of refracting and reflecting glass prisms are used in lighthouses, traffic lights, signal-lights on railways, automobile head and tail lamps, airway beacons and landing-lights, and throughout all the extensive realms of beacons and signals.

The most powerful light in use in the United States at the present time is in Navesink lighthouse on the highlands of Navesink overlooking the lower bay of New York. Its beam of 9 million candlepower, visible 22 miles at sea, is a powerful example of the great contribution of electric light. It is fitting that this lighthouse was the first in this country to use a Fresnel lens and the first in which electric light was installed. The first lens was installed in 1841 and in 1898 carbon arcs supplied by an electric dynamo replaced the last of a long line of fuel burners.

It was natural for electric arcs to enter the field of powerful light-beacons and for filament-lamps to invade the realms of minor lights wherever electrical energy was available. For the great seacoast lighthouses it was practicable to install a generating plant. As gas- and oil-engines developed, isolated plants became even more practicable so that electricity became a great boon to this branch of maritime service. The first electric arcs were seriously experimented with in lighthouses as early as 1860 but the first practical installations were made in 1875. During the next decade much research and development took place with the result that toward the end of last century electric arcs served in many great lighthouses along the coasts of the more prosperous countries.

Throughout the development of light-sources an important objective has been to increase the brightness of the light-source and to concentrate it into a small space for better controlling the light. The arc-lamp is very satisfactory in this respect but it requires more attention than filament-lamps. As a consequence of the development of ductile tungsten, the high concentration of tungsten filaments became possible. Therefore, with the exception of the more powerful beacons, thousands of filament-lamps are serving in beacons along waterways and airways. A general introduction of electricity began in about 1916, exactly two centuries after the debut of the famous Boston Light.

All the early beacons of light were "fixed" lights, but it is a fact of common observation that flashing lights have greater attention value. The novelty of a flashing light among the other steady lights of a harbor was recognized as early as 1783 when the first revolving mechanism was installed. To the novelty of a flashing light were eventually added the advantages of characteristic flashes and definite time-intervals between the flashes. Thus each light could be given a sort of personality which was readily recognized even by a ship's master who might be a total stranger to the locality. The characteristics of various navigation-lights became systematized and recorded in instructions issued by the various governments. Flashes of short duration followed by longer periods of darkness are widely used. This method is extended to two or more flashes between intervals of darkness.

BEACONS OF LIGHT

Another method involves the occulting light, a term applied to a fixed light which is momentarily eclipsed but the duration of the eclipse is usually shorter than that of the light. Sometimes colored lights are alternated with dark periods and are even combined with colorless lights. However, owing to the low candlepower of colored lights they are used for short-range signals. Fixed lights are now generally confined to minor light-aids. Among these are some which are colorless in the direction of the fairway of the channel and colored in the other directions, thus signifying danger.

The range of a light-source in any given direction depends upon its candlepower in that direction. The absorption of the atmosphere depends upon the amount of smoke, water-vapor, and fog present and it differs with the spectral character of the illuminant. In general the yellow, orange and red rays penetrate great depths of atmosphere better than the violet, blue and green rays. This is obvious from the orange and red color of the setting sun. However, with common light-sources the chief factor is light-control by means of which powerful beams of light are obtained from very brilliant and physically small sources of light or sources such as filaments specially constructed to fit the optical system.

Obviously after a powerful beam is available, the range of its visibility is determined by the curvature of the earth. Thus the heights of the light and of the distant observer above the level of the sea, or earth, became important factors. The tallest lighthouse in the United States is that at Hog Island, Virginia, which is 191 feet. If its base is at sea-level its horizontal beam of light should touch sea-level at a distance of about 17 miles. The highest marine light under the jurisdiction of the United States is the lighthouse on Lehau Rock in the Hawaiian Islands. It is 709 feet above the level of the sea and is theoretically visible by a person at sea-level about 32 miles distant. To a ship's lookout 50 feet above the surface of the sea the beam might be visible about 40 miles distant.

The effect of height upon the theoretical range of a light-beacon may be computed approximately from simple formulae. For marine lights the range in miles is five-fourths of the square root of the height of the light in feet above sea-level. For example, if the height is 100 feet the square root is 10 and five-fourths of this gives a range of about 12.5 miles. This is the range for an observer whose eyes are at sea-level. Obviously if the observer is above sea-level the same computation determines his range. Then the theoretical distance at which the light may be seen is the sum of the light's range and the observer's range. The range of vision of a person in an airplane in miles is approximately 90 times the square root of his altitude in miles. For example, for a person four miles above the sea, the horizon is about 180 miles away. Whether or not beacons of light can be seen at distances corresponding to the theoretical ranges depends upon their candlepower and the atmospheric conditions. Of course, their important ranges are those in foggy or blinding weather which is a primary reason for developing powerful beacons.

The construction of lighthouse towers on shoals and in deep water is sometimes impracticable or even impossible. For this reason lightships were developed and equipped with sound signals as well as with lights. The first lightship in this country was anchored near Craney Island in Chesapeake Bay in 1820. For centuries small boats had been anchored at dangerous points along channels. Carrying at the masthead a light but no crew these served shipping far better than no lights. The lightship with its varied equipment and a crew to maintain and operate it was a natural development. Now there are many sturdy vessels of steel, manned by crews of 6 to 15 men, located at many points where it is impossible or impracticable to construct lighthouses.

Thus progress in the development of light-aids to marine navigation parallels that of artificial light. Most of it has taken place in the past two centuries. Three-fourths of the earth's surface is covered by water and a large portion of that area constitutes waterways of commerce. What a change has taken place! Wrecks are now seldom due to the inefficacy of lighthouses and other light-aids to navigation. No longer do communities live on a bountiful sea which wrecked ships and sent the wreckage ashore. Times have changed since Robert Louis Stevenson, in describing the coast people of the Orkney Islands stated that "in the leasing of farms, a location with a greater probability of shipwreck on the shore brought a much higher rent."

And times have changed in other ways—to airways. The great ocean of air above the earth is already lined with air-lanes. Here again beacons of light are in partnership with sight to guide the pilot along his route and particularly to his destination. He may ride the radio-beam and land in a blinding fog. This is satisfactory in an emergency but there is no substitute for light and sight for us human beings, dominated by the visual sense and overwhelmingly trusting to seeing. Air-travel having been born during the ascendency of electricity, electric lights serve airplanes, air-lanes and airports completely in many ways. All the experience with light in navigation, signaling, and other practices was available along with modern electric lamps. The records for safety achieved by railroads with their powerful headlamps and particularly their light and electric signals were a challenge to this new competitor in the realm of transportation. At the present moment 735 airports in this country are lighted for night-landing and light-beacons are nearly always in sight, in good weather, along 30,000 miles of airways.

A powerful rotating beacon flashing a beam of a million candlepower every ten seconds, heralds a distant airport to the pilot. Intermediate flashes of at least 200,000 candlepower identify the airport. Inasmuch as the pilot may be flying at a high altitude, the beam is directed somewhat above the horizontal which, of course, is never done in marine service. An auxiliary code-beacon of 5000 candlepower or more is sometimes installed at airports in addition to the rotating one. In these beacons the light from the concentrated filaments of 500-watt to 1500-watt tungsten lamps is gathered by searchlight projectors into proper beams. The beacons are equipped with stand-by lamps which automatically go into service when the one which is lighted burns out.

As the pilot approaches the field he notes the illuminated flying "sock" or other wind-direction indicator. Red lights here and there warn of obstructions. Approach-lights located outside the landing area indicate favorable directions of approach. The boundaries of the entire landing area are outlined by colorless lights not more than 300 feet apart. Green range lights, fifty feet apart and in line with the boundary lights, mark the ends of runways or of favorable landing directions. On some of the larger airports, contact lights, consisting of colorless lights set flush with the ground, parallel the runway at a distance of 200 feet on each side.

The electric circuits are controlled so that one runway at a time is outlined in this manner.

Located out of line with runways are floodlights ready to illuminate the portion of the landing area the pilot will use in landing. This beam follows the movement of the plane but the plane itself is usually kept in shadow so that the pilot will not be blinded by the glare. These and various minor uses of light make flying at night largely a matter of following—and knowing—the lights. This has done much toward perfecting the safety of flying and reducing the fatalities in scheduled flying to about one in many million flying miles at the present time. Even among the rare accidents one due to improper or inadequate use of light is so rare as to be practically non-existent.

This enviable record of safety on the airways, as well as on waterways and railways, does not apply to highways. On the highways of this country the present rate of accidents results in about 35,000 persons killed and more than a million injured annually. If this rate should continue for a lifetime, a sad future is in store for the million babies born this year. On the average 900,000 of them will be involved in a traffic accident on our highways before they die, 100,000 of them will be seriously injured, and 30,000 will be killed! That is a pitiful picture in a civilization which has made a great record of safety on other traffic lanes. Beacons of light in traffic signals, street-lamps and automobile headlamps can do more to alter this picture than they have. Uncounted danger points, and practically all highways outside of cities, towns and villages, are not yet illuminated by fixed lighting. Headlamps on motor cars are essential and the new sealed-beam headlamps are great improvements. But the condition is reminiscent of the relatively primitive lighting when persons carried candles or lanterns as they moved about after dark. And on our highways pedestrians do not even carry lights. As is quite proper, much attention is given to carelessness of drivers and failure of brakes and other parts, but relatively little attention is given by the public and public authorities to an overwhelmingly important matter—seeing. Safe seeing is achieved only through an adequate partnership of light and sight.

On seaways and airways light and sight cooperate to guide the craft to its destination but there is little or no congestion. On railways, beacons and signals have done much to promote safety but here also there is little or no congestion. On highways, beacons have their useful functions but there is congestion and there are narrow channels not always well defined. There are pedestrians, obstacles, soft shoulders, ditches, and other vehicles. Seeing conditions suitable for the age of horse-drawn vehicles are not adequate with legal speeds ten times as great. Concepts of what seeing is and of the conditions necessary for quick and certain seeing by drivers, engaged in operating the motor car and in observing signs and signals, are generally inadequate. The modern beacons of light, such as the sealed-beam headlamp, greatly improve seeing and safety. They reduce glare and illuminate the highway a long way ahead, but they are only a part of the solution of the problem of poor seeing for a streamlined era. The complete solution for major highways is adequate illumination of the highway independent of headlamps and signal-lights.

The proof of this statement arises from our knowledge of seeing which is embodied in the recently developed concepts and science of seeing. But striking verification is also found in the analyses of accurate records of day and night accidents, and of accidents before and after the installation of highway lighting or of improved street-lighting. Black-outs in European cities have resulted in an astonishing number of traffic accidents. The seeing conditions of our highways at night approach closer to those of the black-out than they do to those in the daytime. About 50 percent of the accidents on highways occur after dark notwithstanding the fact that only about 20 per cent of the traffic occurs after dark. Actually the hazard on highways is several times greater at night than during the day, if computed on the basis of vehicle-miles. Owing to the greater severity of accidents at night, the chances of getting killed in a traffic accident are many times greater than in the daytime. These are the simple gruesome results of the war of darkness and of poor seeing conditions against human life and limb.

During a period of intense education toward the reduction of traffic accidents, the percentage occurring at night has increased relatively to those in the daytime. Education is no substitute for poor seeing and the latter is largely due to the inadequacy of light in the partnership of sight. Of the total traffic in this country about 75 percent is confined to 50,000 miles of major highways which have been paved at a cost of many thousands of dollars per mile. Practically none of this mileage is illuminated even though a great improvement in seeing and in safety could be accomplished at a small fraction of the cost of paving. Where lighting has been installed, or new lighting has been substituted for old, accurate records reveal that night accidents have invariably been decreased and in some cases very greatly.

It seems inevitable that recognition of the relation of seeing to safety should eventually increase sufficiently for proper lighting of the major highways to proceed from a public demand as powerful as that which resulted in paving them. The entire cost of lighting the major highways of this country would be considerably less than the present economic loss in property damage, time lost, litigation and hospital bills due to accidents unquestionably arising from darkness, inadequate light or improper lighting. In addition to a saving of hundreds of millions of dollars, great human losses in sorrow and suffering would be eliminated. We abhor war and its tragedies but on our highways poor seeing conditions of an outmoded era are making war on life, limb and property. And the people's general ignorance of the cause and general indifference to the remedies are powerful allies of the prevailing primitive conditions of seeing. Such a record on our highways ill-becomes a civilization that has accomplished so much toward perfecting safety on seaways, railways and airways. Possessing the means to do the same on highways, there can be no satisfactory alibi. We, the people, are guilty.

XIII. LIGHT AND SIGHT

AS YOU READ these lines of printed words, your eyes do not move steadily along each line as you might brush a finger across its length. Your eyes walk along in a series of steps varying in length. They take several steps along each line and between the steps they pause and are quite stationary for a fraction of a second. An analogy is the drinking of water. It is taken in swallows, not poured down in a continuous flowing stream. In reading these lines you actually see words only during the pauses when the eyes are at rest. And between the pauses, while the eyes are in motion, you are not conscious of blurring for you have "learned" not to see excepting when the eyes are motionless. Here again we have a glimpse of the value of infancy and early childhood in learning how to see—how to use the gift of sight. Actually during those early years, seeing involved much learning—and some forgetting. As a consequence, seeing has become fairly automatic and quite commonplace.

We take for granted, or are indifferent to, many important matters involved in seeing. Six tiny external muscles move each eye and guide it along this line of type. They keep your eyes converged upon these words and make your two eyes work together as a team. If you should read continually all day long these muscles would make your eyes travel carefully and critically over a mile of lines of type—and back again. During that time these little muscles would make your eyes take about 100,000 steps. If your legs had taken a step every time your eyes did, you would have walked about 50 miles. Obviously, that would be a hard day's work for legs. Therefore, you need not be surprised that your eyes and you are fatigued from hours of reading or other critical visual work.

No one could read these lines without light, but mere light is not necessarily enough to make this task of seeing—reading—as easy as possible. One of our most important objectives during many years of research with light has been to determine the influence of light upon the ease with which various tasks of seeing can be performed. Such researches have invaded the complex realm of effects of seeing not only upon the eyes but upon various organs, processes, tenseness and fatigue of the entire human being. Reading, or the performance of any other task of seeing, is work just as walking, climbing or running is work. If you read continuously all day long, not only would your eyes have worked hard in taking 100,000 steps and in keeping focused and converged upon the print, but you also would have worked hard. You would have recognized perhaps 200,000 words consisting of about a million letters. All this required not only accurate focusing of the eyes but also critically focusing your attention. Your eyes did a hard day's work, but so did you as a human being operating as a human seeing-machine. Adequate light and proper lighting increase the visibility of the printed matter and decrease the work involved in reading.

While you read you are not conscious that you are more or less tense, which means that you are dissipating energy just as you do in physical labor. You are not conscious that your heart-rate may be affected. You are unaware that your rate of blinking increases as fatigue increases, and as daylight wanes if you are reading by a window or on the porch.

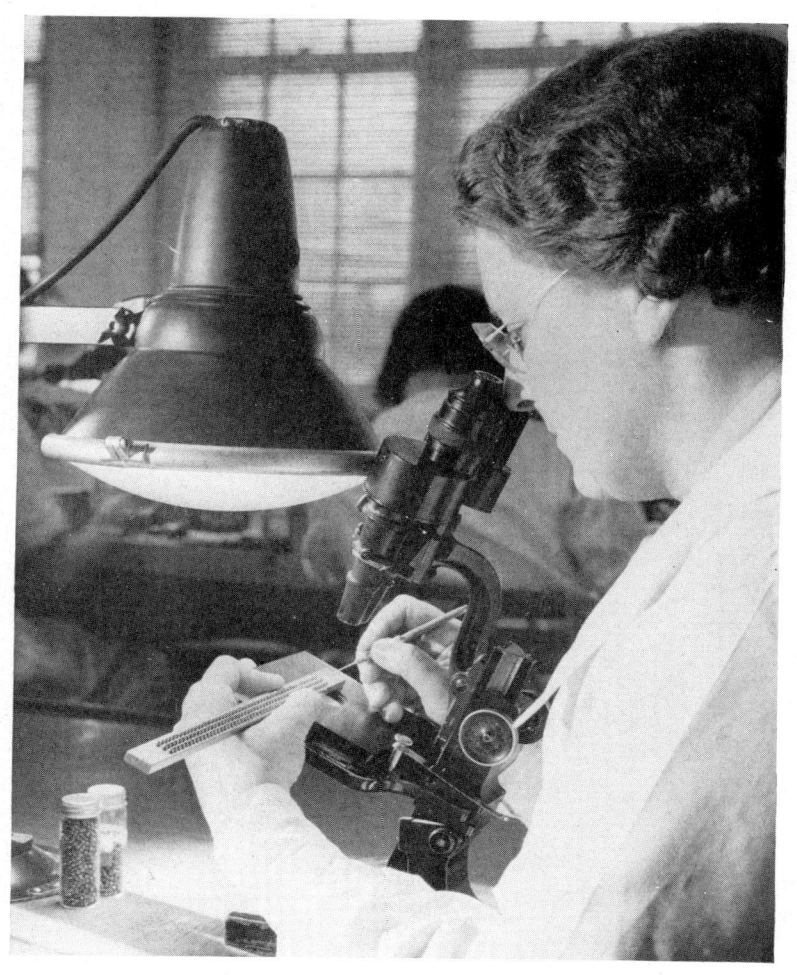

Light-control, illustrated by eyeglasses, microscope, light-source, reflector and diffusing glass, dominates seeing which dominates human activities.

LIGHT AND SIGHT

You may be conscious of strain and fatigue in certain eye-muscles, but you do not know that the pupils of your eyes increase in size as the muscles controlling them become weakened, thus revealing actual fatigue. You do not know that your ability to see decreases measurably as you and your eyes become fatigued. These are effects of seeing which we have already discovered. Undoubtedly there are still others more deeply hidden. We do know that from strain and fatigue due to seeing, human resources are dissipated and we know that certain nervous disorders may arise. How much we pay in unnecessary penalties is not known, but enough has been revealed to emphasize the desirability of utilizing adequate light as a partner of sight to make the partnership do the best job for us at the least cost in human resources.

Reading is an example of countless man-made tasks involving critical seeing for prolonged periods at distances within arm's reach. And by no means is reading one of the most severe visual tasks. Many others involve the recognition of finer details and much lower contrasts in brightness. But all of them involve long periods of strain and concentration in focusing the eyes, and the attention, for near-vision. When we look at objects a few feet away, the eye-muscles are much more relaxed and are quite relaxed when focused upon objects beyond twenty feet. Since Gutenberg invented movable type five centuries ago from which modern printing evolved, civilization has become largely a world of near-vision. This is unnatural when we consider that human eyes, and of possibly more importance, human beings as seeing-machines, evolved outdoors over the course of millions of years during which near-vision was as casual as distant-vision.

Probably no one would forego the pleasure and progress of civilized activities throughout homes, schools, offices and industries. We will accept the unavoidable penalties along with the rewards of being shackled to near-vision tasks. However, it is essential that we ascertain the penalties and how to reduce them. I set myself to that task a quarter of a century ago and with various colleagues, particularly Frank K. Moss, have developed through new avenues of research much of the structure properly known as the science of seeing. Glimpses of our attack and of the results are of importance to everyone in conserving the great gift of eyesight and in reducing the waste of other resources expended in seeing.

Our approaches have been directed along several avenues. They are avenues now but most of them were not even trails in the wilderness when the researches began. Where it was possible we began to study seeing where knowledge of optics and vision ceased, but most of the entire realm of seeing was practically an unknown. Naturally the development of knowledge of seeing involved the study of the contributions which light—the essential partner of sight—could make toward decreasing the penalties of poor seeing conditions and toward increasing the rewards of better, and eventually of best, seeing conditions. Immediately upon confronting this complex unknown, one finds the levels of brightness and of illumination outdoors in the daytime to be enormously greater than those indoors under natural or artificial light. Civilization wrought no such changes in the amount of air, water and food that human beings use. It is true that complaints of deficiencies in these other essentials are obvious, direct and emphatic, but lack of obvious and direct complaints in the case of inadequate light, and of many other essentials to ease, to health and even to life itself, is not proof of the absence of penalties. Nor is it an excuse for indifference to the possible waste in eyesight and in other human resources due to generally poor seeing conditions.

Before discussing some of the revelations of the science of seeing in regard to the efficacy of more light and better lighting, let us glimpse the pitiful picture of eye-defectiveness. I do not refer only to those possessing unusually defective eyesight such as pupils in sight-saving classes and many elderly persons. In such cases, as with persons possessing normal vision, there is a limit to the effectiveness of light. It is the maximal ability of sight. However, in the case of a person with serious eye-defects, there is no excuse for not giving him all the benefit of light which generally means many times more light than he may be using. In general we have found that light helps those most who most need help in seeing. Some progress has been made in providing more light in sight-saving classrooms, but there are thousands of elderly persons who have given up reading and other visual work because they find it difficult to see under the usual levels of illumination available. The eyesight specialist has been slow in recognizing that light, while no substitute for eyeglasses, is a partner of sight which, if adequately available, can work wonders beyond those of corrective eyeglasses.

Civilization should be greatly concerned with the trend of eye-defectiveness. More than a million babies will be born this year in the United States. All but about three percent will come into this world with the priceless gift of normal eyesight. Nearly all of them will retain their socalled normal eyesight until after they start to school. Then they enter the slavery of near-vision including unnaturally critical and prolonged visual tasks amid the meager light of indoors. They enter an unnatural artificial world of inadequate light as judged by Nature's textbook and verified by the science of seeing. As these school-children progress from grade to grade, the percentage of them whose eyes become measurably defective steadily increases. When they graduate from high school about one out of every four will need eyeglasses. When they graduate from college one out of three will need eyeglasses. When they reach middle age about one out of two will need eyeglasses.

Is this natural? A broad view of evolution and adaptation answers emphatically, "No!" If this were natural, somewhere in the course of evolution this would have been remedied. Eyes would have become capable of being used from infancy to reasonably old age without becoming so impaired or defective. There is no comparable increase in defectiveness of any other part of the human being. A great mass of details can be woven together into an indictment of civilization which lifted natural burdens from the backs of human beings and placed unnatural burdens upon their eyes and upon the entire human seeing-machine. Look into the faces of adults that have reached or passed middle age. Their use of their eyes is commonly written there. But to be more certain, look at the statistics of eye-defectiveness sorted out according to occupation. The percentage of clerical workers having eye-defects is much higher than the percentage of common laborers, farmers, or of those in other occupations who are not so shackled for long hours daily to the unnatural tasks of near-vision.

Suppose we could temporarily transfer defects of eyes to defects of legs. As we watch the stream of human beings on a city street, a large percentage of them would be limping on crippled legs. We would note that only a few small children limped perceptibly but crippled legs would be more common among the older and grown children. Every other person past middle age would limp perceptibly, many markedly, and some would be in wheel-chairs. This would be a pitiful throng because the defects would be so obvious. And we might ask, Is this increasing eye-defectiveness unavoidable or preventable? At present the answer cannot be decisive. Civilization is built largely upon the tasks of near-vision and they may be largely responsible. But we do know that these tasks can be made easier by more light and better lighting and there is some evidence that when seeing is made easier, defective eyesight may actually improve. At any rate, the enormous increase in the efficiency of light-production and the consequent decrease in the cost of light make it possible to provide a hundred times more light for our tasks of seeing today compared with a hundred years ago and still leave great savings to be expended in other ways.

These are the glimpses of our reasons for initiating researches in seeing which aimed to determine what light could do to ease the burdens and penalties of seeing. The glory of great achievements in the production and control of light was dulled by a lack of knowledge of how to use it. Lighting-practice had long used the light-sources available and with knowledge of optics produced the controlling lighting equipment necessary. But sound specification of light and lighting for the varied tasks of seeing was impossible without sound knowledge of the relationships between light and sight and without adequate concepts and knowledge of seeing. Now let us glimpse some of the highlights of new knowledge in this important realm of modern science.

TORCH OF CIVILIZATION

In order to appraise the effect of light upon the visibility of tasks and upon ease of seeing, it is necessary to begin with the footcandle. This is the unit of illumination, stranger to most persons, but no more mysterious than such units as the pound or quart which are used every day. Just as other units are defined arbitrarily, so is the footcandle. It is the level of illumination on this printed page when held vertically one foot from a lighted standard candle and perpendicular to a horizontal line joining the center of this page with the flame. However, this definition is not important in itself. It is repeated here merely to give the reader an idea of the magnitude of the footcandle. We are more interested in relative levels of illumination and in relative brightnesses. After all, it is the brightness of this page which is important, and the visibility of these printed words, and the ease with which they can be read, depend upon the level of illumination. Incidentally, the near-black letters receive the same amount of light as the white paper surrounding them. Their brightness is much less than that of the paper because they reflect much less light and the contrast between the letters and the paper makes it possible to see them. Here we have a basic lesson in distinguishing between illumination and brightness.

Outdoors on a green grass lawn during midday in summer the level of illumination commonly approaches 9000 footcandles. Owing to the fact that the grass lawn reflects only a small percentage of the light and the white paper of this page reflects nearly 80 percent, the lawn is as bright under 9000 footcandles of midday midsummer sunlight as this page is under about 500 footcandles. But it is likely that you are reading this page under a few footcandles. In fact, the severe visual tasks of civilization are being performed, on the average, under a few footcandles. This tremendous departure from Nature is further emphasized when we consider that most of our visual tasks reflect much less light than this printed page and, therefore, are much lower in brightness under the same level of illumination.

Looking down the various avenues which have recently been carved out of the unknown wilderness, let us examine sight or vision as a tool. It appears reasonable that the proper conditions under which to use a tool are those under which it is most sensitive. Vision is most sensitive for use in everyday seeing under the conditions which make it possible to see the smallest object with the least contrast in the shortest time. A vast amount of investigation of the partnership of light and sight reveals that these conditions are obtained when the brightness-levels approximate those of an outdoor landscape—woods, fields and lawns—under the full light of a clear midsummer day. These brightnesses are approximately equaled by this printed page when it is illuminated by several hundred footcandles. In other words, sight cannot do its best until its partner, light, has been permitted to produce brightness equal to that of this white paper when illuminated to more than a hundred footcandles. For many other tasks the reflection-factors, as in the case of dark cloth in sewing, are so much lower than those of socalled white papers that the illumination must be increased to more than a thousand footcandles before the optimum brightness is reached. These levels of illumination are enormously greater than those under which the unnaturally severe and prolonged critical seeing of civilization is being done. But they are attainable at the present time by satisfactory lighting methods and at costs which are not out of line with benefits. In fact by properly combining direct light with general lighting where this combination is practicable, it is easy to obtain high levels of illumination.

For a moment let us go to the eyesight specialist for a simple examination with the familiar test-chart containing lines of letters of various sizes. By ascertaining the smallest letters you can read, he determines what is termed your visual acuity and brings it as near to normal as possible by prescribing glasses if necessary. This is a practicable method of determining errors in the optical system of the eye but it falls short of revealing how well you see the various tasks you encounter, particularly those involving low contrast. It is also an interesting fact that if the eyesight specialist determined your visual acuity under different levels of illumination on the test-chart, he would obtain different results.

This is readily illustrated by a typical test upon a group of persons who were wearing proper glasses of moderate corrections. We measured their visual acuity with and without their eyeglasses with the test-chart illuminated by one footcandle and by 100 footcandles. Let us consider their average visual acuity without their glasses to be relatively 100 when the test-chart was illuminated by one footcandle. Wearing their glasses the average visual acuity increased to 123. In other words, the glasses increased the average visual acuity 23 percent. Then we took off their glasses and increased the illumination of the test-chart to 100 footcandles. The average visual acuity was 133. In other words, the increased illumination increased visual acuity more than the eyeglasses did at the one-footcandle level. On wearing their glasses, the average visual acuity increased to 156 when there were 100 footcandles on the test-chart.

This is a striking demonstration of the importance of

adequate light as well as of proper eyeglasses. By no means is it implied that more light is a substitute for eyeglasses. In cases of certain eye-defects, this may be true but while eyeglasses and more light both increase visual acuity, they accomplish the result in somewhat different ways. Eyeglasses are needed to correct optical defects and relieve eyestrain due to them. More light increases the ability of the eyes or decreases the limitations of vision. Eyeglasses serve to "sharpen" the eyes. They increase the ability to distinguish fine detail but they do not influence the sensitivity to brightness-contrast which is the most generally important factor in seeing. Contrast is controlled entirely by controlling brightness whether it is obtained by printing words with black ink on white paper or by lighting a pavement so that an object is seen silhouetted against it. In other words, light is a far more controllable factor than sight and it is the only aid to seeing if eyesight is normal or is properly corrected by means of eyeglasses. Such intimate studies and results of researches which have uncovered many hidden physiological effects of seeing account for the great interest in light and sight which has recently swept throughout civilization.

The printed words on this page are visible or you would not be reading them. If your eyes are normal you can probably read them under a fraction of a footcandle. If you do not have enough light to read them, you move to a place where you are able to read them. But that is not the entire answer. So far you have been concerned with barely seeing, not with easiest seeing. The visibility of these printed words depends upon the size and style of the type, upon other typographical details and upon paper, ink and printing. These are the fixed factors of this visual task. The only other controllable factor is light. Generally you are not satisfied to read when the visibility of the printed matter is so low that the words are barely visible or barely readable. You insist upon more light than that. However, the question to be answered is, How much light is necessary to increase the visibility and the readability of the words to a maximum?

To measure visibility we have developed the Luckiesh-Moss Visibility Meter and units and scales of visibility. By means of this device it is possible to measure the effect upon visibility of such factors as size, style and boldness of type, the contrast between the printed matter and the paper background, and various aspects of light such as footcandles. A discussion of all factors excepting light would be out of place here. It is sufficient to say that many of the inadequacies of type, typography and printing are revealed by measurements of visibility and determinations of readability. In general the influence of footcandles upon the visibility of the words on this page is such that optimum visibility is not generally obtained until the illumination is of the order of 100 footcandles. For small type-sizes such as are usual in newspapers, the desirability of even higher values of illumination is indicated. The size of type used in newspapers is generally little more than half the size of the type used in printing this page. Considering that the paper and printing are far better in this book than in newspapers, much higher levels of illumination are necessary for reading a newspaper than for reading this book with the same ease. Still our researches indicate that the readability of this printed page is not maximal until it is illuminated by more than 100 footcandles.

Now let us consider how we approached the important matter—ease of seeing. This required an invasion of the realm of hidden effects of performing the work of seeing. Every task of seeing may be confronted from two viewpoints—the task and the human being. When we examine the task we find ourselves analyzing the factors which influence the visibility of the task such as this printed page. We have already taken some glimpses of these factors. However, when we think of ourselves as readers, or in general as human seeing-machines performing other tasks of prolonged critical seeing, we may try to analyze the effects upon us. Most of the effects are deeply hidden and are not easily discovered. For example, vitamin A was always deeply hidden in carrots until revealed during the present century. Modern science discovered it and later revealed the penalties of diet deficient in this vitamin, as well as other vitamins.

Applying the same scientific methods, we began to hunt for the unobvious effects of seeing. In many researches the standard task of seeing was the reading of printed matter of specified typography under a controlled environment. In the course of many years we have prosecuted scores of researches with hundreds of subjects to obtain the results and conclusions presented here. Those pertaining to light are amply supported by results obtained by studies of various secondary aids to seeing, but all of them are a matter of controlling light in some manner. Unless otherwise stated, the reading matter was printed with type approximating in size that used in this book, of an acceptable style, and the printing was well done with non-glossy black ink on excellent non-glossy white paper. We shall use the term readability interchangeably with ease of seeing. Subjects generally read for long periods and always repeated the test, sometimes many times.

By means of delicate instruments and automatic recording apparatus it was discovered that tenseness is produced in a human being while performing a critical task of seeing such as reading. A million actual measurements of tenseness were obtained while each of many subjects read for a long period many different times. The duration of the research is indicated by the fact that each subject completed reading a rather voluminous book. Actually the book could be read under a fraction of a footcandle, but the tenseness was decisively decreased as the illumination was increased, during different periods, from 1 to 10 to 100 footcandles. It was also found that tenseness was materially increased while reading under glaring conditions such as produced by an unshaded 25-watt tungsten lamp in view.

The external muscles which converge the two eyes upon these words are not a part of the optical system of the eyes. Their function is similar to the reins which merely make a team of horses do team-work. Delicate measurements of the strength of these tiny eye-muscles before and after subjects read for an hour under controlled conditions showed they were three times as fatigued when the illumination of the printed page was one footcandle as when it was 100 footcandles. Apparently the greater visibility of the printed matter under the higher level of illumination increased the certainty and decreased the strain upon these muscles of convergence.

In another research a million heart-beats were recorded while each of a group of subjects read for long periods under 1 and 100 footcandles, respectively. Under the lower level of illumination the average heart-rate decreased markedly during an hour's reading. The decrease was much less under 100 footcandles; in fact the heart-rate remained almost normal. We do not know what this means in the life and health of modern human slaves to critical prolonged tasks of near-vision, but this research opens a new vista for the heart specialist to contemplate. At least the results indicate the desirability of the higher level of illumination.

Science proceeds to obtain different sets of facts and then attempts to correlate them. This procedure over and over results in extending our structure of knowledge. In ascertaining the influence of any controllable aid to seeing, such as light, we need criteria which can be readily applied. The researches which we have glimpsed are long and tedious, suitable only for the laboratory, but very necessary in laying the foundation for a science of seeing. A far simpler criterion was sorely needed. As a consequence we accumulated data for years on two visible movements—on the change in the size of the pupil of the eye and on the change in the rate of blinking while reading under controlled conditions.

It was found that the pupil increased in size during the course of the day's work and during the course of the workweek. It recuperates somewhat overnight and considerably over the week-end. This increase may be due to the fatiguing of the muscles which keep the iris of the eye from opening wide when the muscle is very fatigued or temporarily paralyzed by a drug. However, more promising than the size of the pupil as a measure of ease of seeing, or of fatigue due to seeing, is the rate of blinking.

Apparently the blink is a kind of temporary relief from strain, tenseness, or fatigue. Of course by blinking, the outer surface of the eyeball is moistened and foreign particles are wiped off. However, we blink from a deeper inner cause. Various persons blink at widely different rates but this does not matter for research purposes if the same persons are used for studying the effect of any controllable aid to seeing such as light. The rate of blinking also depends upon what the person is doing, but this is taken care of easily by having the subjects read non-emotional material. Already the results of more than a score of major researches dovetail very nicely into a consistent and impressive structure. Glimpses of a few of these should suffice to complete a rather convincing verification of the theory that human eyes and human beings perform the activity of seeing most easily under brightnesses and levels of illumination equivalent to the prevailing ones outdoors in the daytime—where human beings and their eyes evolved.

In studying the rate of blinking as a possible criterion of ease of seeing (reading) the average rates were determined for conditions which were respectively easier and more difficult for seeing. For example, everyone will agree that it is easier to read large type than small type. It was found that the rate of blinking is decisively greater when reading 6-point type than 12-point type. All will agree that it is more fatiguing to read after one has read an hour than at the beginning of the hour. It was shown that the rate of blinking is decisively greater at the end than at the beginning of the hour. The rate of blinking is decisively greater when eyeglasses are slightly incorrect than when they are correct. The same is true when normal eyes are supplied with eyeglasses of slight power and of no power, respectively. The same decisive result is obtained while reading with a bare lamp in view and with the lamp shaded. Similar results were obtained in many other researches involving hundreds of subjects and dealing with various typographical factors such as style, boldness and leading of type, various lighting and brightness conditions, and other controllable factors which influence fatigue and ease of seeing.

Here the most interesting fact is that the rate of blinking

is decisively less while reading under high levels of illumination than at low levels. We have proved this for a range from 1 footcandle to above 100 footcandles. The other interesting fact is that the results of more than a score of major researches and many minor ones are so consistent that the rate of blinking while reading is a thoroughly dependable criterion of ease of seeing and fatigue due to seeing. Thus after constructing a sound foundation for the science of seeing through many tedious researches, a criterion is now available which measures the effects of light and lighting upon seeing.

Lighting-practice, which was necessarily empirical and had little or no basis for specifications of light and lighting, is now furnished with means for making such specifications and for testing the results of the installations. By correlating measurements obtained with the visibility meter with those of the "comfort meter" (rate of blinking) it is possible to simplify lighting specifications by means of the far easier measurements of visibility. Tasks such as sewing are found to require very much higher levels of illumination than reading for the same visibility and ease of seeing. The printed matter in newspapers is found to require several times more light to be of the same visibility and readability as that in a magazine which is well printed on high-grade paper. The countless tasks of seeing in the work-world can now be brought to the same visibility by specifying different levels of illumination for the various tasks. And the effect of the kind of lighting—the distribution of light—upon visibility and ease of seeing can be readily determined.

With these new devices and criteria and the knowledge obtained from them, it is found, for example, that seeing on the highway at night is ridiculously poor—and it has a very great responsibility. But the results of inadequate seeing conditions on the highway are merely more obvious and gruesome than in many other places where penalties are being paid because of poor seeing conditions. The science of seeing has revealed impressively that the artificial world of civilization is at best a half-seeing world. We may well admire the great development of artificial light—most of it in the past half century. It is the most important man-made product. But the use of light is still more important than the production of light. Its use touches every human being and all the vital activities of civilization.

The science of seeing is providing a sound basis for recognizing and reaping the rewards from adequate light and proper lighting. It is very complex but it can be reduced to a simple statement insofar as it affects lighting-practice. In general it has verified the validity of Nature's textbook and has proved in still another way that we are children of Nature. There are two sides to the ledger of civilization, debits and credits, penalties and rewards. Artificial lighting has a long way to go before it matches the abundance of natural lighting, but only when it does will the penalties of near-vision and poor seeing conditions be minimized and the rewards of easiest seeing conditions be fully realized. The torch-makers have been far ahead of the torch-bearers chiefly because modern science came to their aid sooner and in greater force.

As we look back over the long road that artificial light has trod, we see the great contributions which organized laboratories have given to its production in the past half century. Similarly the foundations for the use of artificial light in the service of mankind are being established by laboratories organized for that purpose. One cannot intimately view these achievements and the need for more knowledge in many of the empirical practices and activities of human beings, without recalling the plea and plaudit of that great benefactor of humanity, Louis Pasteur.

Take interest, I implore you, in those sacred dwellings which one designates by the expressive term "Laboratories." Demand that they be multiplied, that they be adorned. These are the temples of the future—temples of well-being and of happiness. There it is that humanity grows greater, stronger, better.

XIV. THE LIGHTING ART

THE PERPETUAL PURPOSE of the age-long struggle to produce more and better light has been to use it in the service of mankind. There are three links in the chain—production, control and utilization of light. Naturally the use of light being linked to the production of light, it followed the same course in the history of civilization. But uses of light are more difficult to understand and to appraise accurately. Production and control of light are relatively isolated physical sciences. Use of light involves the complexity of the human being and his efficiency, efficacy, comfort, welfare and happiness. This is also a complexity of economics consisting of some costs which can be computed and others that cannot be.

The costs of lighting a home, a school, an office or a factory can be easily determined. But the penalties of not having more light and better lighting, and the benefits of having them, cannot be appraised in monetary value. They are human penalties and rewards. They involve human resources, human welfare, human sorrow and human happiness. Research is doing something to appraise what can be appraised; but lighting remains largely a matter of habit, budget, and slow but certain improvement. It has not generally kept pace with the tremendous progress in the standard of living and in the efficiency of light-production. However, as we look backward along the course the torch of civilization traveled, a great advance has been made particularly during the past quarter of a century.

Light may seem to be ethereal but it is tangible enough to be controlled and measured. It is easy to follow the interesting course of its production from primitive fires to the powerful electric light-sources of the present time. It is not difficult to understand the various methods of production and the various optical principles of control. But when light is put into use where we live and work with it rather intimately as we do indoors, we find it accompanied by another factor—lighting—which cannot be easily measured or defined. Lighting may be described as the distribution of light and brightness particularly in the field of view; but that description scarcely supplies a satisfactory word-picture. Therefore, it is necessary to try to describe some common examples of lighting.

You are conscious of light upon this page and you could readily measure the footcandles with a light meter. The visibility and readability of these printed words are determined largely by the partnership of light on this page and of the ability of your visual sense. But light upon this page cannot be obtained without a distribution of brightness in the field of view. If there is an unshaded light-source near the line of vision, the glare and the reduction in the visibility of these printed words are obvious. The natural strain and fatigue resulting from reading this printed matter are augmented by the glaring light-source. But other brightness-contrasts which are not jarring enough to be noticeable also unduly increase fatigue and if the reading is continued long enough may produce actual discomfort.

It is relatively easy to provide adequate light on the work but to do this with proper lighting is often difficult and sometimes impossible. Most of the light may reach this page from a portable lamp behind and to the left of the reader. Some of it may come by reflection from the ceiling. So far the lighting may be fairly satisfactory and certainly the direct light from the lamp and indirect light from the ceiling are easily controlled and obtained. But now decoration and furnishing enter and they may be such as to make it impossible to produce the best seeing conditions. This bright page may be surrounded by a relatively low brightness for it may be silhouetted against a desk-top, clothing or carpet of relatively low brightness. Furthermore the walls may be dark because they may consist of deeply stained wood commonly used in libraries. The high contrast between the book and its surroundings is a poor condition for seeing. Even in the course of an hour's reading it causes unnecessary strain and fatigue.

One may be reading this page in a room where all the light reaches it from a large expanse of ceiling as is the case in socalled indirect lighting. If a large part of the distant ceiling is in the field of view this may cause unnecessary strain and fatigue. Outdoors a patch of sky may not be glaring until one starts to perform a critical task of seeing. In a few minutes one may experience discomfort and soon the condition may become unendurable. Thus lighting may be satisfactory for conversation but not for reading. It is seen that the surroundings in the field of view are unsatisfactory if they are too dark or too bright. Usually lighting can overcome the difficulties but decoration and furnishing are inevitably important. They can make the task of providing the best seeing conditions easy, difficult or impossible.

In reading this page you are not annoyed by glossy paper

Studies of blinking, and of extremely minute electrical currents arising from activities of the eye-muscles, reveal unobvious contributions of light and lighting to easier seeing.

which is commonly used when half-tone illustrations are interspersed throughout the text-matter. In such cases the glossy surface acts somewhat as a mirror and the glaring highlights, which sometimes render the printed matter difficult to read, are images of bright areas such as light-sources or shades. No kind of lighting system can prevent this trying condition. The best that can be done is to shift the task or the position to eliminate this socalled specular reflection from the portion of the text being read.

A printed page is a two-dimensional object and the black ink and white paper provide the necessary contrast to make the words visible. Lighting, as distinguished from light, is not so important in making the reading matter visible as it is in making the reader comfortable. However, the visibility of three-dimensional objects depends largely upon the lighting. Suppose you are threading a needle. You turn it to get a highlight around the eye of the needle or you hold it so that you see a bright area through the elusive slit. Actually you are altering the lighting until it is satisfactory for seeing. This is true when one twists and turns a small object and changes his position in relation to a light-source in order to see the details better. A jeweler does that as he examines the works of a watch. And experience teaches many of them to dismantle the fine parts on a sheet of white paper so that they may be seen easily by the contrast of the objects or of their shadows against the white background. These are merely a few examples of countless ones which reveal the influence of lighting upon seeing.

The lighting art is in the middle of three consecutive eras —mere light, more light and much light. The original function of artificial light was to compete with darkness. Primitive man's declaration of independence from Nature was a modest one. But the success of modern science in producing light and in ascertaining its benefits has shown that the proper objective of artificial light is to compete with daylight. This means much light. There could be no lighting art until a century ago. Feeble flames supplied mere light. The candle or oil-lamp was placed near the work or carried to light the way. When light-sources became fixed as in gas-lighting, a crude lighting art was born. Large areas began to be illuminated instead of mere local work-places and some light continued to escape to the surroundings. But the surroundings being farther away than the work they remained quite dark in the feeble light. The level of illumination upon the work still remained about the same—perhaps a footcandle—as in the era of mere light.

Then came the era of gas-mantles and electricity with a considerable increase in candlepower of light-sources. The middle era—more light—began and continued for fifty years. But with enough light to barely see, the footcandles upon the work were increased very slowly as the years passed but progress in lighting systems took place. When light-sources became fixed so that large areas were illuminated, pendent shades began to come into use to re-direct the light and to screen the light-source from the eyes. All the light was directed downward to get it on the work area. The amount of light on the visual tasks was increased somewhat by such a system but the lighting was trying on the eyes. The dark ceilings and other surroundings provided high contrasts as the light-sources or bright portions of the shades were seen against these dark backgrounds. The efficiency of utilizing the light was increased by the use of pendent shades but the seeing conditions remained very poor.

In addition to providing light upon the work, lighting

eventually began to receive attention. Light-sources were enclosed in diffusing glassware which reduced their brightness so they did not cause blinding afterimages. This expedient was erroneously believed to reduce the effect of glare upon the visibility of the visual task, but it did not. As the efficiency of light-production increased by the development of gas-filled tungsten-filament lamps, direct lighting began to be replaced by indirect lighting. This is equivalent to turning the shades upside down and throwing the light to the ceiling. In other words, the light comes indirectly to the work-place by way of the ceiling. Thus the light-sources are screened from the eyes and the large expanse of ceiling becomes the source of light. But it reduces the visibility of a visual task in proportion to the amount of light it sends toward the eyes just as an unshaded lamp does. Obviously in small rooms very little, if any, of the ceiling is in the field of view while one reads or performs most other visual tasks. Therefore, this criticism applies particularly to the larger rooms.

Indirect lighting was a great improvement in some respects but it is not the cure-all it is often assumed to be. The annoyance of harsh and multiple shadows from several sources, as in the case of direct lighting, is eliminated. Shadows are single, soft and vague under indirect lighting. This is satisfactory for clerical work, classrooms, and drafting rooms where things to be seen are largely of two dimensions such as printed matter. But three-dimensional objects are distinguished by highlights and shadows, which are minimized by a single large source such as a ceiling or an overcast sky. However, the greatest objection to purely indirect lighting, excepting in small rooms, is that the ceiling is the brightest area in the room and usually there is no escape from seeing it. Actually the work should be as bright or brighter than any other area if this is possible.

A satisfactory solution was available in Nature's textbook where it had been written since the dawn of creation. No one can study natural lighting outdoors, intimately viewing objects and landscapes, without recognizing the superiority of the lighting on a sunny day over that on an overcast day. When the sky is overcast it is definitely glaring as one performs a task of critical seeing such as reading, provided some of the sky is in the field of view. On a sunny day the sky is far less bright in comparison with sunlit objects, for the latter are receiving several times more light from the sun than from the sky. This combination of direct and indirect light may be termed, balanced lighting. Of course, the sun must not be in the field of view if one is to see comfortably. Carrying this lesson indoors it is only necessary to combine direct light upon the work with indirect lighting. Now the brightness of the visual task may be increased to any value desired and the ceiling is no longer the brightest area in the room. This system of lighting we termed, general lighting plus. The plus lighting is also a means of obtaining high levels of illumination upon the work efficiently and inexpensively. This system of lighting is becoming quite common among advanced lighting installations where it is practicable. The direct component may be obtained in various ways.

Countless lighting problems or conditions cannot be easily described but all can be solved or analyzed fairly well in terms of the major systems which developed in the course of lighting progress. The era of mere light was an era of purely localized light. The portable flame-source was placed near the work and the illumination or brightness of the surroundings was not considered. The users were glad to have mere light. Carbon-filament lamps in pendent shades spaced more or less regularly, or at least over specific work-places, constituted a direct-lighting system. Light-sources enclosed in diffusing glass globes have also been considered to be a direct-lighting system but inasmuch as a large fraction of the light goes upward from them to the ceiling, this system might better have been termed, semi-indirect lighting. Dense glass bowls which screened the light-sources from the eyes and permitted most of the light to escape directly to the ceiling were often considered to provide semi-indirect lighting. As a matter of fact the lighting effect was practically the same as that from opaque inverted reflectors which provided indirect lighting. Then the last and most flexible and efficient system wherever practicable, consists of general illumination supplemented by direct or directed light from a source well concealed from the eyes. Actually in this system, the indirect-lighting component is demoted from a major to a minor role and the direct-lighting component performs the major role.

Years ago when general lighting of large areas began to supersede purely localized lighting, particularly in factories, in many cases the ability of the worker to see to perform his task of seeing was greatly reduced. At that time a lighting system was not designed specifically for seeing but merely to deliver a certain amount of light fairly uniformly on a mythical horizontal work-plane 30 inches above the floor. In fact, little was known of the relations of light and sight or of light and seeing. However, even casual observation revealed that many workers doing fine work needed a local light-source so that they could orient small objects as they wished, or had to, in order to see what they wanted to see. When these light-sources were taken away from them and other more powerful ones were hung high and regularly spaced, they could no longer do their own lighting for seeing. The local sources should have been left at the work-places and the general lighting installed in addition to them. The blessings of general lighting in work-places had arrived but the advantages of direct or localized light disappeared along with the disadvantages of the old system of entirely localized light-sources.

Many researches under the controlled conditions of the laboratory have revealed the advantage of general lighting plus direct or localized lighting. We cannot have good lighting without general lighting. The surroundings must not be dark for the contrast between the work or work-area is trying on the eyes and distracts attention. A glaring source of light in the visual field causes fatigue due to the continual strain of muscles and attention in overcoming the distraction. We have much evidence that dark surroundings are fatiguing in the same way. In addition to this we lift our eyes to the more distant surroundings to relax momentarily our eye-muscles and our attention. It is erroneous to assume that the eyes need rest from the brightness of the book or other visual task and should look at dark surroundings momentarily in order to be rested. This requires re-adaptation to a greatly different brightness which is annoying and fatiguing.

Returning to the matter of level of illumination we may divide lighting-practice into four eras. Beginning with the long era of mere light, we may divide the period since the beginning of fixed light-sources into mere footcandles, production footcandles and humanitarian footcandles. When large areas began to be illuminated by regularly spaced light-sources, such as gas-flames and carbon-lamps, some light was provided over the entire work-plane. The level of illumination was only one or two footcandles so that this was the era of mere footcandles. It still lingers in many places in this country and is still more prevalent in foreign countries.

During the World War when production of factories was being pressed to the utmost, higher levels of illumination were provided in many cases. Careful records of production and spoilage revealed that the value of the increase in production per worker was commonly at least ten percent after paying for the additional light. In other words light went to work without pay and contributed as much in increased production as an increase of ten percent in the number of workers would have produced under the old lighting system. In addition, spoilage of material generally decreased several percent or more. Such achievements with more light and better lighting became common and in many factories and other work-places the level of illumination was increased from a few footcandles to 10 and 20 footcandles. Thus there was inaugurated an era of lighting in the work-world which may well be termed, production footcandles. Measured in terms of the manufacturing operations of the United States a ten-percent increase in production due to good lighting would be approximately equivalent to a million workers, a billion dollars in wages and six billion dollars worth of manufactured products.

In general, careful researches under laboratory conditions generally revealed that production of useful work, such as the rate of reading, ceased to increase appreciably when the level of illumination was raised to 20 or 30 footcandles. The resulting contribution of more light and better lighting to total production and decreased spoilage in the work-world was very great. But it was erroneously assumed that further increases in levels of illumination would be fruitless. However, it did not seem that this relatively low level of illumination, compared with the footcandles and brightnesses outdoors, provided all the benefits light was able to contribute. Further researches on the relationships of light to seeing, and on the effects of seeing upon human eyes and human beings, revealed that production was an inadequate measure of the beneficence of light and lighting.

Inasmuch as extensive and highly controlled laboratory researches yielded conclusive evidence that workers, fatigued by a day's work, often work faster and with greater concentration than at the beginning of the day, the futility of production as a measure of seeing was further emphasized. These results were consistent with those obtained in other researches. It seemed obvious that when increased production is accomplished by workers whose ability to produce has been lessened by fatigue, there is a combination which might operate against the welfare of the workers. Neither is the rate of production nor the quality of work done a measure of seeing conditions or of the condition of the human seeing-machine at the close of a work-period. The clue to such results is found in the willingness of eyes and workers to draw upon their reserves to compensate for poor seeing and for fatigue. Runners draw upon reserves of energy and will-power in their closing sprints. In the cases of eyes and workers, they pay the price of willingness and reserve ability to sprint even at the finish. Workers and their eyes are penalized because there is little or no evidence of the severity of their visual tasks in the records of production; also because they do not complain directly, when taxed by prolonged abuses, until they approach the point of exhaustion. The penalties are deeply hidden and unnoticed until their effect becomes obvious in some manner. This might manifest itself in eye-defectiveness, ill-health, accident and what not.

Eventually the science of seeing revealed the desirability of at least 100 footcandles for clerical work and much higher levels of illumination for many tasks of seeing. This led to new concepts of fatigue and waste of human resources. It also led to the proper definition of the efficiency of a worker. His production became not merely a matter of useful work done per hour or per dollar. It also took into account the waste of human resources in useless work or expenditure of energy due to seeing conditions below those for easiest seeing. These losses cannot be appraised in dollars but a new philosophy or attitude entered into lighting-practice. The era of humanitarian footcandles had arrived. Some lighting installations are already supplying 100 footcandles of general illumination. Some installations of general lighting plus direct or supplementary lighting are already supplying hundreds of footcandles upon the work. The work-world in general is illuminated with less than five footcandles but the new philosophy of humanitarian footcandles born of, and backed by, the science of seeing is now rapidly spreading.

Great progress has been made in safety devices and in accident prevention in industrial plants but no safety measure is better than good seeing. Proper and adequate general illumination reveals obstacles and hazards and localized light can provide for easy seeing and decrease fatigue, both of which tend to decrease accidents. A decade ago experts of insurance companies estimated that as many as 15 to 20 percent of the industrial accidents were due to faulty lighting. This would mean an annual toll due to this cause of about 3000 persons killed and 250,000 injured. The economic loss to the employer was estimated to average $200 directly and $1000 indirectly for each accident or more than a quarter of a billion dollars annually. These estimates of the experts should now be revised upward because in the past decade the science of seeing has revised, radically upward, our ideas of adequate light and proper lighting.

This is an appropriate place to suggest some practical levels of illumination. The ideal levels as revealed by the science of seeing are hundreds and even thousands of footcandles depending upon the character of the visual task and particularly upon the size and contrast of details and of the reflection-factors of the objects or their backgrounds. The ideal levels of illumination are ideal objectives toward which to progress. In general they are the levels of illumination and of brightness of outdoor landscapes. To achieve these throughout the artificial world where the best seeing conditions are important is not generally practicable at present. However, 100 footcandles are easily obtained with modern illuminants and lighting systems and there are installations of direct lighting in existence for special purposes, such as surgery and fine inspection, of 1000 and 2000 footcandles. There need be no fear that many visual tasks will be over-lighted. The best practical answer to the question of desirable footcandles for prolonged tasks of critical seeing is that they be as far above the present meager levels as practicable. In other words, the immediate objective should be to increase footcandles above present levels which may be crippling eyes and are certainly causing eyestrain disorders and unnecessarily wasting physical and nervous energy. Inasmuch as the problem becomes one of economics and practicability, it is well to give particular attention to the prolonged tasks of critical seeing. Based upon measurements of visibility and considering economic, practical, hy-

THE LIGHTING ART

gienic and humanitarian aspects, conservative minimum recommendations may be briefly expressed as follows:

100 footcandles or more

For very severe and prolonged tasks, such as fine needlework, fine engraving, fine pen-work, fine assembly, sewing on dark goods, and discrimination of fine details of low contrast, as in lace-making, weaving, darning and inspection.

50 to 100 footcandles

For severe and prolonged tasks, such as proofreading, drafting, difficult reading, watch-repairing, fine machine work, average sewing and other needlework.

20 to 50 footcandles

For moderately critical and prolonged tasks, such as clerical work, ordinary reading, common bench-work and average sewing and other needle-work on light goods.

10 to 20 footcandles

For moderate and prolonged tasks of office and factory and, when not prolonged, ordinary reading and sewing on light goods.

5 to 10 footcandles

For visually controlled work in which seeing is important, but more or less interrupted or casual, and does not involve discrimination of fine details or low contrasts.

0 to 5 footcandles

The danger zone for severe visual tasks, and for quick and certain seeing. Satisfactory for perceiving larger objects and for casual seeing.

In connection with these footcandle recommendations which are not ideal but are generally practicable, it is interesting to note the effectiveness of footcandles upon seeing. The effectiveness of a footcandle is not fixed but varies within wide limits. For example, if the level of illumination is one footcandle, the addition of another footcandle causes a significant increase in visibility and in ease of seeing. But one footcandle added to 10 footcandles causes only a slight improvement in seeing. Actually any level of illumination must be doubled in order to produce an obvious and significant improvement in seeing. From many varied researches the scale of footcandle effectiveness, in which each higher level produces about the same improvement in seeing as any other step does, is approximately as follows:

1, 2, 5, 10, 20, 50, 100, 200, 500, 1000

About 25 million children attend the schools of this country. There and at home they subject their eyes and themselves to prolonged critical seeing. They form habits and develop eye-defects which go with them into the work-world and through life. At six years of age children have just about mastered the use of their eyes. They are able to orient the eyes together and to converge them accurately upon the things they must see. They have entered the slavery of near-vision. The rapid increase in eye-defectiveness as they pass from grade to grade demands attention and this continues in college. For example the class of 1934 at our Naval Academy began with 647 members who had presumably passed stringent physical examinations including eyesight. At graduation in 1934 the number had been reduced to 464. Of these, 12.7 percent—one of every eight graduates—was rejected by the Navy owing to defective vision. Where they studied the light was inadequate and the lighting was improper, judged by very conservative standards.

A majority of the classrooms in the schools of this country have levels of artificial illumination not exceeding 5 footcandles. This is meager for normal eyes. It is still more so for young eyes and for defective eyes. The minimum level of illumination recommended in the codes of school lighting by a group of technical societies was 3.5 footcandles in 1918 and is 15 footcandles in 1940. An intermediate code recommended a minimum of 8 footcandles. Incidentally it is interesting to note that the minimum was about doubled in each successive revision. These are meager levels of illumination from the viewpoint of our present knowledge of seeing but the trend is in the right direction. Quite a few classrooms now have 20 footcandles but the average in this country is about 7 footcandles. Attempts have been made to measure the effects of increased footcandles in terms of scholastic achievement and the results have been favorable. But even such researches are not free from emphasis of money saved when the real penalties to school-children are far beyond appraisal in dollars.

Recommendations for sight-saving classrooms are 30 to 50 footcandles and some of these have reached 30 or 35 footcandles. However, actual measurements of visibility by pupils of sight-saving classes and pupils with normal sight, reveal that the former should have much more than two or three times more light than the latter who should have much more light than they now have. It is impractical to have localized light on each desk in ordinary classrooms in addition to general lighting. For this reason indirect lighting has represented the best practice so far. However, if modern fluorescent lamps were screened from the eyes and much of the light were sent downward, and the rest upward to the ceiling, much higher levels of illumination could easily be obtained.

Schools cannot be justly blamed for all the eye-defectiveness and other penalties of poor seeing during childhood. Children study and read at home. Notwithstanding the great advances in interest in better light for better sight and in improvements in lighting in the home, it is probable that children's eyes are abused as much at home as at school. Fortunately more light and better lighting in the home are readily obtainable from portable lamps which can easily supply 20 to 50 footcandles for prolonged critical seeing. Special portables can supply several hundred footcandles for such tasks as sewing. And shades concealing all light-sources go far toward obtaining proper lighting.

Fortunately the portable lamp with a shade which was closed at the top has quite generally disappeared along with fringes and frills. Shades with open tops permit light to escape to the walls and ceiling, thus providing some general illumination and some brightness of the surroundings. The direct light from the lamp comes efficiently to the book or other visual task. But modern semi-indirect portables are still better. A single high-wattage lamp furnishes more light per watt than the equivalent wattage in smaller lamps. It is concealed in a diffusing-glass bowl and this in turn is concealed by a decorative shade with white lining. These portable lamps provide excellent lighting for the task and the surroundings. The lighting may be said to be balanced between general illumination and direct light. With a proper balance of this sort, high levels of illumination are pleasant and comfortable. I read nightly in a library of moderate size with three 300-watt portables serving myself and others; and there is not the slightest impression of over-lighting. Why should there be, with levels of illumination which are very meager compared with lighting on the porch or in the shade of a tree in the daytime? We do not think of over-lighting in these cases. Years ago when we knew less about lighting, a recommendation of three 300-watt lamps in a modest library of a home would have been considered preposterous. Thirteen of these 300-watt portables and about an equal number of other portables serve our family with convenient light and fairly satisfactory lighting wherever there is a suitable place to perform the critical tasks of seeing in our home. In addition, suitable fixtures on walls and ceiling supply abundant light wherever desired and decorative light wherever appropriate.

These are a few glimpses of different kinds of lighting and of the minimum footcandle-levels which should be in use. However, the chief purpose has been to show that lighting is just as important as light. In fact, adequate levels of illumination cannot be practicable and comfortable without much attention to lighting. Furnishings and also walls should not be dark either because of low reflection-factors or from lack of sufficient light. Lighting and seeing conditions cannot be satisfactory amid dark surroundings. Besides, this is an age of enlightenment which has obviously extended its influence to lighting, decoration and furnishing. These glimpses should aid the interested reader to study lighting effects on every hand and to analyze them. In fact, all that we see is lighting effect whether it is an object, a printed page, a room or a sunset. A variety of moods can be introduced into a room entirely by lighting effects. But that is another chapter.

TORCH OF CIVILIZATION

As one sits in the comfort and protection of home, however humble it may be, it is strikingly obvious that civilization has advanced far beyond that primitive period when the light and heat from a crude fire first made a cave a home. Even where electric lighting is used with indifference, the convenience of switches and outlets, and the blessings of more powerful light-sources, are self-evident. We may ponder the reason for the perpetual tendency to progress toward greater convenience, ease, comfort, safety and welfare. In the development of artificial light to its present high state of efficiency, the underlying force is obvious. The visual sense dominates the usefulness and happiness of human beings, and it demands light. Science has provided the means generously and is revealing the need for adequate light and proper lighting. But applications lag behind the possibilities. Lack of consciousness of the penalties of poor seeing conditions conspires with natural inertia and indifference to prolong the eras of mere light and mere footcandles. After many years spent in the midst of activities directed toward the production, control and use of artificial light, the inevitable lag of applications of light behind great improvements in production and control becomes very obvious and pronounced. One looks back for encouragement, for the conquest of darkness by mankind is something to be proud of. There is much encouragement in the many excellent lighting installations of the present time, for they are lighthouses in a half-seeing world.

As one sits before the cheerful fireplace and looks about him at the marvels of modern lighting, his thoughts span the long age from primitive man to the present high achievements of the torch-makers and the torch-bearers. But he cannot avoid the fact that even in this modern age of in-

THE LIGHTING ART

expensive, convenient, controllable and efficient light much of the artificial world has not emerged from the eras of mere light and mere footcandles. Naturally he summarizes the tragic waste of human resources—eyesight, energy, health, life and limb—due to inadequate and improper use of light. Even the monetary losses are impressive in an era of staggering expenditures for socalled welfare. Accidents in homes, on highways and in factories mean waste in property damage, loss of time, idle machines, and unproductive activities. Poor seeing conditions in the work-world mean decreased production and increased spoilage. The waste preventable by proper use of light amounts annually to many billions of dollars. It is a staggering invisible tax on indifference, inertia and negligence. Its magnitude is the difference between the costs of poor lighting and the profits of good lighting.

XV. PAINTING WITH LIGHT

OUR EYES ARE more than optical mechanisms which make it possible for us to see objects accurately. They are doorways through which we gain impressions. An artist expresses himself in a painting, a sculpture or a great spectacle and this expression, passing through our visual doorways, arouses our sensibilities, emotions and sentiments. It becomes an impression. In this realm of emotion and feeling we find another measure of the progress of human beings beyond the primitive state. And in following the story of light in the service of mankind we find that it inevitably becomes a medium of expression. Everything we see is an expression of light. All objects are molded and colored by it. The expression of anything—a human face, an interior, a building, a desert, a mountain or the sea—is influenced by light and lighting. What is done with artificial light as a medium of expression depends upon ability to control it and sensibility to use its powers in this direction.

Primitive human beings picked up bits of colored earth, glittering fragments, colorful pebbles, and stones of significant forms. They admired and treasured them for themselves and as human sensibilities developed, such objects became media of expression. They bedecked themselves with some of these baubles and the art of jewelry began. Groupings of colored pebbles and glittering fragments were crude beginnings of inlay and mosaic art. With colored earths and vegetable juices they painted themselves, the walls of their caves and their crude utensils. Thus the art of painting began. They squeezed soft clay into various shapes and made utensils and ornaments. All the arts had a similar lowly beginning from which they grew as knowledge and feeling developed. Always the interest at first was in the specific objects. Gradually the interest evolves into the uses of these materials as media of expression.

During all those uncounted centuries in which various materials were evolving into media of expression, resulting in painting, sculpture, mosaic, architecture and stained glass, artificial light played only an incidental role. Not until the present era of safe, convenient and controllable artificial light did interest pass beyond the stage of the specific object—the flame or lamp. Throughout many thousands of years oil-lamps and candles played important roles in ceremonies and in this sense were media of expression. But as long as light-sources were flames, their use in this manner was confined to themselves. Lighting effects were so limited that they were scarcely considered. With the advent of electric lamps the sources became powerful and filament-lamps could be concealed or used in any way desired. The era of light as a medium of expression was born. Painting and modeling with light became possible on a large scale. However, those engaged in the various arts who had the sensibilities to utilize this new medium were slow in recognizing its possibilities. The lighting artist had to be developed to utilize light as a medium of expression.

All arts which we enjoy visually are dependent upon light and lighting. A sculpture is modeled by the lighting. The sculptor chisels highlights and shadows. The designer of a molding or a cornice leads lines of light and shade wherever he desires them. He cannot even fix the expression of the object, for it varies as the lighting varies. The painter applies the media of his art, but the color is in the light which falls upon his painting. He can only fix the outlines or forms, for the values and the colors change with the lighting. The decorator applies his color scheme but he cannot fix it. The mood or expression of the interior depends upon the quantity, quality and direction of the light which reaches the various surfaces. The colors and values, and the direction and character of the shadows, change with the lighting. The furnishings of a home are fixed in expression in proportion to their absorption of light. But even here lighting can ease the blunders and soften the harshness.

Everywhere we turn in a home, or anywhere else, we see lighting effects—major overwhelming ones and countless minor ones. The lighting artist uses light as a medium of expression, painting and modeling with it. In most places light should play two roles simultaneously. These are obvious if we consider eyes as organs of sight and as doorways for impressions. It is difficult to discuss the subtlety of the lighting effects with which we live intimately. The subject can be presented properly only through the medium of light. The medium of words is inadequate. Therefore, only the more striking effects are easily described.

One cannot view the sunsets without noting something of the expressiveness of light. Likewise, by observing a familiar landscape throughout the day, and on different days, one cannot fail to note many expressions and to feel those moods. The charm of dawn with its faint diffused light, delicate colors, indefinite shadows and tenuous mists slowly merges into a gayer mood as the sun rises. The birds sing for good reason. The elongated shadows are now well defined and objects are well modeled. The sun is still relatively weak

Painted with mobile light, this Fountain of Life was vitalized at night into ethereal beauty attainable only by this relatively new medium of expression. (San Francisco Exposition)

and the diffused light from the sky subdues the shadows. The sun mounts toward the zenith and the shadows shorten and grow harsher. The mood is far different from the earlier ones. We may even associate the short harsh shadows with the heat of midday. Compare two paintings of a desert, one with short shadows and one with long ones. We carry our experiences with Nature's lighting into our artificial world. We cannot escape the imprint of light and lighting effects outdoors nor our instinctive reactions which are the remnants of this imprint upon our countless ancestors.

The sun passes the meridian and shadows begin to lengthen. Variety of lighting effects is introduced by clouds. When a cloud suddenly obscures the sun, the well-defined shadows disappear. The shadows are now vague and objects are not strikingly modeled. The same setting on an overcast day loses much of its interesting variety. The shadows are vague and most of the modeling is gone. This alone teaches us that purely indirect lighting is generally uninteresting, particularly in large interiors. It teaches us that we want shadows in those interiors where the expressiveness of light is important. And the more pleasing shadows are not the harsh deep ones of sunny midday but those of Nature's landscapes earlier or later in the day.

As the afternoon progresses, the shadows lengthen and soften. Usually the landscape becomes more interesting until eventually the mood of sunrise is repeated at sunset, but without the vagueness of the morning mists. And these moods are modified by our thoughts and attitude. Sunrise is full of promise. The day is passing. Has that promise been fulfilled? Thus our own mood may alter somewhat the mood of Nature. Twilight arrives and the veil of darkness deepens. Stars may pierce it and the moon may rise. Other moods are these. In fact, the day outdoors is a pageant of moods, usually one slowly modulating into another. It is a textbook of lighting effects which, transferred into our artificial world, becomes a textbook of painting and modeling with light.

Ever since architecture became a recognized art, the evolution of ornamentation has been influenced by Nature's lighting. It is obvious that ornaments such as moldings, capitals and cornices were developed for light coming generally from above as it does outdoors. All one needs to do to prove this is to note their unnatural appearance when lighted from below. The architect has created lines of light and shadow where he desired them. In sunny climes there is some evidence of a daintiness of ornament and a shallowness of relief as compared with regions of greater cloudiness. In the former case, the intense sunlight and relatively little skylight cause undue harshness and darkness of shadows in deeper ornamentation.

Thus we learn fundamental lessons from Nature which make it rather easy to provide lighting effects that are natural or artificial. There is no need to follow Nature in lighting effects or in painting with light in any of the novel usages. But where human beings live and work for hours it is unwise to depart too far from naturalness in the basic or overwhelming factors. For example, the decorative scheme which is natural is to have light ceilings, moderately light walls and somewhat darker floors. This is natural but we may then depart, as we do, in countless details and make an interesting indoor world. So it is with lighting. The most pleasing fundamental lighting effect is to have general illumination as from the sky and localized light as from the sun. We may introduce as many portable lamps, lighted ornaments and minor lighting effects as we choose. However, the overwhelming effect to be satisfying to live with must be fundamentally natural.

In interiors various moods or expressions may be created by controlling the distribution and color (spectral character) of the light. These may be so subtle that they are more felt than seen. The differences in the slight tint of lamp shades make subtle alterations in the mood. The character of the shadows obtained from frosted or clear lamps, even though they are concealed by shades, may be subtle or obvious, respectively. Demonstrations of lighting effects can be made in any room of a home which has fixtures and portable lamps or even with the latter if at least one of them provides a powerful upward component of light. Flooding a room with indirect lighting results in a much different expression than when the lighting is produced by one or more ordinary portable lamps. Thus we make great changes in the mood or expression of a room by very simple expedients. These changes are interesting. They provide variety and suit the lighting to the occasion. No decorative scheme can do this.

Light accomplishes this because it is mobile. This is the outstanding characteristic that light possesses as distinguished from the media used in the other decorative arts such as painting, sculpture, architecture and decoration. This characteristic of mobility it shares with music and in this sense it is ethereal as music is. Actually it is far more so. This is why we speak of painting or modeling with light. It can be done by flipping switches. Lighting need not be monotonous if sufficient attention is given to its power of mobility. It even relieves decoration, furnishing, ornaments and architecture of their monotonous fixedness. Modern electric light is the most flexible and effective medium of all those expressive ones we live with.

To the extent that these powers of light are recognized, they may be utilized effectively in home, church, theater, ballroom, club, restaurant and all places where we are released temporarily from the purely utilitarian activities of our lives. The various rooms of the home may have lighting effects to suit the occasion or activity. Light predominantly on the table in the dining room with some light on the ceiling produces a simple and satisfying effect. Where we read we may have light predominantly on the book with some general illumination for eye comfort, but the room as a whole may be somewhat subdued. In the living room, portable lamps here and there with some light scattered to the ceiling, but fairly subdued for conversation, conspire to produce a suitable effect. Then the room can be flooded for a crowd. On the porch there should be enough light to see facial expressions for conversation but on the whole the lighting should be quite subdued to a restful mood. In the ballroom we may have a flood of gay light from glittering chandeliers to enhance the gowns and the jewels. In the church the lighting may easily fit the architecture or denomination. Light is so readily controlled that it may be showered down and the ceiling and walls may remain quite subdued. And restaurants of various kinds can be painted with light as their character demands. Nothing can do as much as lighting so easily and inexpensively to create the mood appropriate to the place and the occasion. Viewed in this manner, modern electric light-sources are Aladdin lamps indeed!

As we look at motion-pictures we find a textbook of lighting effects if we open our consciousness to them. The producers of these adopted light from the stage where it has been used effectively. But motion-pictures in the silent era did not have the spoken word to aid in telling the story. All the powers of light were eventually drawn upon. In the production of the motion-picture you may see light used suggestively and dramatically, creating moods and helping to tell the story. This use of light sometimes reaches great heights of perfection. And then you witness the picture in the theater under the most primitive seeing conditions. Amid dark gloomy surroundings the relatively brilliant screen is trying on the eyes. The theater is kept dark, due to the erroneous conclusion that the picture can be seen better. But this is an illusion adequately proved by the science of seeing. It is not difficult to provide some brightness over the front part of the theater in the field of view surrounding the screen without sacrificing details and contrasts in the picture. Other subtle effects of light can be used to suit the mood of the picture.

The foregoing are glimpses of painting and modeling with light in the more subtle aspects in the realms in which we live intimately, and particularly in those which should be dominated by naturalness and ease. There are many other uses in novel, striking, spectacular and frankly artificial realms. The possibilities in these directions are numberless and unlimited. They may be used everywhere as secondary effects and in suitable places as primary effects. Many things, and even spectacles, are overwhelmingly more striking at night, when painted and modeled properly with controlled artificial light, than in the daytime. Among these are fountains, gardens and expositions. Into the mobility of water the mobility of light may be perfectly blended. In the garden, interesting spots may be highlighted and the deep shadows do their part. And expositions as a whole have become great spectacles of controlled light.

TORCH OF CIVILIZATION

The modern exposition at night represents a tremendous step since Murdock devised a display of gas-flames early in the last century. And it is interesting to note that practically all the advance in this realm of painting and modeling with light took place after the advent of electric light. In fact, the great expositions represent the progress of the lighting artist in learning how to use this new medium. Just before the close of last century, expositions were festooned with strings of bare lamps and buildings were outlined with them. Interest was still confined to the light-sources themselves. The idea of painting surfaces with light had not been definitely born. Early in the present century outline-lighting gave way to floodlighting. Buildings were flooded with light from concealed sources hidden on the ground, on roofs and elsewhere. The subdued lighting was a pleasing relief from outline-lighting. Beautiful architecture remained alive at night and became even more impressive as a whole. Areas were painted with light for the first time on a large scale.

Colored light was scantily used because light-sources were not efficient enough to produce adequate quantities of colored light by means of colored filters. Great scintillators did come into use for the larger spectacles of light. They were powerful searchlights arranged so that their beams of colored or colorless light radiated in a fan-shaped pattern. This was a spectacular centerpiece of the exposition, for the light-beams painted huge tinted rays on the dark night sky. Here and there a fountain or tumbling water was illuminated by mobile colored light.

As the decades passed, light-production by electricity progressed so rapidly that the possibilities of using light as an expressive medium greatly increased. Painting with light became a full-fledged reality. Recent expositions have used

PAINTING WITH LIGHT

light lavishly in this manner and in other expressive ways. Great areas and entire buildings are now flooded with colored light from concealed sources. Light of various colors can now be made more efficiently than colorless electric light was produced in its earlier years. A variety of electric light-sources is now available providing various subtle tints of light besides the distinctive colors. Glitter from light-sources, metals and glassware is combined with the flooding of large areas and great buildings. Expositions now are superb spectacles of light at night which seem to express mankind's joyous independence of Nature. Here civilization has greatly outdistanced Nature in the control and use of light. Even the superb sunsets with their symphonic quality are sometimes dwarfed by man-made spectacles. Perhaps when the lighting artist has developed further, his productions may acquire more of the quiet power of these great natural light-paintings. But man's artistry seems to have to pass through the stage of garishness. Fortunately his greatest achievements in painting with light have emerged from this stage.

After this brief survey let us further examine the reasons for the powers of light as a medium of expression. Let us examine a painting done with pigments. A socalled white pigment is only 30 or 40 times brighter than a socalled black pigment under the same level of illumination. These two pigments represent a very limited range in contrast but the greatest range attainable with pigments. The brightest object or area in a painting can be only about 30 or 40 times brighter than the darkest object or area if both receive about the same amount of light. In an actual landscape the sky is thousands of times brighter than a deep shadow and the sun

TORCH OF CIVILIZATION

is millions of times brighter. Thus we see the extreme limitations of pigments. Light has no such limitations.

Next let us examine a colored or colorless transparency against the sky or a background of diffusing glass behind which there is a light-source. The deep shadows may be opaque and if viewed in a dark room will be of an extremely low brightness. The highlights or bright areas can be very bright. This brightness will depend entirely upon the brightness of the background against which the transparency is viewed. The brightness of the brightest area may be a thousand times brighter than the darkest area. Thus the range in contrast may be enormously greater than that of a painting. Some of the power and vitality of the motion-picture on a screen is due to the fact that light is projected through a transparency. The range of contrast may be much greater than that of a photograph printed on paper. The same is true of the lantern-slide. And the image of a landscape focused on the ground glass of a camera is vivid with brightness-contrast compared with the printed photograph.

These illustrate very well the extreme powers of light. In painting with light a powerful vitality is imparted by the control of light which greatly outranks that of pigments. There is also the matter of purity of color. As a pigment becomes purer or more saturated in color its reflection-factor decreases. In other words fairly pure or saturated colors are generally dark. There is also a dilution of the color by the colorless light reflected from the actual surface of the pigment. Practical colored lights can generally be purer or more saturated in color than reflecting pigments. And their brightness in painting with light is merely a matter of the wattage of the lamps used. Therefore, more striking colors and more powerful colored effects can be obtained with

PAINTING WITH LIGHT

light than with pigments. In other words the range of colors and of values on the pigment palette is very limited compared with that of the light palette.

It is easy to see this difference in a stained glass window. A painting of it is a weak imitation. The same is true of a painting of a diamond. The glitter is far beyond the range of pigments. Fireworks are pure gems of light. The bursting rocket is a jewel of light, and as such it exemplifies the powers of light as a medium of expression. Paintings or colored photographs of these are rather dead by comparison.

It is interesting to note the effect upon a painting of controlling the distribution of light. A landscape with a relatively bright sky or with some sunlit clouds is a definite fixed expression when the picture is more or less uniformly flooded with light. But if a lamp in a reflector is held near the area of sky or clouds, this area will receive several times more light than the foreground. The normal range of contrast is thus increased several times and the vitalizing effect is apparent. An interesting demonstration of the great increase in the range of contrast by perfectly controlled light can be readily made. A photograph of the painting is first taken and from this negative a transparent positive is made. If this positive is placed in a lantern-slide projector and the image is projected in exact superposition upon the painting, it is obvious that the range in contrast is greatly increased. The highlights will receive much light through the relatively transparent parts of the positive. The deep shadows will receive very little light through the dense portions of the positive. As a consequence a striking vitality is given to the painting by this great increase in range of brightnesses or values.

The other outstanding power of light is its mobility. This

can be illustrated by using the analogy of music. A painting of a landscape or sunset, for example, is comparable to a chord prolonged indefinitely. By means of pigments a momentary expression is fixed. But mobile light can be something like a melody—a succession of light and color of infinite smoothness if desired. The restless colors of an opal might be likened to the songs of birds. The sunset might be compared in magnitude and in variety of moods with the renditions of a symphony orchestra. Throughout Nature is found an endless variety of musical analogies, but they are only analogies. There is no physical relation between music and light. They are related only as they arouse similar feelings and emotions.

It is difficult to have a lighting effect without familiar or definite forms. Therefore, it is difficult to appraise a lighting effect entirely by itself, for the form or object involved arouses certain associations. Painting with pigments is a perfect analogy. A landscape, a portrait or any other painting is fundamentally a lighting effect. It consists of reflected lights, shadows and colors. These create the form but after doing so the subject or form commonly dominates our appraisal of the picture or our reactions to it. We see the picture primarily as a form or scene enhanced by light and shade and embellished by the magical drapery of color. Artists in this field of art have done little toward subduing form and substituting vague form, meaningless in itself. Such a painting would attempt to paint purely an expression of light. Certainly the public generally would not understand nor would it be likely to accept such attempts. But this is not necessarily true of productions with a relatively new medium such as light.

PAINTING WITH LIGHT

Painting with light has the great power of mobility which the artist's pigments do not possess. The elusive mobile colors of the opal are examples of vague undefined form and mobility of light. These can be reproduced and varied with infinite variety by mobile light. I have projected great mobile patterns before large audiences and with sufficient variety from rapidly scintillating glitter to slowly changing vague patterns. It is evident that modern human beings are entertained, pleased and even moved by these examples of mobile light. And they are in their infancy in this realm compared with their experience with music which has been presented to civilized mankind in an organized manner for ages. Even the fundamental physical basis of modern music is a thousand years old. Would a primitive savage appreciate a modern symphony orchestra? Even a great majority of civilized beings prefers modern jazz or swing to the exquisite art of the symphony. Perhaps the savage would prefer the music obtained by shaking a rock in a tin can. Appreciation of music and other arts is a matter of education over long periods.

High appreciation of the expressiveness of light cannot be achieved by any shortcut. All the arts must pass through the cruder stages. Certainly the expressiveness of light cannot be justly judged by public appreciation or by many present practices although some of the latter have reached considerable heights of artistic expression. A recent example of painting with light on a large scale where the architecture was more or less unified was the exposition at San Francisco known as Treasure Island. Here A. F. Dickerson demonstrated the heights to which the lighting artists can rise even though the forms or subjects were more or less established independently. However, there was close cooperation between the other established arts, and the lighting art glorified them superbly and brought even more glory to itself.

If poetry is to be believed, the symphonies of light rendered by Nature in the sunsets, in the aurora borealis, in the moonlight, and in other sky-effects of great magnitude have deeply impressed poets. These are persons with highly developed sensibilities who not only see, but respond to what they see in feelings and emotions which they express in appropriate sentiments. If their reactions are to be accepted at their face value, the melodies of light rendered by precious stones, in ice-crystals, in flowing water, and in the iridescence of bird-plumage please their finer sensibilities. If they are sincere, mobile light is a seductive agency that need not be left to the accidents or whims of Nature. It may well be developed into an art—even into a fine art—just as by refining the usage of crude materials of Nature they became the expressive media of other arts and of some of the fine arts.

In utilizing the mobility of light it is fair to give the medium every advantage. Sometimes it requires the elimination of other competitors or at least the reduction of the handicaps of their dominance, as in decorative schemes and architectural forms. If in a dining room one wishes to use the mobility of light, the architect must aid in providing a suitable setting and perhaps a glass ceiling. Then with proper installations one can alter the mood at will. One may have a flood of cool daylight, the glow of the sunset, the cold colorfulness of glorified moonlight, or purely artificial effects unrelated to Nature.

On the stage, light has always had competitors which were better understood. They had been playing roles for centuries before artificial light rose from its infancy to the present heights of a powerful controllable medium of expression. In the drama, words and action are completely understandable. Regardless of the effectiveness of light it could never supersede those other media in emotive value. But it can do much to enhance them by providing specific effects and general moods. In the wonderful harmonies of music and dance, they naturally overpower the effectiveness of light. They speak familiar languages. But light has done much to enhance them and it can do still more in providing settings more ethereal, spiritual or dramatic than scenery and mere lighting. With such established competition, light must play a secondary role.

Wherever other factors are dominant, the proper function of light is to aid them and to provide atmosphere and enhance the mood or setting. At night at an exposition it can assume a major role. Without lighting effects all would be in darkness. The task of light is to resurrect the architecture and other elements—the entire physical setting. It does this and by appropriate painting and modeling with light it enhances and glorifies the whole in an ethereal manner of its own. In the daytime most of this magical drapery of light disappears and the products of the other arts become the fixed and limited expressions of media with which we are familiar under unpremeditated lighting.

There are many other applications of painting with light and of the mobility of light where light can be made supreme because conventional arts and forms can be greatly submerged and eliminated. In these, light may be fairly judged on its own merits as a medium of expression. In these as well as in harmony with other arts lighting can become a fine art in the hands of the lighting artist with ability to control it as an artist controls pigments and with a similar fineness of feeling.

Modern artificial light is a relatively new medium with new possibilities arising from its unique powers and characteristics. It can create colors, contrasts and brightnesses far beyond the limitations of other media. Its effects can be controlled. They can be changed at will. It possesses the powerful characteristic of extreme mobility. Painting or modeling with light need not be fixed or static. One effect may follow another continuously or discontinuously. The torch-makers have created possibilities far beyond Nature. The achievements of the torch-bearers in this direction are only limited by their opportunities, their own skill and their artistic sensibilities. In this field the torch of civilization passes far beyond the purely utilitarian aspects of lighting and even far beyond the ceremonial use of light. It enhances settings and it creates beauty itself. Swift and silent light reveals its finer subtle qualities. It can make our individual worlds interesting and pleasing, and with its magical drapery it can beautify much of the artificial world of mankind. It emphasizes in another way the value of modern man-made light and of our gift of sight and of color-vision.

XVI. CHALLENGING THE SUN

WE LIVE BY the grace of sunlight, but not merely because its heat makes the earth habitable and its light enables us to see. We live by the grace of sunlight because it creates living things out of lifeless matter and we feed on those living things. Life in everything that lives is sustained only by a continuous supply of energy. We obtain this from food and our food consists of plants and animals. In the last analysis the plant kingdom is the fundamental source of energy for the animal kingdom, including human beings. And the fundamental source of energy for plants—and all living things on earth—is sunlight. Therefore, we live on sunlight or, at least, by the grace of sunlight. In other words, the earth imports the energy which Nature transforms into food. We in turn transform this food into energy which maintains growth and continually makes repairs—for a time. Death marks the cessation of this transference of energy as birth symbolizes the beginning.

As we watch the trees budding in the spring, we are witnessing Nature's factory going into production after the winter shutdown. Lifeless matter, through the agency of sunlight, is again being converted into living things. For the successful operation of this process several substances, such as carbon dioxide and water, are essential and the temperature must be suitable for the plants to exist. The most important process in this miraculous transformation of lifeless matter into living things is termed photosynthesis. This is a relatively simple word for such a complex process. Certainly it is a modest one for the most important chemical reaction in the entire world of living things. Through the action of sunlight upon the green coloring matter (chlorophyll) of plants, carbon is separated from the carbon dioxide of the air and hydrogen is separated from water. These two elements are formed into new combinations which are termed, hydrocarbons. Growth consists of an accumulation of these, which are in reality stored energy to be released when used as food. Thus plants store up energy for their own use in growth and germination and for the direct and indirect use of the entire animal kingdom. And sunlight is not only all-important to this fundamental life-process but to other known ones and probably to many still unknown.

For countless centuries the sole objective of the torch of civilization was the conquest of darkness. But recently the science of seeing has shown that artificial light should be a competitor of daylight, not of darkness. Thus from the relatively minor task of dispelling darkness, the torchbearers are turning toward the more important one of reproducing the outdoor levels of brightness for the artificial world of civilization. The conquest of darkness continues, but the new goal is to provide light and lighting for easiest seeing. This means not only reproducing natural lighting conditions under which human beings and their visual sense evolved outdoors, but even improving upon them, if possible, for the specific new tasks of seeing created by civilization. But even when this objective is reached the story of light in the service of mankind will not be completed. Already we see another goal—artificial sunlight for life-processes as well as for the tasks of seeing. Just as primitive beings challenged darkness, modern science chal-

Man's latest challenge to the life-giving sun is this high-pressure mercury arc, radiating an enormous wattage from a tiny capillary tube of quartz.

lenges not only the light-giving sun but the life-giving sun as well.

The early history of the earth was an azoic or lifeless period. During those ages the sun showered the earth with its energy but this energy was not stored until life began on earth. When the earth cooled sufficiently, its crust became solid and huge quantities of water-vapor condensed to form lakes and oceans. Eventually the necessary elements and the proper environment were available to support living things. Somehow life began and sunlight, supplying heat, light and ultraviolet energy began its life-giving role. It is not surprising that sunlight, the overwhelming factor of the earth's environment, became intimately entwined in life-processes. It showered upon the earth throughout the uncounted billions of years of the early lifeless period. It is only natural that living things, living upon energy, were evolved to utilize it and to store it—and to be enslaved by it. Throughout the fundamental plant kingdom the daily and seasonal cycles of sunlight have made life-processes cyclic during the day, the season, and the years. Sunlight not only gives light but sustains and dominates that life from birth to death.

How and where life began on earth need not concern us here. From a simple beginning an enormous number of different kinds of living things now exists. A great variety of environments is found over the earth's surface. Living things evolved by the process of adaptation to fit these different environments. From the tropics to the arctics the temperature varies greatly. The daily duration of sunlight changes with latitude and with the season. Valleys, hills and mountains provide different exposures to sunlight. Climate varies within wide limits. These and many other factors provide a great variety of environment so that a great variety of living things now lives on earth. But all, directly or indirectly, depend upon sunlight. With the steady advancement of knowledge, the influence of the various secondary factors are being unraveled. Modern civilization through plant-breeding is improving upon Nature for its specific needs just as it has done in light-production and in other ways.

In many studies of the effect of light upon plants, artificial light is being used because it is completely controllable in duration, intensity and spectral character. Plants are being successfully grown in laboratories entirely under artificial light. In greenhouses, artificial light is being experimented with for augmenting natural light on cloudy days and for lengthening the natural day. Inasmuch as light makes it possible for plants to utilize the carbon from carbon dioxide, this gas is supplied artificially in well-controlled experiments instead of depending upon the natural supply of it in the atmosphere. In our complex civilization which demands certain plants or their fruits throughout the year, hothouses are already playing a prominent role. In some of them artificial light in addition to natural light already appears to be economically practicable. However, it is possible that eventually plants may be bred which, in a completely controlled environment, can be economically grown entirely under moderate levels of illumination from light-sources which efficiently supply radiant energy of the most effective wavelengths for the process of photosynthesis.

One may visualize the possibility of hothouses of the future not enclosed in glass but actually insulated from the cold of winter. Thus the saving in fuel might pay for the light, and the growing plants would be under complete control. There are obvious advantages in such control in timing the maturing of the plants or crops to fit the market exactly. The great strides in light-production during recent years have resulted in a real challenge to the sun. In the growth of plants, light or visible radiant energy seems to be all-important. At least there is little evidence that ultraviolet energy is necessary, although it may be eventually revealed that it may have special applications. At any rate the variety of efficient producers of light and ultraviolet energy now available provides for a variety of possible future demands and uses. When more is known of the relation of radiant energy to plant growth, the ideal sources for these purposes will become well-defined objectives of light-production.

The new fluorescent lamps produce visible energy more efficiently than even the latest tungsten-filament lamps. These seem to be promising for experimental work in plant growth because reasonable levels of illumination can be obtained without unduly heating the plants. The new water-cooled high-pressure mercury arcs already successfully challenge the sun because very high levels of illumination, transcending those of tropical sunlight, can be obtained with less heating effect. Most of the infrared energy is filtered out by the circulating water. The heating value of this could be utilized by circulating the water wherever desired. Incidentally, in a non-glass insulated hothouse the artificial sunlight might supply enough or most of the heat necessary to maintain the proper temperature, while supplying the radiant energy for the life-processes of the plants. With abundant water and carbon dioxide, and possibly with plants specially bred for the purpose, luxurious and economical growth may be attained independent of natural sunlight.

TORCH OF CIVILIZATION

From the viewpoint of man's progress toward independence from Nature the growing of plants under completely controlled artificial light, alone or in conjunction with natural sunlight, is an interesting challenge to the sun. That it will be done for costly and timely crops of flowers and vegetables there appears to be little doubt. How far it will invade the plant kingdom which furnishes the great bulk of the food for human beings is purely a matter of economics of the combined factors. Plants can be raised under natural light outdoors. However, the artificial world of civilization keeps a large and increasing percentage of human beings indoors. Clothing, congested cities, indoor occupations and the winter season have conspired to rob many human beings of much of the sunlight which their ancestors were exposed to outdoors even a century ago.

It is ridiculous to assume that in the short time since civilization has become largely an indoor world, human beings have become properly adapted to the artificial conditions and immune to the beneficence of sunlight. It is far more reasonable to assume that such a powerful environmental factor as sunlight since the beginning of life on earth is essential to the best of health through the best functioning of life-processes. Medical science has made great strides in the cure, and even in the prevention, of disorders and illnesses. But it is no reflection on that science to recognize that it is in its infancy and much remains to be discovered and to be understood. This is the situation even to a greater extent when healthy or near-healthy persons are considered. Why they remain healthy or become ill is a still greater unknown because it is always difficult, or often impossible to invade it by direct research. Considering all aspects of the matter, in the light of rather scanty knowledge, it is natural for thoughtful human beings to have faith in natural sunlight or its artificial equivalent. This approach through logic, combined with some direct evidence and much indirect knowledge, long ago convinced me that the indoor world of civilization should be illuminated with artificial sunlight —life-giving as well as light-giving. And if ultraviolet energy of proper wavelengths could be a by-product of lighting for seeing the additional cost might eventually be insignificant.

Aside from sun-worship, primitive races and early civilizations turned to sunlight as a tonic or adjuvant, for disinfecting and curing of wounds, and for the cure of certain disorders and diseases. It is true that their approaches were more instinctive than scientific but they also possessed powers of observation of results. Greek physicians acclaimed the curative value of sunlight and the upper classes, already pampering themselves in an indoor world, exposed themselves to sunlight in the belief that they were benefited. Hippocrates, the father of medicine, built a sanatorium high on a south slope of a mountain, in which he featured a solarium. Four hundred years before the Christian era he recommended sunbaths for persons afflicted with what is now known as tuberculosis. Other Greek physicians treated skin diseases and weak and flabby persons with sunlight. Throughout Greek and Roman practices sunbathing was recommended and practiced somewhat systematically. Of course, it was difficult then, as it is now, to separate the effects of sunlight from the effects of fresh air, rest, exercise, nourishing food and other factors which are involved, depending upon the case. Thus scientific proof of the efficacy of sunlight is difficult to obtain in the case of ill persons and even more so in the case of socalled healthy persons.

With the fall of the Roman Empire, the treatment of diseases with sunlight went into an eclipse as civilization itself did. It was not particularly revived in the Middle Ages but about two centuries ago it began to receive serious attention. Sunlight began to be used for wounds, for exposed cancer, for treating foods, for curing meats and for treating certain kinds of tuberculosis. By the beginning of the present century sun-therapy was ready for more scientific study and application, and soon the curative value of sunlight became established for certain diseases and disorders. Electric arcs became available for better control of light and ultraviolet energy in scientific studies and systematic applications. Experiments on animals as well as upon human beings began to establish a foundation of knowledge.

In 1903 Finsen received the Nobel Prize for his work with sunlight, particularly in the treatment and cure of tuberculosis of the skin. He had done much to establish the potency of ultraviolet energy in affecting the health of human beings. Now sunlight—or its artificial equivalent—is quite generally recognized as a helpful agency in the cure of certain diseases, as an aid in the preservation of health and in the prevention of disease, and as a tonic which at least increases the feeling of well-being. Perhaps it is safe to assume that sunlight generally plays a supporting role of more or less significance, depending upon the particular case of disease or disorder. But it is specific in the cure and prevention of rickets and it is contended by some of the leading specialists in this widespread deficiency in the bone structure of young children that the only complete substitute for natural sunlight is artificial sunlight. Both natural and artificial sunlight increase calcium metabolism with the result that better bones and teeth are developed in children. But in adults, whose bone-structure is complete, the same processes take place. Sound bones and teeth must be maintained. Perhaps diet can supply all that is necessary—perhaps not.

Sunburn is caused by ultraviolet energy of various wavelengths, even those much shorter than are present in sunlight. Tanning is the result of sunburn and it is produced most effectively with the least sunburn by the long-wave ultraviolet energy just beyond the violet end of the visible spectrum. For the maintenance of health by exposure to natural or artificial sunlight, no particular benefit is as yet attributable to sunburn (erythema) or tan. The one is annoying and the other seems to be desired more for esthetic reasons than otherwise. Both are superficial effects of ultraviolet energy. The applications of ultraviolet energy in the treatment of disease have very generally been in large dosages which produced erythema or sunburn. Special equipment such as sunlamps and ultraviolet generators have been available for a long time but sunlamps for public use have been greatly improved in efficiency and safety. However, I have long looked forward to supplying ultraviolet energy for health along with light for seeing. In other words, it has seemed to me that the ultimate combined goal of the torch of civilization was to illuminate the indoor world, where human beings were confined for long hours as in schools, offices and industries, with artificial light supplying the full beneficence of sunlight.

Naturally I wondered if benefits could be obtained without sunburn or erythema. The problem resolves itself in establishing the benefits of mild ultraviolet energy to which human beings would be exposed for many hours daily while working under artificial lighting in the indoor world. Researches under the supervision of Dr. H. J. Gerstenberger,

Director of the Babies and Childrens Hospital in Cleveland, confirmed the possibility. Rickets were cured and prevented in babies, both white and colored, by means of ultraviolet dosages which are only a small fraction of those required to produce a barely perceptible erythema or "sunburn." This is encouraging and, combined with the general knowledge of the beneficence of sunlight and of artificial light, leads to the conclusion that the torch of civilization may complete its service to mankind with a fitting climax as an agency of health as well as a partner of vision.

Artificial sunlight is already serving to preserve the health and increase the production and fertility of poultry. Experiments are being conducted with cattle and other animals. Domesticated animals are victims of the artificial world as human beings are, but not to such a great extent. And besides providing from sunlamps merely the beneficial ultraviolet energy, it is worth inquiring what artificial light can do for them. The eyes of animals are also doorways for impressions as well as optical organs of sight. Most of our domesticated animals evolved outdoors as human beings and plants did. There is no reason to believe that they are benefited by darkness. On the contrary, they may be aided by light as well as by ultraviolet energy. Darkness may possibly be advantageous when animals are being fattened for the market. Enormous fields of research are opened by viewing all living things as creatures of sunlight. The variety of sources of artificial light and ultraviolet energy makes it possible to control these factors in researches. With due credit to the scientific work done in the past, the torch-maker of the present has greatly extended the possibilities of research and practice. Artificial sunlight as a new and powerful natural agency is available for the artificial world. The effect of light and ultraviolet energy upon animals is more difficult to detect than upon plants. Animals are not rooted to one spot. Therefore, possessing mobility, they have had to develop the ability to store health or the factors upon which health depends. In addition, animals and particularly human beings, have intelligence which aids them in many ways. But it is difficult to believe that either storage or intelligence can release human beings completely from the bondage of sunlight, or of its equivalent, as a fundamental environmental factor throughout the evolution of life on earth.

The killing of germs and bacteria by sunlight has long been known. In fact, it has been practiced indoors to some extent by the use of ultraviolet energy. But recently very simple and effective sources of germicidal energy have become available which greatly extend the practicability of such applications of ultraviolet energy. Sterilized materials can be kept in enclosed spaces in which these lamps are operating. It is possible that these sources of germicidal energy may be practicable in the main ducts of air-conditioning systems. Already in certain hospitals "curtains" of germicidal energy are being experimented with for doorways and for cubicles in which babies are kept. Germs are killed as they pass through these curtains but the general effectiveness can be determined only by tedious research. These and many other applications may now be studied with the incentive born of the knowledge that simple effective artificial sources are available in considerable variety. All these specific applications of artificial sunlight, of sunlamps, and of germicidal lamps emphasize the great progress made by the torch-makers. They are far ahead of the torch-bearers for the applications of their products to the realms of living things must be preceded by many tedious researches under controlled conditions in order to settle the hopes and the claims which flourish in the twilight zone of knowledge. Thus the condition which existed for centuries has been reversed. Always heretofore there were many applications of light awaiting improvements in light-sources or the development of new ones. Now the production of sources of visible, ultraviolet and infrared energy has far outrun our knowledge of how and where to use them. They are available to improve our artificial world and to add further steps in our progress toward independence from Nature.

But the myriad specific applications of these new sources of light and radiant energy fade into the background when compared to the general objective of bringing the outdoors indoors for the benefit of shut-in mankind. This goal has inspired me for half a lifetime. Far back in the mists of unwritten history man began his conquest of darkness with the feeble flames of burning materials. Progress was slow for thousands of years, but progress it was. Then modern science gave a tremendous impetus to light-production. Electricity—a new kind of controllable energy—greatly increased the possibilities. The luminous efficiency and the power of light-sources increased by leaps and bounds. Modern light-sources have advanced far toward the ideal objective of the most efficient light it is possible to produce. The conquest of darkness has become easy and the torch-bearers seek new objectives.

I am grateful to the accidents of fate, which generally determine our course for us, for having been associated with the torch of civilization. And it is particularly gratifying to have had an opportunity to play an effective part in revealing that the true purpose of artificial light is to compete with daylight—not with darkness. This is a far greater and nobler role for the torch-makers and for the torch-bearers. It is one that brings maximal benefits of light to the present half-seeing world of civilized mankind. The tasks of civilization become easier and safer—and they are better done. The resources of human beings are conserved. The world about them is enlightened and beautified.

But that is not the end. Sunlight showers its beneficence in life and health. So the torch-bearer dreams of a further and, perhaps, final goal—a complete challenge to the sun. Throughout the indoor world where modern civilized beings live, learn, work and play, radiant energy for health may subtly shower its benefits along with light for seeing. This further challenge to the sun is made with a reverence not excelled by the sun-worshipers of more primitive times. Notwithstanding our increasing knowledge of sunlight as a creator of living things from lifeless matter, we still instinctively worship it, but our reverence is born of knowledge. As the awe of mystery decreases, knowledge beautifies and beatifies sunlight as the life-blood of creation. The torch of civilization challenges, with respect and humility, the eternal torch of creation. Progress toward independence from Nature, and toward perfection of the artificial world of civilization, is achieved by the spirit which issues such challenges. Progress is a succession of successful challenges.